YOU AND YOUR PROFILE

YOU AND YOUR PROFILE

IDENTITY AFTER AUTHENTICITY

HANS-GEORG MOELLER AND PAUL J. D'AMBROSIO

Columbia University Press   *New York*

Columbia University Press
Publishers Since 1893
New York   Chichester, West Sussex
cup.columbia.edu
Copyright © 2021 Columbia University Press
All rights reserved

Library of Congress Cataloging-in-Publication Data
Title: You and your profile : identity after authenticity.
Description: New York : Columbia University Press, 2021. |
Includes bibliographical references and index.
Identifiers: LCCN 2020039615 (print) | LCCN 2020039616 (ebook) |
ISBN 9780231196000 (hardback) | ISBN 9780231196017 (trade paperback) |
ISBN 9780231551595 (ebook)
Subjects: LCSH: Identity (Psychology)
Classification: LCC BF697 .Y675 2021 (print) | LCC BF697 (ebook) |
DDC 155.2—dc23
LC record available at https://lccn.loc.gov/2020039615
LC ebook record available at https://lccn.loc.gov/2020039616

Columbia University Press books are printed on permanent
and durable acid-free paper.
Printed in the United States of America

Cover design: Julia Kushnirsky
Cover photograph: Christoph Hetzmannseder/Getty Images

In fond memory of Henry Rosemont, Jr.

The huge vortices of energy created by our media present us with similar possibilities of evasion of the consequences of destruction. By studying the pattern of the effects of this huge vortex of energy in which we are involved, it may be possible to program a strategy of evasion and survival.

—Marshall McLuhan, "Man and Media"

Men will not act by grand plans or formulations of a scheme of ideas, or even by the impulsion of a vested interest, but in the very first instance by the notion they entertain of themselves— and this picture they draw of their private characters is one to which they will address themselves with assiduity of purpose over many years: no portrait is more intensely drawn, Gideon, than the self-portrait.

—Timothy Mo, *An Insular Possession*

CONTENTS

PRE-FACE

THE FACE IN THE MIRROR

Sometimes in the morning when he shaved, he looked at his image in the glass and felt no identity with the face that stared back at him in surprise, the eyes clear in a grotesque mask; it was as if he wore, for an obscure reason, an outrageous disguise, as if he could, if he wished, strip away the bushy white eyebrows.

—John Williams, *Stoner*

Identity enables us to accept the face we see in the mirror as our own. We need it for coming to terms with the "grotesque mask" that we see there, which cannot be stripped away. We must identify with this face so that it does not appear to us as "an outrageous disguise," or if so, then just for a moment. When we leave the bathroom, we need to trust that the image we project expresses our thoughts and feelings quite naturally, and we need to prepare ourselves for the fact that everyone else will take this face to be precisely who we are.

1

THE BIGGER PICTURE

BAMBOO BAY: THE JOY OF TOURISM

There is a small, almost hidden beach in Macau called Cheoc Wan or "Bamboo Bay." Despite its immediate proximity to one of the most densely populated and heavily touristed areas in the world—the casinos drawing tens of millions of visitors each year merely five miles away—Bamboo Bay is a quiet place. Some older locals come daily to swim in the muddy, trash-filled ocean water. On weekends a few families, mostly Portuguese-Macanese, spend some time here, children playing in the sand as their parents may have done in their own youth, in the old country. The few tourists who do make their way to Bamboo Bay tend to be mainland Chinese or other East Asians. But they do not come to swim or sunbathe. They come to take pictures—pictures of themselves posing in front of the shallow waves coming in, sitting on a rock, or walking along the beach with long hair photogenically blowing in the breeze. These beachgoers do not stay long. They might stop to have a snack at the little café, but then they quickly move on to other attractions.

A European friend, having observed this scene, remarked with both amusement and critical disapproval that the tourists were not properly enjoying the scenery. They were, somehow, oblivious to nature. To him it seemed they were not even having fun, just staging a visit that, precisely because it consisted mainly of choreographing digital photographs, did not really take place (as Jean Baudrillard might have said). Nowadays this kind of criticism is common, and the friend felt well justified knowing many share his point of view.

But is our friend right? Perhaps he does not understand, being a middle-aged European, how tourism, along with all society, has changed—and how it is moving on from an older, "bourgeois" paradigm of "authentic discovery" to a new "democratic" one of profile-building exercise.

The point of tourism today, in a world where all travel destinations are branded, marketed, and staged for visitors, cannot be to explore authentic localities. Tourism today means taking part in a public performance—like going to a show, a parade, or a protest. Postcolonial world tourism no longer means primarily rich white people traveling to "native" places. Increasingly it means people from previously colonized or formerly "second-" or "third-world" countries, like Russia or China, participating along with Westerners in a global travelling "spectacle" (in Guy Debord's sense). Displaying the simple fact that one can travel, that one has the time and money for it—and is granted a visa—is already sufficient reason for doing it.

I travel to make my trips part of my profile, to actualize the "profilic" potential of tourism. It is a demonstration to myself and to others that I, too, am a traveler. Like others, I too travel the world. The taste to pick a fashionable destination and the capacity to present the particular appeal of this destination to others further contribute to and raise the prestige of my profile. By projecting my travels to others, I curate my identity—no matter whether I am from Asia, Europe, or somewhere else.

[margin handwritten note: Possible Thesis]

Tourism today is a profile-building activity. Travel destinations—and almost every place in the world has become a travel destination by now—provide resources for a profile-based identity, or "profilicity."[1] Tourists make use of these resources. They generate identity surplus value out of the *profile value* supplied by the tourism industry. In tourism, concrete profile-identity work consists in taking and posting photos. The taking and posting of images increases the profile value not only of the tourist but of the destination as well. All participants can experience this creation of value as enjoyable. Apparently our middle-aged European friend did not yet understand the joy of tourism under conditions of profilicity.

PHOTO EDITING IN THE *NEW YORKER*

Producing images of oneself—of one's face or body, of one's activities or possessions—in order to present them to others is at the heart of profile-based identity work. Social media has allowed an unprecedented number of individuals to engage in this work at an unprecedented scale. The presence of social media in people's lives has expanded explosively: millions spend several hours each day "interactively" participating in the merging roles of producer and audience. As a consequence, photo-editing apps have become exceedingly popular. They are an important tool for manufacturing profiles, and thus profilicity.

At the time of writing, the Chinese company Meitu (meaning "Beautiful Picture") produces some of the most commonly used image-editing apps in East Asia. According to Jiayang Fan, in a *New Yorker* article published in December 2017, "Meitu's apps generate some six billion photos a month." Fan goes on to describe in detail "China's Selfie Obsession"—as her article is titled. Not only are people constantly taking and posting photos of themselves, and watching and commenting on other people's photos, they are also spending a lot of time staging and editing these pictures. Fan—who is herself, as the British would say, "of Chinese extraction"—reports: "I asked a number of Chinese friends how long it takes them to edit a photo before posting it on social media. The answer for most of them was about forty minutes per face; a selfie taken with a friend would take well over an hour. The work requires several apps, each of which has particular strengths. No one I asked would consider posting or sending a photo that hadn't been improved." The article goes on to accurately relate the preoccupation with taking and presenting selfies in East Asia to a flourishing cosmetic surgery industry and a widespread and intense celebrity culture. Cosmetic surgery appears as a "medicinal app" that prepares the body for being photographed—it is a kind of biological photo edit prior to taking the actual photo. Celebrity worship, on the other hand, sets up a horizon of style. It provides everyone with a variety of profile models that provide orientation for self-shaping and self-presentation.[2]

As the term "obsession" in the title indicates, the *New Yorker* article clearly regards the preoccupation with the presentation of self-images as pathological. The Chinese, it seems, are crazy. And they are not only borderline out of their minds but also morally wanting. Fan launches two ethical criticisms against them. First, she depicts the intense interest in selfies as a form of narcissism, as a vain overindulgence with one's own image and an unbecoming fascination with one's beauty. Second, she regards "China's selfie obsession" as an indication of a lack of individuality and authenticity.[3] She illustrates her criticism by relating a story about a corporate event at Meitu that she attended.

At a Meitu party, hundreds of minor and major stars were chatting and snapping away on their cellphones. Meanwhile Fan, with her critical eye, reflected on the situation. Her disapproval of the bonfire of vanities she witnessed there is symbolically expressed in recounting the following scene. An older woman, the wife of a janitor as it turned out, was ushered out by security guards, obviously regarded as an unfit intruder. Fan poetically describes her: "I caught sight of an older woman, perhaps in her seventies, standing and watching the young dancers with an expression of rapt, unfiltered joy. Her face was creased and leathery, but her mouth, agape with wonder, gave her a childlike look. She was the only person there who wasn't holding a cellphone, and she was dressed plainly." The woman's exclusion from the party brings about an epiphany: "As the guards succeeded in ejecting her, I realized that she was the most beautiful person at the party."

Fan establishes a striking contrast between the purity of the older woman and all the other partygoers, She is "unfiltered," her emotions and expressions are of a "childlike" simplicity, and her clothes are "plain." Moreover, she is not entangled in the net of modern technology, the *only one* not holding a cellphone— and thus is without the machinery of inauthenticity at hand. Therefore she is, for Fan, in sharp contradistinction to the fakeness of the other party guests, the only genuine beauty.

In her final verdict, Fan continues her plea for authenticity by accusing Meitu's photo-editing apps and their Chinese users of undermining individuality and individual diversity: "Meitu and the trends it epitomizes seem to be moving China in the direction of homogeneity. A generation of Chinese, while clamorously asserting forms of individualism that would have been unthinkable for their parents and grandparents, is also enacting a ghastly convergence. Their selfies are becoming more and more similar, and so are their faces." Readers of the *New Yorker* are left with the conclusion that, through the proliferation of social media and photo-editing apps, the Chinese have become all but completely unmoored. They are indecently vain and inauthentic. By implication, then, "we" Americans or Westerners are warned, lest we be infected by the same image craze taking hold of China. We must not lose our morally grounded sense of true beauty, which lies in "unfiltered" natural purity. We must not rob ourselves of individuality and become, as the Chinese are quickly spiraling toward, a homogenous mass devoid of uniqueness and diversity.

Fan's article quite correctly points out major problems attached to social media use, such as the stress, anxiety, and addiction resulting from hyperconcern with self-presentation (manifesting itself in extraordinary investments of both time and money in new technologies) and the capitalist commodification of beauty. But from a philosophical perspective, her text is highly problematic.

It is problematic, to start, that Fan suggests the "selfie obsession" and related phenomena of cosmetic surgery and celebrity worship are specifically (mainland) "Chinese" phenomena. The same phenomena are equally common in, for instance, South Korea, Japan, and Singapore. But they did not originate in these places. Long before photo-editing apps, both cosmetic surgery and a celebrity industry were already prevalent in North America. Teeth whitening and face-lifts, for instance, were practices almost expected of aging people in the United States long before many in China had ever heard of such procedures. Capitalism, too, along with the commodification of beauty, predates both the recent economic surge of China and the advent of social media.

The core problem of Fan's article—shared by many current critiques of social media—is, however, that it is unable to understand the "selfie obsession" in terms of profilicity.[4] It wrongly depicts it as a primarily cultural ("Chinese") issue and not a social and psychological phenomenon of identity construction that has global dimensions. As an immediate consequence of this cultural categorization, the article demonstrates an equally problematic bias toward the value of "authenticity" and assumes that truly authentic individuals and genuine beauty exist, both of which are now polluted by social media. Along with this assumption, highly questionable idealizations of authenticity are presented, and staunch good-bad dichotomies emerge (such as natural vs. artificial).

To be sure, obsessive selfie taking and selfie editing happen. And, yes: selfie taking and editing are hardly "authentic." But does it make sense to decry selfie taking as inauthentic if it was never intended to be authentic in the first place? Why measure it against authenticity? It seems that the actual function of Fan's article is to defend the ideal of authenticity at a moment when it is most threatened. Fan's essay attempts to conceal the imminent breakdown of this false ideal. It seeks to save authenticity at a time when it is losing its foothold in society due to its own inconsistencies and anachronisms. The vehement defense of authenticity in the face of an increasingly omnipresent profilicity has the purpose of assuring ourselves that we can still be authentic at a time when in fact we too *have already become wildly profilic.*

Jiayang Fan's idealizing depiction of the true beauty and natural authenticity of the elderly woman at the Meitu party is questionable, and it ought to be questioned. But the bigger issue— one that opens up a view of the bigger picture—is this: Are Jiayang Fan and her job at the *New Yorker*, where she published her article, really all that different from the people at the Meitu party and their lives?

Fan's condemnation of the Chinese selfie-obsession and the resulting uniformity of self-images in China also comes with her

Twitter handle and a picture: a profile picture of author Jiayang Fan herself. This picture is not an edited photo. It is a digitally altered portrait based on a photo or drawing. All essays in the *New Yorker* are accompanied by such images of their authors in the exact same format. To use Jiayang Fan's terms: these pictures show a "homogeneity" and a "ghastly convergence." The author images evoke the standardized connotation of "cool," creative, original, young, intellectual people as represented in animated clips or movies. The alterations to her photo align Jiayang Fan's profile with the profiles of all the other contributors to the magazine, and thereby with the profile of the *New Yorker* as a media company. Here, the same profilic mechanism so disparagingly described by Fan at the Meitu party is at work—arguably working overtime. Both Meitu and the *New Yorker* align the profiles of their representatives with one another so that, taken together, they support the profile of the companies. This operates in the other direction too, of course. By being aligned with the *New Yorker* profile, Jiayang Fan's own profile and those of her coworkers are raised, just as working for or with Meitu can be a profilicity boost for those who do so.

Moreover, when Jiayang Fan visited the Meitu party and marveled at the old lady without a cellphone, didn't she, Fan, have one in her own hand? She did. At least symbolically. Her entire presence at the event resembled a smartphone; picturing and heavily editing it and its participants (for more than an hour, we assume) for her own media audience—readers of the *New Yorker*. In her report Fan metaphorically alters the appearance of the older woman precisely so that this "unfiltered" woman comes to represent the authentic life that Fan wants to show her readers (and her editor). The image of the "unedited" elderly woman presented in Fan's essay is in fact just as manipulated as the hundreds, if not thousands, of pictures posted by the Meitu party guests on their own social media accounts.

And how about Jiayang Fan's social media profiles—which the Twitter handle beneath her portrait in the *New Yorker* directs people to? Like most readers of this book, and of course its authors, she has several: in addition to Twitter, she is also active on Facebook and LinkedIn. On these public platforms, a good number of Fan's photos are shown. Most of them are beautiful. It is difficult to tell if they are edited or how much time may have been spent choosing the one that was "just right," but none of them seems to correspond well to the ideal of unfiltered authentic beauty that Fan's epiphany at the Meitu party revealed.

Just as many other critics of social media, selfies, and associated phenomena, Jiayang Fan simulates authenticity as a counterpart to their supposed inauthenticity. This "edited" authenticity is put into the service of furthering the profilicity of the critics or the media companies they represent. In this way, the critics reproduce and proliferate the very same profilic conditions that they critique. They operate under conditions of profilicity but, paradoxically, still display an ideal of authenticity that they performatively contradict in this very display.

In comparison with their critic, the obsessed Chinese selfiers are rather straightforward with regard to their "fake" images. Of course almost everybody knows that almost everybody uses photo-editing apps. It is, like using makeup, by no means a secretive act of hidden manipulation. It is plainly there for everyone to see. Everyone does it, and everyone knows it and is expected to do it. As Fan mentioned: "No one I asked would consider posting or sending a photo that hadn't been improved." In China—or, to put it more accurately, in the global world of social media today—many users do not aim at presenting authenticity in the first place. The tourist taking selfies at Bamboo Bay does not pretend authenticity. And if authenticity appears, then it is often clearly staged, like someone posting on Facebook a photo of an "authentic" local dish. Here, authenticity is put in the service of profilicity.

Criticisms of social media tend to disregard its non- or transauthentic orientation and inappropriately set up a "pure" authenticity standard as the only correct option. Ironically, since these criticisms themselves are produced under conditions of profilicity, they do not (and *cannot*) meet their own authenticity ideal. Their authenticity can be deconstructed and revealed to be staged and inauthentic. The very calls to preserve our supposed authenticity only show that the age of authenticity has lost its credibility.

Interestingly enough, to return to cultural issues, qualms about the inauthenticity of social media seem to be a somewhat "Western" problem. Europeans and North Americans who feel deeply attached to the "age of authenticity" tend to romanticize it and succumb to nostalgia in a "Facebook Society."[5]

SINCERITY, AUTHENTICITY, AND PROFILICITY

In earlier times, identity was typically assigned by the social roles one was born into. Along with birth came not only one's gender but also one's tribal or ethnic identity, one's social class, one's profession, and one's religion. Identification then typically consisted in committing to the roles people found themselves in by embracing the norms and internalizing the values attached to these roles. This is what we call, following Lionel Trilling, "sincerity": a mental and social method of achieving identity based on sincere role enactment.[6] The family was often the core social unit within which sincere identity formation was experienced, developed, and confirmed.

The image of a traditional Chinese family in figure 1.1 illustrates the power of role-based identity. It shows how, literally, roles assign places and positions. Females are supposed to be on the right, males on the left. Dress indicates gender, age, and social status. Importantly, role designations indicate a bodily regime as well; they determine who gets to sit and who gets to stand, the length of one's hair, or, throughout many centuries in China, the length of a woman's feet. Without intellectual and emotional commitment, such often brutal physiological and behavioral, or "cultural," regimes could have hardly been maintained in society or endured by individuals. For the practice of

FIGURE 1.1 Chinese family portrait, ca. 1910. David K. Jordan website, https://pages.ucsd.edu/~dkjordan/chin/familism.html. Photo published in Edwin J. Dingle, *Across China on Foot: Life in the Interior and the Reform Movement* (New York: Holt, 1911).

such regimes, it was most useful that people actually regarded them as morally, religiously, or philosophically correct. And the most powerful social and psychological tool to bring about such an affirmation is self-identification. If, for instance, a woman identifies fully with the social role ascribed to her by the Confucian society within which she grows up, she will be able to regard the crippling of her feet not only as morally good but also as part of her "self-cultivation." External role-enactment, even if it involves binding one's feet, can work smoothly once people find their identity in an internal commitment to it. When looking at the people depicted in the photo, one can imagine that they may cope with the immense role pressures of their family life by imposing a strict regime of sincere role practice on themselves and one another. In this way they may never even consider the possibility that, to a stranger, their whole appearance can look like an "outrageous disguise."

In modernity, society became more dynamic. Social mobility increased, and people began to exercise a higher degree of choice regarding, for instance, their profession, their marriage, or their religion. This posed a challenge to traditional role allegiance. It was less evident that one needed to commit to the roles one was born into when alternatives could be realized. Increasing personal agency became not only possible but desired. Identity then became a problem. It was no longer almost ready-made at birth but something to be discovered. Traditional role identities prescribed by society began to appear as external facades imposed on people whose real self was to be found somewhere underneath. The conception of the social role as a "mask" covering up one's true identity became a prime metaphor along with the newly emerging quest for what now seemed to be the foundation of identity: authenticity. Again following Lionel Trilling, we take authenticity to be a form of identity based on "the idea that somewhere under all the roles there is Me, that poor old ultimate actuality, who, when all the roles have been played, would like to murmur 'Off, off, you lendings!' and settle down with his own original actual self."[7]

The image of an authentic self as the true face of a person that comes to the fore once one's social masks are taken away is still popular. In authenticity, one's face is expected to accurately express one's actual self. A mask that is no mask, one's true self has to be found or created. That this may be an impossible task is indicated by the suspiciously frequent use of tautological phrases such as "truly authentic" in self-help manuals on authenticity.[8] How can we trust authenticity? Did we present our real face to others, and did they show their true faces to us? Who can say for sure? What does an entirely original face look like? And if it looks *like* something, is it entirely original? What authentic hairstyle genuinely represents your true self? Such questions are difficult to answer. Moreover, not only self-help manuals but also more elaborated philosophical guides on how to become authentic eventually face a core paradox: once one follows the advice to "make one's own path," one is already following a path recommended by others.

Authenticity, like sincerity, has its problems. But, like sincerity, when widely applied as an identity-shaping method, it becomes convincing, credible, and powerful. It has been supported by a vocabulary, a rhetoric, an ethics, a politics, and an economy of individualism that made people believe that identity springs from personal originality, creativity, and autonomy. The protection of the assumed unalienable dignity of the authentic individual became almost a first commandment in (post-)Christian societies. Being tied to identity formation, authenticity was widely internalized. True identity value, it was assumed, could come only from being authentic. The modern woman would no

FIGURE 1.2 One's "real" face behind a mask. Image by Victor Santos
on Pexels.com, https://www.pexels.com/photo/woman-about-to
-wear-half-face-mask-2263189/.

longer need to identify sincerely as wife, mother, and daughter. Instead she could cope with the pressures of competing in a hypermodern capitalist economy by discovering her calling, becoming independent, finding a partner uniquely suited to her, raising the most special children, and, of course, staying true to herself throughout.

Just as sincerity lost its grip on society and individuals with the shift toward modernity, authenticity is now fading away along with more recent changes. Authenticity relies heavily on personal interaction between people. Authentic individuals mutually confirm their identity value, and to do this, they must know one another and be at the same time in the same place. In the virtual world we inhabit today, such "real life" interaction has become less and less important. Personal contact between seller and buyer is often obsolete or irrelevant when making economic exchanges. In times of mass media, as outlined by Walter Benjamin nearly a century ago, artworks are typically not seen in person and by only a few but, as in film, are projected to anonymous mass audiences.[9] Copies have replaced originals. Contemporary democratic politics resemble popularity contests where politicians, like entertainment celebrities, compete for the votes of huge public electorates.

Today, society has switched almost entirely to second-order observation. This means, in line with sociologist Niklas Luhmann's usage of the term, we do not simply look at people or issues directly but rather at how they are seen publicly by others. To judge a restaurant, we look first at its reviews on Yelp!—and later judge our experience in reference to what we read. We have developed the ability to judge products in terms of brands, and people in terms of their profiles. We observe first how things are seen. Learning to see in this way, we also learn to show ourselves in this very same manner. We form identity through curating

profiles. Profiles are images of ourselves presented for second-
order observation. By looking at them, others can see how we
like to be seen as being seen. Thus we create and show pictures
that look like the one in figure 1.3.

Here is no pretense of authenticity, no attempt to represent a
mask that is no mask. It is clear to those who understand a picture like this that it is neither taken nor posted spontaneously.
It is not meant to document an "authentic" moment in one's life
to be stored in an autobiographical album or as part of a deeply
reflective self-narrative. It is meant to communicate with "anyone" (which can, strangely enough, include all those in the photo).
Such pictures are contributions to identity assembly. They are
publicly presented for validation. If the photo is seen and liked,

FIGURE 1.3 People jumping simultaneously at a beach.
Photo by Peopleshot, https://www.1001freedownloads.com/free
-photo/people-jumping-on-the-beach.

those who posted it get the go ahead to continue displaying the personas they presented.

SUPERHOST: WELCOMING PROFILES

Recently, we booked a house for a month in Sweden on Airbnb. Monthly bookings on Airbnb needed to be paid for at the time of reservation and were not refundable. After the booking was confirmed, the host got in touch. There was an error and the price information was incorrect, she said. Normally she rents the house for at least twice the rate we already paid. Could we cancel?, she hoped. It was fine by us. We told her, however, we could not do this ourselves because we would lose all the money we'd already paid. She said that she could not cancel either: cancellation on her side would make her lose her "superhost" status for one year. She would rather allow us to stay for a month and lose money than let her profile suffer. Of course we would be extremely welcome to stay at her place, she added, no matter which rate we paid. . . .

In the liberal West, the Chinese Social Credit System has been thoroughly condemned. This system—which is currently in various trial stages with different versions being tested in different areas—assigns a credibility rating to people based on, for instance, their repayment of loans, their traffic violation record, or their record on minor public misdemeanors such as jaywalking, littering, or smoking where prohibited. It is typically portrayed as a dystopian Orwellian surveillance monster, as reflecting the authoritarian nature of the Chinese government and demonstrating its lack of respect for individual freedom and privacy. Many critics do acknowledge that similar systems already exist in the West (in the form of credit ratings, police records, etc.), but their integration into one state-controlled whole, it is alleged, makes a crucial difference.[10] It gives too much power to the state, is too invasive, and impedes human autonomy.

In China, public opinion about the Social Credit System is not at all negative. Research has shown surprisingly high approval ratings, which we also found when speaking to friends, colleagues, and students.[11] The system, it is argued, helps improve public trust in a society where it is perceived as critically lacking. Rather than insisting on privacy rights, Chinese people tend to emphasize an urgency for making business interactions and public behavior more reliable, more functional, and more transparent. From a bourgeois Western perspective, such an attitude seems problematic: Are Chinese people really willing to compromise their individual rights and subject themselves to constant supervision just so that people's manners and traffic congestion get better?

One rarely hears such qualms about Airbnb in the West. Here it seems perfectly okay for the millions of renters to distinguish between hosts and superhosts. And not only this: as our own booking experience shows, those advertising themselves on the platform may also willingly and actively implement this distinction. Of course, there are economic reasons for doing this. A superhost will get more customers than others and may be able to charge more as well. Along with this capitalist rationale, we feel, identity is at stake. The tone of her messages suggested to us that our Swedish superhost had internalized her status to such a degree that she found the idea of losing it not only economically but also personally uncomfortable. We felt that her whole Airbnb persona—the way she interacted with us through the website—was, from start to finish, put in the service of verifying her superhost profile. Superhost is not merely a business category; it can deeply effect identity.

These two examples, the Chinese Social Credit System and the Swedish Airbnb booking, will inevitably remind anyone who has seen the *Black Mirror* episode "Nosedive" of how it depicts a society in the near future "where people can rate each other from one to five stars for every interaction they have, which can impact their socioeconomic status."[12] Actually, the pervasive interpersonal rating system in the TV show applies primarily to public interactions, like purchases or events, including parties, but not to "authentic" personal interaction. The protagonist's brother, as well as two other characters (a truck driver and a man in jail) she meets at the end of the story, represent alternatives to "rated personality." In effect, "Nosedive" sets up a stark contrast between public personas focused on ratings and profiles, on the one hand, and interactions between "true" and "free" individuals who do not submit themselves to the social rating mechanisms, on the other. The episode eventually sets up a liberation scenario, warning of a destruction of human authenticity through social media use and ratings, and appeals for a return to authenticity before it is too late.

If we take "Nosedive" to be a criticism of new media and ratings, then it, too, performatively contradicts itself. *Black Mirror* is a Netflix show, and Netflix is a key actor in the digitalized, medialized, and thoroughly ranked and rated hypercapitalist world that "Nosedive" warns against. The means of the production, and commodification, of communication enabling and sustained by the show represent anything but the authentic lifeworld it offers as a contrast to a rating- and ranking-based tomorrow.

Moreover, the show wrongly suggests a stark choice between a nonranked intimate sphere of "true" and "free" human relations within the family and among friends and a public sphere of interactions based on mutual ratings. It implies that you can no longer have the former if you get involved too deeply with the latter. Yet it is easy to see that while in the society we inhabit today such incongruity between different kinds of interactions—more and less intimate—exists, the two are by no means incompatible. Which Airbnb customer really wants to get to know their host "authentically"—like they might know their siblings, friends, or lovers? And which Airbnb hosts would be better off if they were always their "true self" when dealing with a different person every other night, saying what they really think about guests and actually answering the question, "How are you today?" In fact, most of us use ratings and rely on algorithms that churn out rankings, in the tourism industry, in financing, in academics, in gaming, for insurance, for shopping, for social media—you name it. And we are rather comfortable doing so on a daily basis. In all these spheres, people orient and identify themselves or others with the help of ratings and profiles, but this does not necessarily prevent them from still having "real" relatives or friends as well.

"Sincere" relationships among group members and "authentic" relationships between friends continue to be there in times of "profilic" social media and ratings and rankings. These three identity modes can and do coexist, despite their incongruities. They can coexist, like older and newer technologies. Even in a digital world, we still use mechanics when pushing a button.

In a society where we need to interact with people whom we have no time, no desire, and no need to know authentically or sincerely, we often know one another through profilicity. This works. No identity technology erases the others altogether, and none of them gets identity "right" or is without problems. But there are shifting hierarchies among them, along with social and historical shifts. As a high-profile TV show, "Nosedive" put its pitch for authenticity in the service of its own profilicity—this pitch helped the show to successfully curate the Netflix brand

and to achieve very high ratings: a whopping 95 percent score on Rotten Tomatoes.[13] No matter how keen on authenticity the makers of the show may have been, they inescapably operate in and for a media environment fostering profilicity, including their own. Where second-order observation is pervasive, profilicity is the most advanced identity technology. In many areas of society today, being successful, or simply being, relies heavily on profilicity. We are in it together.

THE RIOT HIPSTER

Politics today often takes place in the form of meticulously planned and staged mass events, not unlike sports or entertainment. A Group of 20 summit is a good example: a kind of political Olympics, held regularly at different places all over the world. Celebrity politicians and their dealings are the core of the event, the mass media zoom in, the hospitality industry gets to work, extra contingents of police and security arrive, and, of course, protesters regularly flock to the scene.

One particular photo gave an impression of how the G20 Summit 2017 in Hamburg, Germany, was experienced from a protester's perspective: it shows a young man with a hipster beard taking a selfie—with his fancy iPhone—in front of a group of masked men burning things on the street. The photo of the man was taken by an Austrian journalist and then posted on Twitter and published online by the German news outlet *Der Spiegel*.[14] It went viral and became a meme, known as the "Riot Hipster": "Twitter user @JimmyRushmore tweeted the photograph with the caption 'That feeling when you're overthrowing capitalism but just can't resist taking a selfie on your iPhone 7.'" The tweet garnered "upwards of 71,000 likes and 40,000 retweets within three days."[15] Soon, "photoshopped images featuring a cutout of the man began circulating."[16]

The satirical variations of the meme echoed the critique of the riot hipster expressed in comments on social and traditional mass media. In line with the quoted Twitter caption, the selfier was accused of abusing a serious political issue, along with images of violence and destruction, for vain self-promotion.[17] He was also chastised as an ideological hypocrite. After all, if he purchased the expensive iPhone in his hand, he had supported the very capitalist economic system that he was protesting against.

Political activism, too, it seems, has become a stage for self-presentation. Just like the politicians at the G20, protesters use the event as a photo-op to show themselves in a light they desire to an audience they want to impress. The riot hipster was taken to represent a betrayal of the real cause: protesters should not mimic the phony politicians whom they stand up against. Instead of being concerned with shaping their public image, they should be sincerely dedicated to a political quest and express authentic concern.

This may not be as easily done as said, though. How should it be possible to publicly present a political cause, or a social critique, without at the same time curating one's personal profile and without using capitalist communication tools and platforms? What kind of camera did the Austrian photographer use when covering the protests? He, too, took a photo to further his own profile as a photographer, presumably selling it to *Der Spiegel*, and thereby "abusing" the political event for his own professional self-promotion. How about "Twitter user @JimmyRushmore"? He boosted his Twitter profile enormously by his critique of the riot hipster and became, by default, a self-promoting photo poster as well. And how about those who proliferated the meme with their parodic adaptations of it? An endless chain was established through persistent postings and repostings, all done, if not with capitalist iPhones, then with equally capitalist Twitter or Instagram accounts, *Der Spiegel* reports, or photo-editing apps. Where is the "real protester" in this chain of postings and self-presentations? Where is the protester whose only concern is the issue and not herself? How could any pure cause, if it existed, be observed and shared without at the same time transforming it into a self-presentation aimed at attracting attention, getting likes, or otherwise promoting one's own profile? And how could such self-presenting and self-profiling activities take place today without being insolubly tied to a capitalist political economy?

The "real issue," including issues in politics and the economy, is not a nonpersonal and merely "objective" cause but the formation, curation, and presentation of identity. Political issues and economic structures become significant and are perceived as vital once they are merged with the quest for identity. In this way, they are internalized and emotionally charged. They really mean something to us. Identification, in the form of public self-profiling, makes politics relevant not only for the riot hipster. And it can provide marketing opportunities in the economy, as for an Airbnb host.

The way in which individuals and collectives pursue identity is an integral part of the way society functions. People, including the readers and writers of this book, shape their identity by proffering profiles and then hoping for their social validation. This is "profilicity." Political organizations, economic corporations, and nation-states all make use of it. In a society where profilicity has become dominant, individuals and social systems apply it in their everyday operations. Identity work, in the form of work on our profiles, is the real issue.

THE CAUSE IS THE PROFILE

From the perspective of sincerity, profilicity is insincere, and from the perspective of authenticity, it is inauthentic. This is only logical. The selfie-taking riot hipster who protests for the sake of boosting his own social media profile can appear as a traitor to the cause: his focus on self-presentation may indicate only his personal vanity rather than his authenticity; and his ownership of an iPhone may signal that his demonstrated opposition to capitalism is insincere.

From a descriptive perspective, however, sincerity, given its contradictory demand to internalize external social roles and to regard them as second nature, is also insincere. And authenticity, given the built-in paradox that one can learn how to be authentic only by following others, is inauthentic as well. How authentic are those who present themselves as authentic protesters, and how sincere are those who demonstrate their sincere devotion to a cause? Is a merely authentic concern for a cause, or purely sincere commitment to it, really possible? The nineteenth-century German philosopher Max Stirner suspected any dedication to a cause to be an inauthentic form of self-denial. Truly authentic people would have no cause at all other than their own self, he stipulated.[18] We suspect something different: the more intensely one identifies with a cause, the more "self-ish" the cause becomes.

In the 2009 "Climategate" case, private correspondence between climate scientists at the University of East Anglia was hacked and exposed. It was alleged that the correspondence showed that the scientists had conspired to repress data showing that global warming was not taking place. After the allegations had been shown to be false—the scientists had not committed any data fraud, and temperatures were actually rising—a friend who is an ecological activist expressed his relief. He was happy to hear, he said, that the climate scientists had not been lying. He thereby also unintentionally revealed a paradoxical happiness about climate change. Shouldn't he have been rather sad about the fact that it was once more confirmed that scientific data showed that the Earth is heating up?

Later in this book we will turn to the strange case of the allegedly self-inflicted hate crime by actor and black and gay rights activist Jesse Smollett, and to a reaction of one of our colleagues to it. This colleague, being very much in favor of minority rights and causes, expressed her disappointment about this hate crime not actually having taken place, since she much preferred Smollett not to be exposed as a liar. The two cases follow the exact same paradoxical logic. Behind an ecologist's delight about the news that climate change is really happening and a civil rights activist's frustration that a reported hate crime apparently did not occur lies a strong identification with a cause. Identification with the cause becomes so central and primary that, strangely enough, one prefers news that the problem is really as bad as one fears it is—since this affirms the value of the cause, and thereby of one's identification with it. If climate change or civil rights should turn out to be no longer an issue, the identity of those identifying with these causes would be undermined and deflated. One's profile—built and maintained with sometimes a lifetime of effort, and in which one is thus deeply invested—would lose its social validity and become obsolete. The stronger the identification with the cause, the more the care for the cause also becomes the care for oneself. Needless to say (but perhaps actually not so needless, otherwise we would not say it), this mechanism is the same for many ideals, principles, views, and values, both progressive and conservative, left and right. Islamophobes would be utterly frustrated by a lack of Islamist terrorist attacks.

Causes are tricky. From the perspectives of sincerity and authenticity, sincere devotion and authentic concern for a cause show that one takes the issue seriously—that it is the "real deal." From a perspective outside of sincerity and authenticity, it seems that the opposite is the case. The higher the degree of identification with a cause, the more one's identity itself becomes one's real cause. Today, in a society where profilicity is a widely applied method of identity formation, both individuals and collectives use issues to shape and market their profiles—the left as much as the right, Green activists named Greta as much as antipolitician politicians named Donald. A high-profile cause helps improve personal and collective profiles. Under conditions of profilicity, just as with sincerity and authenticity, people and organizations circle around causes like moths around a flame.

OPINIONATED

As sentient meat, however illusory our identities are, we craft
those identities by making value judgments.
—*True Detective*, S01, E08

Morality has commonly been understood in terms of being or doing good. Under conditions of profilicity, it is becoming increasingly clear that another definition may be more pertinent. Here, morality consists largely in *communicating* what is right. Or we might alternatively put it that in profilicity, what we say is the morally most visible and significant aspect of what we are and what we do.

Different methods of identity give rise to different moral regimes. Under the conditions of sincerity, various kinds of "role ethics" flourish.[19] The virtue of a person or an act is typically assessed in relation to a role performance. Is she a devoted daughter? A dutiful wife? Striving for goodness consists in striving to become honorable, and being honorable means committing oneself to one's place within a community, such as a kinship group, religious congregation, military unit, or sports teams. It is important not only to enact one's roles in a proper manner but also to publicly evaluate role fulfillment. One can also show role-based ethical commitment by denouncing others, for instance, for not being a good daughter or wife.

In authenticity, along with its inward turn on the quest for identity, a shift from role ethics to an individualist ethics takes place. Now, the dignity and the rights of the "single individual" are of prime importance. Is he fostering the unique individuality of his children? Is his work original? The current human rights discourse, with its focus on personal freedom, reflects this turn to authenticity. For sure, values of sincerity are not entirely neglected, but they tend to be regarded as problematic when they do not make room for pursuit of authenticity. A regime of authenticity requires constant concern with and emphasis on uniqueness, creativity, and autonomy. One must not only strive for these values but also voice one's support for them. Otherwise it is difficult to find recognition, to distinguish oneself, and to accrue moral value of one's identity.

A profile is public. Accordingly, under conditions of profilicity, morality is, similar to sincerity, first concerned with performance rather than with what may be hidden behind its surface. What counts is what is seen, and importantly, what is seen as being seen. The power of profiles is improved by sharing opinions and judgments. The morality of profilicity can be expressed as "political correctness," "virtue speech," or "virtue signaling," but also by violations of these, if this is what one's audience is known to prefer. Profilic morality consists in proclamations complying

with a targeted public opinion. There is no specific need to indicate "originality" or "autonomy."

Profiles are addressed to a larger, personally unknown
public—to the "general peer." Unlike in sincerity, where those
whom one knows best are in the privileged position to confirm
one's identity, in profilicity those whom one does not know personally count the most. Reviews of an Airbnb host by her family members or friends have little legitimacy, and the academic
peer review process is supposed to be "double blind" (author
and reviewer are not supposed to know each other). The general
peer is anonymous and in this sense supposedly objective, in a
way. This peer does not consist of idiosyncratic views of individuals, and especially not the biased views of close relations.
Public opinion is not the sum of the genuine opinions of each
and every person; it is what everyone knows to be the opinion
that is generally regarded as right. In this we find a crucial difference between authenticity and profilicity and their respective
ethics: authentic morality appeals to the inner conviction of
individuals, whereas profilic morality appeals to the judgments
of second-order observation. It rewards cleverness in assessing
what is *seen to be seen as* good—and the ability to express oneself
in accordance with it. Unlike sincerity, however, what is good
cannot be derived from the expectations attached to fixed social
roles. Traditional roles (such as the "dutiful wife") seem to have
lost much of their moral force, insofar as they continue to exist
at all. Instead, the good is subject to ever-shifting moral trends
that vary greatly from scene to scene.

In profilic morality the distinction between what people
really think and what they say publicly becomes obsolete. Since
the public realm is so important in profilicity, it is not a very
effective excuse to maintain that a verbal violation of moral
norms was "completely out of character." In other words, an

appeal to authenticity does not communicate well. Under conditions of profilicity, the surface is by default the real thing. The ethics of profilicity is concerned with the presentation of the self, and it is this presentation that requires curation. The superior person is the one whose opinions—on Twitter, in peer-reviewed papers, or at political demonstrations—collect the most likes. What anyone "authentically" thinks is beyond the horizon, and therefore not interesting, because, as the poet says, beyond there lies nothing, or at least nothing we can call our own.[20]

FROM BRAND TO PROFILE

Virtue speech is an essential feature of identity work on one's profile. Without a moral dimension, the profile of a person or of an organization appears incomplete. Today, not only religious practitioners or political figures are expected to have moral profiles; artists and academics must also have them. Companies and corporations certainly need them, too. Morality contributes powerfully to self-branding, or better: self-profiling.

The notion of "branding" is becoming increasingly dated. It is too one-dimensional and static. Brands traditionally indicated a manufacturer ("Ford") or a fictitious character like Uncle Ben or Aunt Jemima vouching for a product and supplying it with an identity. A brand used to be just about the presumed quality of objects and the social status they indicated—how sincerity-based this was! A car brand would suggest the class of the man who owned it, and a good housewife could confirm her role commitment by purchasing "quality" brand-name rice. Profiles reflect a much livelier and more interactive type of identity than traditional brands. Buying a Tesla, for instance, isn't just about driving an expensive electric vehicle, it carries a much richer set of values and marks investment in a certain "lifestyle." A Mac does not indicate one's social class in the traditional sense but helps reflect one's personality. Since they manufacture and market profiles, companies today must focus on curating them; they must remain dynamic, connect with their customers, and "care for" the world. They need to "communicate" and "interact" with the public and establish social validation feedback loops.

Companies today need to manage the production of their corporate identity almost more urgently than the production of their goods or services. Old-fashioned advertising is only part of the story. A profile cannot be curated merely through commercials and billboards. Companies must appeal to the general peer and aspire to be seen as, for instance, protecting the environment, supporting local communities, or embracing diversity.

Employees, like the "Mac geniuses"—the technical support staff behind the "Genius Bar" at an Apple store—are just as important elements of a company's profile as the products sold and the customers who buy them. Today, employees are required to perform identity work alongside their managerial and manual responsibilities. They display the identity of their company, which in turn becomes part of their own profiles. The profile symbiosis between employers and employees is increasingly obvious in almost every sector of the capitalist economy, including university education. While Walmart has their "greeters" wearing vests stating in big yellow letters that they are *our* people" and by virtue of this "make the difference," at a university, faculty members take on the same function. Professors, just like Mac geniuses or Walmart greeters, participate in profiling their institutions and must profile themselves accordingly.

Universities today test how invested their future academic employees are in profile work by making them write "diversity statements"—a short essay where the applicant is expected to express support for a "diverse" learning environment.[21] Schools thereby not only prepare teachers for engagement in profile-building virtue speech but also clearly signal that employment will be offered only to those who put their own profiles in the service of the profile of the institution that is going to pay them. And, like Walmart greeters, university professors readily oblige. Does this mean their diversity statements are written just to further their own profiles? If so, is that a bad thing? In profilicity, it is important to be opinionated. People need to have a clear stance on a wide range of issues. The reasons for doing so, however, can remain completely opaque.

KEEP IT REAL: THE PARADOX OF PROFILICITY

All identity modes are necessarily paradoxical—and they are useful not despite but precisely because of this characteristic. They serve to make the incongruity of human existence appear congruent. We need them to convince ourselves and others that our face is more than a mere biological coincidence further shaped by the additional coincidences of our life experiences. In fact, we inhabit bodies we did not chose, are subject to all kinds of psychological experiences that are in large part beyond our control, and need to enact multiple persona that are often in contradiction with one another. Moreover, there is no obvious match between our specific bodily shape or sex, our thoughts and feelings, and the social expectations we need to respond to. Human existence is helplessly multifarious. Nevertheless, identity needs to be achieved. We somehow need to become one and the same individual.

Sincerity achieves identity by paradoxically claiming that the social roles we find ourselves in are determined by nature, by the gods, or somehow morally correct and without alternative.

We might feel that we do not fit into a role well, but then we have ourselves to blame, not the role, and we need to try harder. The role is always right. Authenticity paradoxically claims that we can be original and independent, and find identity therein, even if this originality and independence must be copied or learned from somewhere else. Profilicity fully acknowledges that profiles are somehow "fake," they are staged—like the photo of several people jumping simultaneously at a beach. Or like a résumé or portfolio submitted for a job application. Everyone knows that these are created for a desired effect, often with the help of purchased tools or professional advice, and specifically tailored for each new attempt. And yet in profilicity, too, as with any other identity technology, once we present an identity, we are required to live up to the expectations associated with it, no matter how "fake" it is. In sincerity, we need to commit to a role. In authenticity, we need to prove how special we are. In profilicity, we need to be invested in the identity presented to the "general peer."

Profilicity operates in "social validation feedback loops": a picture posted on a social media platform, or a portfolio submitted to an employer, is a request for acceptance.[22] We humbly project our profiles and hope for positive reactions. If the reactions are negative, we can try something else, but if they are positive, there is a need to follow up on the initial proposal. Positive acceptance generates validation promises on both sides. The addressee validates the profile, but in return the profile has to be confirmed by the sender. Social media accounts are feeds requiring constant curation and updates. We are accountable for curating our social media accounts. Similarly, if an employer hires us on the basis of a professional profile, our profile is thereby validated, but continued validation is also expected from us.

In profilicity, then, validation interdependencies emerge. Social media users validate each other's profiles. These profiles are quite worthless, however, without validation feedback loops; on their own they simply have no validity. As projections, they are in need of being reflected and perceived to become real. And, in a highly accelerated society such as ours, validity is short-lived. A profile does not remain valid if it is not continuously confirmed. In today's academia, for instance, papers not cited by other scholars count little on one's CV. In fact, a mere slow-down of validation, like a declining number of "likes," can already indicate devaluation. Profile validity is fragile and unstable. The "fakeness" that lingers on behind the validated profile must be carefully erased. Otherwise it might rise to the surface. What is cool can become uncool at any moment. Profilic revaluations may happen at any time.

The paradox of profilicity bears a resemblance to fashion.[23] Fashion is always artificial, but once it becomes fashion it just seems natural. As soon as one fashion is replaced by the next, however, its artificiality comes again to the fore. We must do our best to "keep it real" as long as we can.

PICTURE PERFECT

Profilicity is not new. It existed long before the internet and did not succeed because of social media. To the contrary, social media propelled itself to the center of capitalism by exploiting the potentials of profilicity. By providing platforms for the production of profilicity for almost everyone, social media accumulated an enormous amount of financial value, outperforming almost every other sector of the economy.

A first surge of profilicity was made possible by early forms of the mass media, like books, newspapers, and journals. These media relied on the copying technology of print. Through print, images of, among other things, artworks became widely accessible and known. One no longer had to go to a big city with many churches, or to be an aristocrat, to be able to see a significant number of paintings. Along with the proliferation of printed images of paintings, the notion of the "picturesque" became popular and an influential aesthetic ideal in eighteenth- and nineteenth-century Europe. Given the increasing familiarity with an always growing range of pictures, a shift in perspective took place. Instead of comparing a picture of a landscape or a person with an actual landscape or person, one could now compare actual landscapes or persons with pictures. A reversal of the traditional hierarchy between the present and its representation took place. Rather than measuring the beauty of a picture by comparing it with "reality," one could now measure the beauty of "reality" by comparing it with pictures. This is what "picturesque" means: meeting the beauty standards of pictures, or being "picture perfect."

The logic of profilicity follows the reversal of the hierarchy between presence and representation entailed in the concept of the picturesque. The picture in fact becomes the real thing: that which is actually of interest and most valuable. In profilicity, the profile is the real thing. Profiles precede essence.

2

PROFILICITY

The Venetians of old time who made as great a mystery of love as of state affairs, have been replaced by the modern Venetians, whose most prominent characteristic is to make a mystery of nothing.

—Giacomo Casanova, *History of My Life*

GIVING AN ACCOUNT OF ONESELF: A VOCABULARY OF PROFILICITY

Postmodernist philosopher Judith Butler sees human identity as multifarious, without a defining essence. We continuously reconstruct our identities in response to what circumstances we find ourselves in. In her book *Giving an Account of Oneself* (2005), Butler also explores ethical aspects of her take on selfhood. The title means to be understood in two senses: on the one hand, people establish selfhood by recounting their lives. They tell their personal stories to themselves and others and thereby form a conception of who they are in the form of an "account." On the other hand, selfhood is also an ethical endeavor. Achieving identity amounts to becoming responsible for what one does and who one is. Selfhood makes us morally accountable.

Butler affirms that the accounts we give of ourselves are never complete. There will always be aspects of selfhood that are unknown and unknowable, that cannot be adequately expressed, or perhaps do not make sense. Ethical bonds emerge out of assuming accountability for them anyway, despite their imperfection. Moreover, we are held accountable for aspects of our selfhood that are not under our control. While many of our psychological, bodily, and social features are not of our own making, they nevertheless shape us. To assume an identity, we must also take on some form of responsibility for these. All this is particularly so since people exist in relation to others. We relate to others through giving these accounts of ourselves and allow them to relate to us. Identity is assumed and communicated in presenting incomplete and partially uncontrollable accounts of who we are to others.

Giving an Account of Oneself was first published in 2005, when social media was still in its infancy. Butler thus had not yet considered a third possible meaning of the title: to establish identity by means of personal profiles that are addressed and accessible to others—as with social media accounts. Arguably, this third meaning of "giving an account of oneself" has now eclipsed the other two in importance. Narrative and ethical dimensions of "giving an account of oneself" are still vital aspects of identity, but they are increasingly incorporated into the larger task of projecting self-portraits to a general public. These projections take on the form of an account or profile. Profilicity means assuming identity through public accounts of oneself. By presenting their profiles, people tell others and themselves who they are, and they are made accountable for it.

As with "account," some of the vocabulary that we use to analyze profilicity is related to social media. We do not thereby mean to imply that profilicity is a mere effect of social media. As mentioned, we think it has a much longer history. Nevertheless, just as the theater provided a rich metaphorical toolkit for Erving Goffman's analysis of the presentation of selfhood, we find the realm of social media, where profilicity undoubtedly flourishes, to be a valuable terminological reservoir.

Second-Order Observation: Four Dimensions

RACHEL: The real reason I didn't want to run with you is because the way that you run is just a little . . . [makes crazy motions with her body].

PHOEBE: So?

RACHEL: Well its embarrassing, people were looking at us like we were crazy.

PHOEBE: Why do you care?

RACHEL: Because they are people.

PHOEBE: But people that you don't know and will never see again.

RACHEL: Yes, but still they are people with eyes.

—*Friends*, S06, E07

SEEING WHAT OTHERS SEE

Many definitions have been given to characterize modernity and how it is different from premodern times: in terms of industrialization, capitalism, a Protestant work ethic, the shift from community to society; or alternatively, as the information age, social acceleration, risk society, and so forth. Niklas Luhmann added two items to the list: functional differentiation and second-order observation.[1] We are specifically interested in the latter and regard it as a key concept for understanding profilicity (see disclaimer in note).[2]

For Luhmann, the transition from the primacy of first-order observation to pervasive second-order observation took hundreds of years until it was eventually accomplished in the twentieth century. Figure 2.1 shows one specific instance of the transition happening much faster—within a mere seven years.

The two pictures, posted by "The Theme Park Guy" Stefan Zwanzger on his blog (thethemeparkguy.com/blog), were taken at the very same spot at a Chinese theme park, the first one in 2010, and the second in 2017. They show people watching a performance. In the first picture they observe it in the mode of first-order observation—they look directly at it. In the second one, everyone adopts second-order observation—that is, everyone except the small child in the foreground, who is apparently not yet well-versed in observing observations. Rather than

FIGURE 2.1 People in a theme park in Shenzhen, China. Photo from Stefan Zwanzger's Theme Park Guy blog, entry of December 5, 2018, http://www.thethemeparkguy.com/blog/view.html?bid=21. Reproduced by permission of Stefan Zwanzger.

watching the performance directly, the audience in 2017 looks at it through their cellphones, thereby seeing it as it is being seen, or will be seen, by those who will watch the show as posted on a social media account or other online platforms.

It might be tempting, following a common critique of cellphone and social media use, to analyze the two pictures in terms of a decay of authenticity. As with the case of photo-editing apps, however, this is not our intention here. Our point is simply to provide a concrete illustration of second-order observation. As opposed to seeing and being seen directly, second-order observation sees something, or oneself, as being seen. It observes something, or oneself, indirectly, by observing it from the perspective of other observers. Thereby the complexity of the observation is significantly increased—as is shown by the difference between the attention and tension in the faces of the 2017 audience as opposed to the relaxation and joy of the 2010 spectators. In second-order observation, both the object and its observer are taken into account and are simultaneously considered. It is not so easy.

In his *Introduction to Systems Theory* (2013), Luhmann states that at the end of the twentieth century basically all social systems have adopted second-order observation: "The observation of the observers—that is a shift from a consciousness of reality to a description of descriptions, or the perception of what others say or do not say—has become the advanced mode of perceiving the world in modern society. This is true in all major functional domains, in academia no less than in the economy, in art as much as in politics." More simply put, this is to say: "You get your information on the facts merely by looking at what others have to say about it." This is, indeed, how we know about global warming, economic trends, Oscar winners, or the latest controversies in politics. Truly, "We no longer need to know what the world is like once we know how it is being seen and once we are capable of orienting ourselves in the realm of second-order observation."[3]

Every academic, for instance, knows that we do not need to actually read our colleagues' work to know about their academic stance and standing. We simply check where they published, whom they quote, and by whom they are quoted, and maybe we also look at their H-index (a numerical score indicating the impact of a scholar's works based on counting how often they are cited) on their Google Scholar profile. As professional academics, we orient ourselves according to the conditions of systemic second-order observation. On its terms we identify one another just by looking at our academic profiles. The observation mode of today's academics parallels that of contemporary theme park goers.

SEEN AS BEING SEEN (OR: THE MISDIAGNOSIS OF NARCISSISM)

Second-order observation is complex. Looking at the world indirectly through mechanisms of second-order observation does not mean that we do not also look at it directly. We look at pictures of people and at accounts of the facts, and we also look at people and facts themselves. We look at both levels. As academics, for instance, we not only check publication lists or citation metrics. From time to time, we still read an actual article or book. But often we cannot but read this article or book in the light of the author's academic profile. The two perspectives of first- and second-order observation are intrinsically intertwined and hardly separable. Second-order observation incorporates first-order observation—and shapes it. Even if we see things directly, we still tend to see them in the light of how they are being seen.

Importantly, under conditions of second-order observation, we see ourselves in this complex fashion as well. Just as we look at others with consideration of how they are seen, we also must consider how we are being seen. At least we need to do so if, to quote Luhmann again, we operate "in the advanced mode of perceiving the world in modern society." The *advanced* mode of observation looks at something by taking into account that it is seen and how it is being seen—that is, by taking account of its profilic dimensions. The observer—or being seen—is always part of the equation. And once we are "orienting ourselves in this realm of second-order observation," our own self-observation, too, will be profile-oriented.

When applied to one's self-image, and thereby to one's identity, the concern with being seen has been depicted as a form of "narcissism." Moral objections to a preoccupation with one's own beauty or appeal to others have a long history—as the very term "narcissism" indicates. In the Greek myth, Narcissus comes to a sad and final end as a result of infatuation with his own image. In Christianity, too, as in many other religions and ethical traditions, vanity is regarded as a most serious moral flaw. It is seen as a pathology expressing sinful selfishness. This makes sense, particularly in the role-based social contexts of sincerity. Here, people are valued for their level of commitment to their roles (as, for instance, a loyal soldier, devoted priest, or dedicated mother). Being overly concerned with oneself and one's own image can easily be regarded as detrimental to a sincerity ethos. It threatens to subvert role commitment and unduly promote pride and even self-interest.

A modern version of the moral condemnation of narcissism was presented by Christopher Lasch who, as a cultural conservative with leftist communitarian leanings, could be regarded as a representative of an early wave of New Sincerity.[4] Lasch chastised post–Second World War America as having fallen prey to a *Culture of Narcissism* (1979), as his bestseller was titled. Current moral condemnations of selfie-taking and related social media phenomena represent a new variation of the very same age-old moral trope. From our own perspective, such moral posturing is misplaced. Rather than being a case of mass narcissism, the concern with one's self-image and profile reflects first and foremost the social proliferation of second-order observation. It has taken hold in all social systems, including the "intimacy system" of personal relations. To perceive that one is seen, and how one is seen, is only rational in a society where second-order observation prevails. In fact, it represents an advanced mode of perception that is more complex, more socially attuned, and therefore more mature than clinging to the problematic notion of some authentic appearance, or personal identity, which is supposed to exist independently of being seen. Arguably, the idea that there is such an original appearance of oneself, unseen by others, totally unaffected by society's gaze—or, in other words, the idea that one can exist in society without vanity, with no concern at all for how one appears to others, devoid of any reputation—can be regarded as much more vain and selfish than simply accepting that one's own image emerges only through the observations of others.[5]

I SPY: SEEING WHAT OTHERS DO NOT SEE

In German, the children's game "I spy" is called *Ich sehe was, was du nicht siehst*—or, I see something that you do not see. This nicely captures another aspect of second-order observation. When observing something as seen by observers, we also observe these observers. And by observing them, we can see not only what they see, and how they see it, but also what they fail to see—like the philosopher Zhuangzi observing how a mantis catching a cicada fails to see that it is simultaneously being hunted by a magpie.[6] We thereby become critical observers. Indeed, second-order observation is inherently critical. And this is important: it makes modern society critical—although probably not in a sense the eighteenth-century Enlightenment thinkers worked to develop.

The notion of second-order observation can well be regarded as founded on the "Copernican Turn" that Immanuel Kant intended to implement in philosophy. Kant considered all philosophy (or rather all metaphysics) prior to his own a failure since it had not generated any reliable knowledge—unlike the emerging modern natural sciences. This failure was, Kant believed, methodological. Traditional metaphysics had attempted to gain insights into metaphysical truths (such as truths about God) without sufficiently considering the means by which such truths are arrived at, namely, reason. Although he did not use these concepts, Kant's Copernican turn was in essence a plea to switch from first-order observation to second-order observation in philosophy. Rather than focusing right away on the world that we want to understand, we need to start investigating the faculty by which we understand the world in the first place. This is, for Kant, the meaning of "critique": a reflection on how something can be known—or "seen." Reason must clarify what it can see, and, importantly, what it cannot (e.g., God). In this way, modern second-order observation is closely tied to critique: a critical consciousness of the limits of seeing emerges.

Second-order observers are highly critical. Once we realize that we do not watch the world directly but as it is presented to us, we are in a position to question how and why it is presented in the way it is being presented. This is not really possible in the mode of first-order observation where the world appears as a matter of fact. In second-order observation, facts are replaced by presentations of facts. This difference is crucial. In second-order observation we are aware, for instance, that a photo has been staged, edited, and displayed for a specific purpose. We learn to judge if this presentation is accurate, or in accordance with expectations or norms. When we look at photos, of, say, an Airbnb posting, we develop a critical understanding of how and why these photos were made and presented. This allows us to critically interpret them. Of course we will expect that they are somehow "truthful" (and do not, for instance, show a different property from the one advertised), but we will also understand that the sun will not necessarily be shining when we get there, even though it is shining in the photo. And we will understand that we can never see the whole house or apartment in the photos. A photo needs to be taken from a specific point of view and can show only so much. It can show only one specific spot at one specific time. And this means it can show something only by not showing something else.

The inherently critical nature of second-order observation can be illustrated with reference to the comment function on many traditional and social media sites. Below a YouTube video or online news report, we find critical comments on the material, and critical comments on these critical comments ("replies"). These comments typically put the video or article in perspective. They comment on what, for instance, the video shows, and often on what it does not show as well. Thus a multiplicity of perspectives is generated, and therein a consciousness of perspective emerges. "Orienting ourselves in the realm of second-order observation" represents an *advanced* mode of perceiving the world in modern society" precisely because it means recognizing a perspective as a perspective. And there is critical potential tied to this recognition. Under conditions of second-order observation, a critical awareness of perspectives evolves.

SEEING MULTIPLICITY AND INCONGRUITY

Insofar as it is critical, in the sense of reflecting on the conditions of the possibility of seeing and presenting something as real, second-order observation is rather Kantian. However, it moves far beyond Kant in an important way: by developing a consciousness of perspectives and blind spots, second-order observation acknowledges that there is no "transcendental" structure (of reason, or anything comparable to reason) that serves as the common foundation of all perspectives. In second-order observation, there is no ultimate unity that encloses or informs all perspectives. Possibilities for perspectives are endless. There is no central perspective, and there is no final word.

The multifariousness, openness, and incongruity of second-order observation are also visible on the web. There is no central website that unites all others, or provides a summary of their structure, or gives a final account of their content. There is no comment on all comments that ultimately closes all threads and brings them to conclusion. There is no set of photos on any Airbnb posting that can present the whole place to be rented just as it is—and no one expects that. Luhmann points out:

> Any observation also produces at the same time something invisible. . . . There are only shifts between what one sees and what one does not see, but there is no comprehensive enlightening or scientific elucidation of the world as the totality of things, or of forms, or of essences, that could be worked out piece by piece, not even if this task would be regarded as infinite. . . . In contrast, in the classical theory, the prevalent notion was that more and more knowledge could be collected and not that in order to present something specific something else needs to be obscured.[7]

In contemporary second-order observation, as opposed to its earlier predecessors, it is understood that there is no final verdict, no overarching consensus, no ultimate end, and no single "grand perspective" that includes all others. According to Luhmann, this was not yet the case in the old world. Here, or in what he calls "the classical theory," "a common given world was presupposed in the form of nature or creation" (102). Second-order observation did exist—people would inform themselves about the world, for instance, by listening to what priests or people who could read would tell them—but this did not necessarily result in critical reflections on why people were told what they were told, or in realizing a multiplicity of perspectives. In contemporary all-pervasive second-order observation, it is well understood that more and more information does not lead to a complete and final set of information but, to the contrary, to an increasingly diverse multiplicity of information.[8] More and more incompatible perspectives arise. Complexity increases to the extent that one realizes that under conditions of second-order observation we will never get to see "the full picture"—simply because there is none. You cannot read the internet to the end. It has no final page.

Full-fledged second-order observation is not linear or circular but network-like or "rhizomatic," to use a metaphor coined by Gilles Deleuze and Félix Guattari. Negatively speaking, second-order observation fractures the world and makes it impossible to reduce it to one binding perspective, or rationality, or type of reason. Every second-order observation establishes its own rationales, but it does so in relation and in response to other perspectives. In the academic system, no final consensus on the truth emerges, and in the political system, there is no final agreement that establishes once and for all the arrangements of best government. Similarly, there is no definitive profile of oneself that sums up one's identity for good. Under conditions of second-order observation, profilic identity work never ends since no profile can fit all contexts and purposes. To the contrary: profilic identity has to be reshaped and re-presented continuously in accordance with the increasingly multifarious and incongruent expectations on how one needs to be seen as being seen. *common*

Second-order observation is pervasive throughout contemporary society. Profilicity is a technology for achieving identity under its conditions.

The General Peer

Being seen is different from being-seen-as-being-seen not only with respect to how one is seen but also in terms of whom one is seen by. For me to be seen directly, someone needs to be present and see me with her own eyes. In this case, I normally know the person who sees—if not personally, then at least through my also seeing her at the same time. We are both present, making us peers in that presence, and see each other eye to eye.

For both sincerity and authenticity, the presence of peers is important. That I am a good father, or a good teammate, or a good teacher needs to be confirmed by my children, my teammates, or my students. They are in a privileged position to validate my identity. In fact, that I can enact my role at all depends on their presence, and on their acknowledgment of my performance of that role. The self-presentations of the Scottish Shetland Islanders in their everyday life, as described by Erving Goffman, consisted in staged performances of, by, and for present peers. Similarly, the authentication of my authenticity must come from someone who is also authentic, and this normally includes some form of presence. Accusations of the inauthenticity of social media typically point to the merely virtual presence of others (and oneself) in the online world. Here, it is assumed, the lack of physical presence makes others somehow less valid in serving as peers.

Under conditions of profilicity, the criteria of validity for serving as a peer change rather drastically. When the point is no longer to be seen but rather to be seen as being seen, then the actual presence of a peer becomes less important. It is taken for granted that my immediate peers see me anyway. My public profiles are not really addressed to them, so they do not really count as relevant observers. The success of an academic publication is not measured by the acclaim I might get from my former students or departmental colleagues. In fact, people one knows well are often explicitly excluded by the so-called double-blind peer-review process (where an essay is evaluated by academics before it is published while authors and reviewers of the essay remain unknown to one another) to make sure that there is no personal bias. The same is true for, let's say, a restaurant review on Yelp. Ratings and rankings by friends or family members do not (or should not) count because they are regarded as unrepresentative of the general peer. Profilic identity value depends not on being seen by those who are present but, to the contrary, on being-seen-as-being-seen by those who are not present, who are not here with me, who are not my family members, coworkers, or classmates. Like the academic peer-review process, the general peer review process, too, is "double-blind": we orient profiles toward those we do not know personally, and who do not know us.[9]

The general peer resembles the *general will*, or *volonté générale*, in that it does not refer to any actual and particular individual but to a transpersonal collective. Jean-Jacques Rousseau coined the notion of the *volonté générale* in order to indicate something other than the mere sum of the individual preferences of particular persons. For him, politics needed to be grounded in the common interest of a community that might well transcend the specific personal desires of any single member. The general will does not need to be consciously known by each and every person. It is determined by common sense—and thus not by individual sense.[10] In fact, particular interests may easily obscure or try to manipulate the general will. Therefore it needs to be protected against interference by individuals whose wills are too strong and who might therefore have a "conflict of interest" with the general will.

The general peer, similar to the general will, is an impersonal abstraction. It can manifest itself only in larger quantities, not in singular instances. The popularity of a YouTube video or a Google Scholar profile is not, and cannot be, measured by the authenticity or sincerity of the individual responses to it but only by the aggregated number of clicks or the citation metrics it boasts. The statistical data generated by posts and profiles do not tell us what anyone in particular thinks or has thought. They are not, literally, "artificial *intelligence*" but rather, as Elena Esposito says, "artificial communication."[11] They show what happens in society rather than in the mind. Similarly, the general peer is not constituted by individuals and their particular ideas or feelings; it is, instead, a collective communicative performance. It can be measured in data, but it does not reflect personal consciousness.

If you have ever seen *American Idol* or a similar a talent show on TV, you watched the general peer in action—in the form of a jury of celebrities guiding and shaping public taste.[12] Such jurors are "real"—after all, it's a reality show—but they all participate in a staged public performance. Nothing about them is simply authentic or sincere. They act out their TV personas as a "front stage" theatric representation of the general peer, consisting of different genders, races, and temperaments.[13] In this function they cooperate with the studio audience typically seen behind them. Together, the judges and the audience display approval and disapproval of the contestants. They symbolically manifest a wider and more dynamic dimension of the general peer. The judges in conjunction with the studio audience invite those who watch the show at home to join in with them. Via the staged judges and studio audience, TV viewers can enter the picture and unite with the general peer. A talent show is a public performance that enables anyone to align themselves with the general peer and engage in a staged form of mass profilicity. The general peer remains anonymous to the actual contestants, and the contestants present only a public profile of themselves while remaining personally unrelated to the general peer.

Peers are system specific. Each social realm has its own general peer (and there are subsets within these groups). When judging musical performances on *American Idol*, the *American Idol* general peer has to be imagined. When reviewing a paper submission for an academic journal, one is asked to envision the academic general peer. In fact, journal editors often remind their reviewers of this. You should check your personal biases and instead adhere to the expected standards of your research community. These standards, however, are hardly ever concretely defined since the general peer, being an abstraction, defies concreteness. The *Review of Contemporary Philosophy* explicitly acknowledges the power of the abstract general academic peer by stipulating to potential contributors that it will accept only papers promising decent publication metrics: "This journal considers only manuscripts having a high integrative value in the current Scopus- and Web of Science-indexed literature."[14]

The general peer is the audience to which profilic identity is presented. It is impersonal, is nonpresent, and—as peers do—varies from context to context.

Social Validation Feedback Loops

In a discussion on the news website Axios, Sean Parker, the first president of Facebook, revealed the "thought process" behind the construction of this major social media platform.[15] Parker said that he and the other creators of Facebook were trying to find a way to "consume as much of your time and conscious attention as possible." In other words, they wanted to construct a medium that would get people addicted—at least this is what Parker suggested when he continued to explain: "And that means that we need to sort of give you a little dopamine hit every once in a while."[16] The addictiveness should be as widespread and mainstream as possible, and not be built on something illicit or morally questionable such as pornography or gambling. As Parker candidly stresses, the idea was about finding and "exploiting a vulnerability in human psychology." Parker, however, is not a social scientist or philosopher, and it is therefore unsurprising that he fails to mention other important dimensions of his pursuit. More appropriately, he should have said that he and his colleagues were looking to exploit not only a psychological but also a sociological and existential vulnerability. Ultimately, the "vulnerability" they homed in on was the human need to build identity—and to do so under postsincere and postauthentic conditions. This is what Facebook set out to do: provide a global online forum for everyone in the world to perform their profilic identity work.

When speaking about a "dopamine hit," Parker implies that Facebook mainly operates as a provider of neuro-physiological triggers. This, again, seems too narrowly conceived as an explanation for what Facebook actually does. In Parker's own words, beyond providing physiological triggers, Facebook is also a communication engine: people get hooked to it "because someone

liked or commented on a photo, or a post, or whatever. And that's
going to get you to contribute more content, and that's going to
get you, you know, more likes and comments." Eventually, Parker
moves from the physiological to the social realm and suggests
the concept of a "social validation feedback loop" to sum up what
Facebook is and does. This concept, we think, is an excellent
description of Facebook. Moreover, it is a core aspect of profilicity. Personal identity needs to be socially validated. Under conditions of sincerity or authenticity, this validation can come from
present peers—such as family members and personal friends.
Under conditions of profilicity, one must appeal to the general
peer for identity validation. As it is well known, on Facebook,
the notion of "friend" took on a whole new meaning. It switched
from first-order to second-order observation friendship, in which
we share and assess profiles that are oriented toward general,
rather than present, peers. By providing a platform for the general peer to assemble, social validation feedback loops could
take off.

"No portrait is more intensely drawn . . . than the self-
portrait," writes Timothy Mo.[17] Not only are people captivated
by drawing their own images, they have an equally intense
interest in observing reactions to it. Beyond the mere physiological experience of a dopamine "high," positive reactions to
one's publicly presented self-portrait, or, to speak with Goffman again, to the "presentation of self in everyday life," are crucial for the emergence and maintenance of self-identity. This is
why the addiction is so strong, and far more than merely physiological. It is possible to continue to be oneself without the next
nicotine, alcohol, or even heroin fix. Indeed, one may even
seem to be more oneself without these. But it is much harder to
continue being oneself without validation of one's identity,

especially since we continuously form our identities precisely through such validation. Facebook and other social media sites flourish because they provide new technology for social-psychological identity formation. This technology operates on the basis of second-order observation and self-projection toward the general peer, making it perfectly adapted to conditions of profilicity. While dopamine may play its part in how Facebook and similar networks function, social media thrive within the much wider and more complex framework of social-psychological structures and function on a much broader scale than mere brain chemistry. The social validation function that Parker rightly sees at the heart of Facebook's addictive effects offers as its reward more than a mere feeling. It offers affirmation of our *identity*, of who we are. This makes the addiction extremely powerful.

Social media users' identity work consists in a feedback loop of posting, liking, commenting, or "whatever," to paraphrase Parker. It is simultaneously work on one's self-image and work for the general peer. By commenting on someone else's profile, we contribute both to the validation of that profile and to the projection of our own. Every comment can draw further comments. On social media, every "user" (interestingly enough, the term "user" is also a reference for drug addicts) is both a profilic self-presenter and a constituent of the general peer. This makes social media strikingly different from traditional mass media like books, TV, or movies. There, the roles of presenter and audience are separate. Social media, to the contrary, is "interactive." It achieves a higher level of personal involvement and provides a more intense forum for identity work. It makes everyone a participant in the mass production of profilicity. Profilic identity work establishes social validation feedback loops where the roles of profile-presenter and general peer merge.

Accounts

To function well in today's economy, you need to have a bank account—along with PayPal, Apple Pay, Alipay, or WeChat accounts. To have a social life, and a career, it is increasingly indispensable to have social media accounts. These accounts are necessary to assembling profiles. An account is a virtual space owned, or rather occupied, by a person, a company, or an organization, like an apartment in a huge building. We present profiles within the confines of such accounts.

As Judith Butler points out in *Giving an Account of Oneself,* personal accounts also assign responsibility. By becoming an account holder, one becomes accountable just as much in social media as in banking. Ownership of one's profile and social media identity, similar to ownership of wealth and financial identity, involves subjecting oneself to rules and regulations, to social institutions, and to behavioral and normative expectations. A social media account functions similarly to an ID card or social security number in the political or legal sphere. It is a basic form of identification that allows one to assume a preformatted profile (name, date of birth, gender, nationality, and so forth) and at the same time also imposes responsibilities on the individual. As a citizen of a state, one can be taxed and fined. Social media accounts, just as citizenship or a bank account, can be revoked by the relevant authorities for violation of the terms of holding that account. Personal and institutional profiles are ascribed to account holders within the social system, by the authorities or company that acts as the provider of the account. Thereby the profiles presented "on (the front) stage" through an account become morally, legally, and economically chargeable to their holders. And thereby the organization that provides accounts is extremely powerful, politically, economical, and existentially. If you want to make a lot of money, or exert a lot of control, you should become a provider of accounts.

An "account" indicates a social space and format for the generation and presentation of identity profiles. Outside of such an account, profiles cannot be effectively put together or communicated to others. All social systems operate through such accounts. In the political system an account is "opened" with a birth certificate. As a student or professor, the university supplies me with a university ID. Once an account within the educational system is set up, a person's academic profile can be established.

Profiles

A profile is a type of self-image that is not just seen but seen as being seen. It is made and presented intentionally for this purpose. Under conditions of sincerity, I can act in accordance with my role and present myself, for instance, as a dedicated researcher to my colleagues. Then, hopefully, they will see me in this way and thereby confirm my identity. Under conditions of authenticity, I can express my inner self by biking up Mount Rainier. Eventually, hopefully, my friends will recognize my uniquely adventurous personality. In profilicity, I may do all the same things, but I need to broadcast them as part of my profile for them to count in a relevant way. This can be done by listing my achievements on Academica.edu or tracking my bike ride and posting it on Instagram.

A profile is an obviously selected and edited form of self-presentation that is undertaken for the sake of self-presentation. I present who I am in accordance with the format and aims of the account. Everybody recognizes the profilic conditions of the production of these profiles because they appear in public forums populated by the general peer. Here, everyone is tied into the same "social validation feedback loops" and produces their own profiles in the very same way.

Profiles are identity projections that are communicated under conditions of second-order observation. Since practically all social systems today function with second-order observation, most of us need to work on the level of such identity projections: we introduce and evaluate one another through profiles. Whenever we open an account, literally on a website or figuratively in a professional context, we need to project our profiles in order to become identifiable and assume an identity.

Profiles are just as multifarious and incongruent as social roles under conditions of sincerity. Each different social context requires a different profile in a different format. Unlike traditional social roles, however, profiles are hardly concentric or in correspondence with one another. In traditional social contexts, professions were often inherited and roles in the family and the profession were related. A Tinder profile, however, has very little bearing on an Academia.edu profile, and vice versa. In a highly differentiated society, profiles need to be highly differentiated as well. To achieve identity in various social areas, professional and private, competence in profile diversity is necessary.

Feeds

Many websites are no longer page oriented. They instead comprise feeds. The internet is dynamic and hungry, devouring information as soon as it is fed. The feed allows viewers to consume quickly as well.

According to Niklas Luhmann, social systems can be identified on the basis of the "code" with which they operate. In the legal system, for instance, communication is generated on the basis of the simple code legal/illegal. And in academia, we discuss whether something is true or not. Right? The codes of these two systems are relatively stable. Of course, things that are legal may eventually become illegal, or vice versa—for example, drinking and driving, or smoking marijuana. And in the academic system, a lot of that which was once true is now false, and the other way around. Nevertheless, there is a certain stability on the two sides of the code in both the law and the sciences. It took a long time to legalize marijuana, and it is not now foreseeable that drunk driving will ever become legal again. This is decisively different in mass media—and even more so in the forms of social media that evolved in their wake.

Luhmann hardly noticed social media, since it had not evolved much by the time of his death. He did write a book on the systemic dynamics of mass media, though: a first edition of *The Reality of the Mass Media* was published (in German) in 1995.[18] Here, he defines the code of the mass media system as information/noninformation. This code is rather peculiar due to one specific characteristic: once information has been communicated, it is immediately transformed into noninformation: "A news item run twice retains its meaning, but it loses its information value."[19] This most crucial feature of the mass media system, the immediate self-reversal of its code through communication, is carried on into social media. Therefore, through their code sharing with the mass media system, they may be regarded as an evolutionary development of mass media. It is crucial to stress: information, in this sense, does not simply indicate an item of "meaning." I can look at the same picture of a cat again and it still makes sense in the same way, but it has lost its information value because I have seen it before. Precisely because of this split between "sense value" and "information value," mass media and social media work unlike many other systems, such as law or academia. This is also what makes them so hungry. Information immediately destructs itself and needs to be replaced by new information. And so many websites are now feeds.

The self-destructive mode built into the information/noninformation code distinguishes mass and social media from, for instance, law and academia. But it makes them similar to another highly important social system in today's world, the economy: "Just as the economy . . . generates the never-ending need to replace money spent, so the mass media generate the need to replace redundant information with new information: fresh money and new information are two central motives of modern social dynamics."[20] The economy is a restless system because it compels us to make money just so we can spend it. To make it count, we need to give it away. The theoreticians Paul Virilio and Hartmut Rosa have made social acceleration the core concept of their respective analyses of modernity, showing it to be an effect of how the economy and media system function. Along with the evolution of mass media into social media, this acceleration has once more accelerated and now been brought not only into every person's wallet but also into their cellphones and computers. It has become a most integral aspect of human experience in modern society.

The web feed is the pacemaker of contemporary life. Along with the acceleration mechanisms of other social systems, such as the economy, online feeds regulate the heartbeat of social experience. Given the close ties between profilicity and social media, this means that personal identity, too, must be fed. Our profilic self-portraits demand more intense attention than ever before. In sincerity and authenticity, identity needs to be maintained and developed, but it is not subjected to the same feeding frenzy as in profilicity. Profilic identity, on and off the web, is to a large extent constituted by information, not simply by meaning. It needs to be constantly updated. A publication list that has no recent publications is worthless. A résumé that is blank for the past year will not get you a job. A new trip, a new activity, a new feeling are crucial to maintaining an active and presentable personal profile.

Memes

The concept of a meme was originally introduced by Richard Dawkins in *The Selfish Gene* (1976), the book that made him famous and which has become somewhat of a meme itself. Here Dawkins, an evolutionary biologist, coined the term "meme" in analogy to "gene." A gene is a biological unit that replicates itself and thereby plays a central role in the reproduction of life. Dawkins thought that a similar element must exist in society, or "culture" (as he tended to say somewhat imprecisely), and that this must be equally crucial for social evolution. Thus he originally conceived of "memes" as cultural items such as certain skills or ways of doing or making things, or as artistic creations, such as melodies, that could be imitated and thereby replicated to spread over time and space. The term soon became popular beyond its academic usage and was eventually applied to "internet culture" as well. Today, in loose connection with its original meaning in Dawkins's work, it indicates "an idea, image, video, etc. that is spread very quickly on the Internet."[21] In an interview with the magazine *Wired* in 2013, Dawkins expressed his approval of the evolution of his concept: "The meaning is not that far away from the original. It's anything that goes viral. In the original introduction to the word meme in the last chapter of *The Selfish Gene*, I did actually use the metaphor of a virus. So when anybody talks about something going viral on the Internet, that is exactly what a meme is and it looks as though the word has been appropriated for a subset of that."[22] Interestingly enough, the notions of "meme" and "going viral" both connect the realm of social media with biology. They connect the body with society and point toward the phenomenon of identity. Identity is physiologically embedded and can be proliferated and extended by "spreading one's genes." It would be tempting to say that the biological identity formation and procreation that occurs through genes finds its social-psychological counterpart in the identity formation and procreation that occurs through memes in "culture," and especially on the internet. Just as humans have a biological urge to affirm and extend themselves by passing on their genes, they seem to also have a social urge to pass on their memes to others. In this way, the proliferation of profiles, on and off the web, could be regarded as an attempt to create identity memes with the intent to spread them as far as possible. This would explain the "orgasmic" experience of seeing one's "idea, image, video, etc." going viral.

Next to giving joy, the successful spreading of one's memes is perhaps perceived as particularly satisfying because it can promise relief from the constant burden to feed one's profile. It may seem that once one's profile has gone viral the pressure to constantly create new information would cease. One is already seen as being seen. However, this hope is often not realistic. Just as making a lot of money usually does not quench the thirst for riches, the hunger of the profile is not likely to end just when it has tasted success.

Casting

When Erving Goffman described self-presentation in daily life using terms from theatric performance, he said little or nothing about an aspect of the production that has since gained much prominence in TV and cinema, namely, the casting process.[23] For Goffman, who worked in a sincerity-based community, casting was not really an issue because most actors had already been assigned to roles by birth or by other coincidences, such as semi-inherited social status. There was little necessity, or possibility, of choosing to play a certain character; the point was to effectively enact the social role one found oneself in.

In TV and cinema, as well as in postsincerity society, things changed and the jostling for roles became more competitive. In addition, due to technological reproduction, the audience became much larger than it had been in traditional theater and was no longer actually present to witness the performance. It took on features of the general peer. This, too, made casting more relevant, since appealing to an audience became more competitive as well. To be sure, theater also had its celebrities, but not on the global scale we now see with the movie industry. Today, actors tend to be more important than their roles. As a celebrity, an actor's profile value is conferred to the movie. Casting is a profile symbiosis: it designs the profile of a movie, while being cast shapes the profiles of the actors.

Under conditions of profilicity, identity work takes on features of casting. The focus is less on how to play a preassigned role well, and more on how to choose wisely which role to play. To choose a travel destination, for instance, can be a way of casting oneself. When deciding between going to Florence or Florida for the holidays, one may (also) consider the different effects the respective trip will produce on one's social media account. In sincerity, as well as in traditional theater, actors had to adapt to their assigned roles. In today's movie industry, as well as in profilicity, it becomes more important to be able to cast oneself successfully into a marketable script. And particular markets, for instance, the academic job market, may well value the public profile and profilic fit of an applicant higher than his or her professional skills.

Curating

"If you don't have a persona, it's hard to be a person," say Giovanni Formilan and David Stark in an intriguing study on contemporary electronic musicians.[24] With a number of case studies they document how artists in this music genre tend to make use of multiple aliases to perform in different styles and as different personas. DJ Wey, Louis, DJ Python, and DJ Xanax are four artistic personas of one and the same real-life person, Brian Piñeyro from Queens, New York City. It is even typical for an artist to change from one such persona to another (and perhaps another and another) during the same event.

Electronic musicians, as Formilan and Stark's analysis shows, are identity virtuosos who manage to enact a variety of personas. Different relationships are developed between these personas, the artist's own person, and the audience. A highly dynamic identity framework emerges: multiple "moments of identity" become possible, modulated by the degree of dedication to the persona by the artist and the audience. If, for instance, Brian Piñeyro feels personally attached to DJ Python during a show, and the audience is intensely involved with the interplay between him and his persona, then an "engaged" moment of identity takes place. Alternatively, Brian Piñeyro may develop a distance from DJ Xanax and the audience may have no interest in the person behind the music and attend exclusively to DJ Xanax. In this way, an impersonal "anonymous" moment of identity is constituted.

Through the complex relationship between the three poles of person, persona, and audience, identity is experienced via the presentation of personas. This is why it is impossible to be a person without assembling a persona—or, better, various personas. And, as Formilan and Stark point out, this is the case not only for performers of electronic music but for everyone. Artists may be especially good at creating and presenting distinct personas, but "developing a convincing persona has become . . . a must for everyone who wants to participate in social exchange" (3). It is socially useful to "maintain and manage a good many personas," and this is also true beyond art and the internet, because their "simultaneous enactment . . . permeates the social dimensions of most of us" (3–4). We all need to cultivate identity virtuosity.

Formilan and Stark use a highly pertinent word to describe the kind of identity work that goes into constructing and presenting personas. Personas are "*curated*." Under conditions of profilicity (Formilan and Stark call it "projected identity"), a persona is "intended as a test put out into the society and continuously revised, updated, refined. Out of this process, identity develops as a curatorship" (9).

A curator, in a common contemporary sense of the word, is the person in charge of an (art) exhibition. The word goes back to the Latin verb *curare*, meaning to "take care of." A curator manages public exhibitions. This includes the selection of what is shown, how and when it is displayed to whom and where, and the context of its presentation. As a caretaker, though, it is implied that a curator will also *care about* what it is exhibited. It will mean something to her. Like an artist, she will, to a varying extent, identify with and be attached to what she shows to other people. She will be emotionally invested in an exhibition, worry about it, and perhaps love it or hate it. This implies that she also *cares for* it. She will be constantly involved with it. The relation is ongoing and demands continuous attention, supervision, and, if necessary, interference. Curation means taking care of an exhibition in all three senses. The relation between persons and the personas they show in public is very similar to that between curators and their exhibits.

Importantly, while taking care of an exhibition in such an encompassing way, a curator remains, to use Goffman's term, "back stage." This signals a *distinctive distance* between what is exhibited on the "front stage" and the exhibitor who works behind the scene. A curator is *not* an exhibitionist exposing himself. The person is, by definition, distinct from the persona. In this way, as Formilan and Stark highlight, "curation is ultimately a non-authenticity process" (9). Under conditions of profilicity, the difference between persona and person is *understood*—by both person and audience—in the same way as the difference between a curator and what she exhibits. Both the curator and the audience are aware of this difference. Despite the attachment and identification involved and acknowledged in exhibitions, authenticity is, in a strict sense, never intended in curatorship. It is therefore nonauthentic but not inauthentic.

The notion of curatorship is pertinent for understanding profilicity because it expresses nonauthenticity rather than inauthenticity. Persons manage their personas and profiles, are emotionally invested in them, and are constantly involved in staging their presentation. Personas and their profiles are exhibited like public works of art; they must be taken care of, cared about, and cared for.

THE TIMELINESS OF PROFILICITY

With the help of the vocabulary just outlined, it is possible to see how and why profilicity is in a position to outdo sincerity and authenticity as an identity technology today. It is the right time for profilicity to flourish.

(this Thesis)

In a highly diverse society, it is important to be able to curate different personas that work in various and often unrelated social spheres. In a highly accelerated society, it is important to make identity flexible. Profiles can easily do this: we can have several at the same time, and they can all be constantly "fed"—that is, changed, updated, or deleted.

Profilicity corresponds to today's "transparency society" and "surveillance society" where we are constantly monitored. Profiles are intended for exhibition to the general peer and are subject to the categories and labels that algorithms and artificial intelligence impose. But because they are intentionally curated and made to be shown, it is a misconception to regard them as lethal threats to privacy or autonomy. They do not reveal any innermost core, nor do they abolish agency altogether.

Modern society is "democratic": it invites public participation and evaluation. Individuals expect to be heard and seen. Profilicity is inherently democratic as well. Profiles provide opportunities to constantly engage in evaluation, to express opinions and judgments, to rate and rank, and to thereby interact with and contribute as a constituent of the general peer.

Diversity

From the perspective of authenticity, Brian Piñeyro and his fellow electronic musicians could be denounced as inauthentic—as posers, fakes, or sellouts. Rather than expressing who they really are, they produce certain show effects to please an audience in as many ways as possible, curating the different personas they put on stage. And they do so to become famous and make money. From a sincerity perspective, they could be condemned as narcissists, fascinated by their own images and vainly displaying their insincere self-projections. But it is inappropriate to conceive of what is going on in the electronic music scene in terms of authenticity or sincerity. This music scene is neither inauthentic nor authentic; it is nonauthentic. It is likewise neither insincere nor sincere but rather nonsincere. These performances are concerned with neither authentic self-expression nor sincere fulfillment of roles. And in this way they resemble so many other "scenes" of contemporary social life.

Formilan and Stark succinctly point out the convergence of identity virtuosity in the electronic music scene with the social structures of our times: "As individuals participate in diverse contexts (i.e., multiple working environments), they project a number of diversely curated personas onto each of them" (10). *This* is, seen in a wider perspective, what can be learned from identity performance in electronic music: the multiple working environments of today's society require the capacity to develop appropriate personas for each of them. From a theoretical perspective, this means that in a highly differentiated society, the most useful identity technology is profilicity. Sincerity and authenticity do not work that well here. They are not flexible enough and do not allow for enough self-diversification.

In a sincerity-based society, the social persona of an individual is determined by available social roles. Once one is born into the role of daughter, it is expected that one will develop a persona in accordance with this gender role. Multiple personas are possible—daughter, mother, Christian, shopkeeper—but they all ought to correspond to patterned roles. In an authenticity-based society, everyone is expected to find or create their own original self. Again, multiple personas are possible, for instance, one may have an especially creative self and be capable of being original in different ways—as both landscaper and Olympic figure skater—but these personas are all supposed to be rooted in the same true self. In a highly differentiated society, such dedication to a supposedly unified underlying self is no longer functional or even credible. Instead, people are required to develop the flexibility to adapt to different "working environments." One can be a postdoctoral fellow at a university during the day, a girlfriend in the evening, a DJ later that night, and a soccer player the following weekend. These identities are not expected to significantly overlap or remain stable in the long run. The postdoc contract will end in a year or two. The boyfriend may not be that committed and leave even sooner. The music scene will change, and new musical personas will have to be developed. A twenty-nine-year-old woman knows that she won't be able to play soccer on the same level or with the same team in five or six years. And each of these changes happens more or less independently of the others. Little overlap between these roles is expected.

In a highly differentiated and accelerated society, personas cannot follow stable role assignments or be grounded solely in unique and coherent selves. Instead, personas are generated in the form of flexible profiles. The "diversely curated personas" adapted to "multiple working environments" that Formilan and Stark speak of are neither role-based nor self-based. They are profilic personas. They seem inauthentic or insincere only when evaluated from the extraneous perspectives of authenticity or sincerity. Nor are they psychopathological schizophrenics. Formilan and Stark write: "It is then crucial to stress that, although projected identities entail multiple personas, they are not *fragmented* identities, since that phrase could suggest that there is some core identity that has been broken into pieces that might or might not be put back together" (11). This, too, is a crucial observation that helps to distinguish profilicity from sincerity and authenticity, and, accordingly, the profilic persona from the role-based and the self-based persona. Under conditions of authenticity, it is presumed that different personas all ought to represent the same self. To a certain extent, this is also the case in sincerity, given the relative interconnectedness of social roles with one another. There is a connection between the roles of daughter, mother, Christian, and shopkeeper. They are tied together by the same "ethos," and accordingly, the emotional and intellectual commitment toward them is grounded in an overarching rationale or narrative. Under the conditions of profilicity, there is no presumption of "some core identity" informing all personas. To the contrary, such a presumption can easily become problematic. To be a good DJ at night, it may well be advisable to bracket the postdoctoral and girlfriend personas for a while—and vice versa. In profilicity, the illusion that identity is grounded in one's self or in a unified ethos is no longer maintained. Instead, identity is shaped more freely, and it is contingent on contexts. I may have certain musical talents— unrelated to my academic interests and relationship status— and given the accessibility of a music scene, I can build up one or more profilic musical personas. And, lucky me, I live in a postsincerity and postauthenticity society, so I do not need to justify myself for potentially violating an overarching ethos that may consider it unbecoming for an academic, or a loving partner, to perform at a techno club early into the morning. I also do not have to ask myself if I have become crazy or "broken into pieces" because my inner experience as a DJ persona is totally at odds with how I felt and behaved as a professional academic only a few hours before my show. Profilic personas, unlike role-based or self-based personas, should not be considered fractured simply because they are multiple and flexible. Their multiplicity and flexibility do not reflect a broken self or a shattered ethos but rather a form of identity adapted to highly diverse society.

Transparency, or Algorithms: The Mirrors of Profilicity

Transparency used to be a positively charged word. Corporations were accused of hiding their profits from the tax collector, making secret deals with one another, or concealing the horrendous working conditions of their employees—so they ought to become more transparent. Politicians were accused of implementing covert strategies, conspiring with the enemy, or being motivated by illicit funding sources—so politics, too, needed transparency. University professors were accused of shady networking, veiled harassment of students, or covering up plagiarism. Here, too, more transparency was in order. Transparency was supposed to rein in economic corruption, fight political manipulation, and clean up professional misconduct. The internet could help. More and more information would be made available and shared widely, so that eventually everyone could be held accountable. Just as Wikipedia would make knowledge transparent and accessible to everyone, WikiLeaks would reveal clandestine dealings and transactions to the world. In the economy, in politics, and in academia, people were supposed to make their profiles public, declare their income and tax payments, disclose information about professional relationships and sources of information, or simply leave the office door open whenever a student was present—all signs of embracing the value of transparency.

But that mood has shifted, and the value of transparency has come under attack by a powerful countervalue: privacy. It seems the more transparency we get, the less privacy we have left. Therefore a new need arose to balance the positive notion of "transparency" against its more sinister inverse aspect. Making use of the rich heritage of dystopian twentieth-century literature, iconically represented in George Orwell's novel *Nineteen Eighty-Four*, the notion of "surveillance society" was put forth.[25] Alongside the increasing presence of surveillance in everyday life—from airport security to traffic cameras—an increasing awareness of and discomfort with surveillance took hold, and "transparency" lost some of its good name. Reflecting this semantic shift, the Korean German author Byung-Chul Han published a short treatise titled *The Transparency Society* (2015), advertised as a "manifesto" that "denounces transparency as a false ideal."[26] In substance, the text says little more than what had already been said about "surveillance society," but it certainly contributed to further denigrating the word "transparency"—and simultaneously signals as well Han's alignment with this emerging evaluation.

Today, big data is the prime culprit of mass surveillance or "transparency society." Facebook has been accused of invading the privacy of millions of users by allowing their data to be analyzed for commercial and even politically manipulative purposes. According to the American Civil Liberties Union, there is a "danger of tipping into a genuine surveillance society completely alien to American values," and thus "a dark future" looms on the horizon "where our every move, our every transaction, our every communication is recorded, compiled, and stored away, ready to be examined and used against us by the authorities whenever they want."[27]

Whenever "American values" are mentioned, the bells of individualism and authenticity start to ring in the background. Central to these "American values" is the right to private property, most concretely manifested in one's personal space—to be protected against trespassing by anyone, and especially by the government. Our private space can now be invaded digitally not only by the government but also by companies who enter our homes via the internet and other new communication technologies.

We are not just watched, we are manipulated. Everything from steps taken and websites visited to restaurants reviewed, bars frequented, and the quality of birdseed purchased counts as valuable data about us. These data are then used to target us with personalized messages, services, deals, and discounts. But targeted advertising is only the beginning. As machine learning or artificial intelligence becomes "deeper," predictive analytics hones itself into a powerful tool. Utilizing big data, these systems develop ever more personalized diagnoses in order to influence people's decisions. Predictive advertising can reliably get people to purchase new items and services, and, importantly, make them vote for particular candidates. Thus, it seems, surveillance takes away not only our privacy but also our agency.

One of the most popular critics of the surveillance society is Shoshana Zuboff. She expresses a widespread concern when she warns against the use of algorithms to "nudge, tune, herd, manipulate, and modify behavior in specific directions" and denounces such practices as "unacceptable threats to individual autonomy."[28] The threats Zuboff identifies are real. The question is, however, if the "American values" and "individual autonomy" supposedly at stake here were ever adequately protected in the first place. Were these more than mere narratives employed to convince ourselves of a model of identity that once dominated an era? Rather than seeing the success of big data and rise of the "surveillance society" as signaling the end of authenticity and the curbing of our individual autonomy, we might see them as the end of the period in which we could credibly conceive of ourselves in this way. Maybe, given the social and technological developments of recent decades, it no longer makes much sense to speak of human beings as "autonomous individuals"; and maybe we must realize that we exist in a highly complex society and are embedded deeply in its social networks. Therein control, especially by the single individual, is limited. How we look and what we think and feel are highly contingent upon the lifeworld we inhabit, and it seems much of these aspects of life are simply not up to us. Maybe they never were.

The current critics of surveillance tend to speak mostly in negative terms about the effects of new artificial intelligence technologies on individuals and society: surveillance undercuts autonomy and makes everything inauthentic. From the perspective of authenticity, this observation is correct. But this perspective also implies a nostalgia for the authentic self and an idealization of "individual autonomy," neither of which can be fully realized—or ever could have been. This false memory, the desire to "make the self great again," is blind to the shift toward profilic identity. The functioning of surveillance society cannot really be understood if it is measured against the ideal of authenticity. Instead, the rise of surveillance society should be seen in connection with the rise of a different identity technology. For better or worse, surveillance is applied so widely and functions so efficiently today, not because it impedes authenticity but because it works so well along with profilicity.

As Elena Esposito rightly highlights, the algorithms at the center of today's surveillance or transparency mechanisms are "themselves part of the world in which they operate. They observe the world, they view the world from within, not from the outside."[29] Importantly, the way in which society and individuals observe themselves is shifting—from first-order to second-order observations. Big data and associated technologies thrive in part because they are tools of second-order observation. They are intrinsic to an ongoing shift in observation we find throughout society and not anomalous mechanisms flourishing only in economic and political dimensions of society or applied by divergent powers in order to control the world.

The preface of this book presents the image of a man looking dubiously at his face in the mirror. This image stems from the age of authenticity and suggests that we can find, or question, our identity in this way. Looking into the mirror is a first-order observation—we see our face right there. But under conditions of profilicity, we look at much more in order to locate, and explore, our identity. We need to see not only how we look to ourselves but how others see us. The observation of other observers is a more complex operation than simple self-observation, and more advanced technologies are involved in it than a simple mirror. Algorithms and artificial intelligence (AI) help do the job. They are the mirrors of profilicity, and our attention is increasingly focused on them.

Amy Webb defines AI and its algorithms as "automated system[s] that make decisions using data."[30] We can further understand them as procedural and statistical operations simulating the general peer. As Timothy Wu has aptly put it, they are "profile builders."[31] They collect and store data that inform rankings and serve to make determinations such as who is a superhost on Airbnb, which résumés get accepted or rejected, or which criminals can be considered for parole. No first-order observation—looking in the mirror, or looking at a person—can do this. To make these valuable and efficient determinations, we process the much more complex, contextual information available only through second-order observation; and we all rely on such observations willingly, often gratefully, on a daily basis. We (the present authors) check Airbnb reviews and restaurant ratings just as we check the metrics of our publications. This does not necessarily boost our authentic agency, but it does "empower" us as individuals because it allows us to more effectively conduct ourselves and navigate our world under conditions of profilicity.

Since profilic identity relies heavily on public appearance, knowing who we are involves knowing how others see us. We do not find identity merely by looking inward or at our own face. We must look at the faces of others and figure out what they see, and on this basis present ourselves accordingly. In profilicity, moreover, these others are often not present and even unknown—or, as in the case of algorithms and AI, not even human. We curate, assemble, and display profilic identity by entering into social validation feedback loops with such observers.

Under the conditions of profilicity, individual agency is not completely absent. When we surf the internet, borrow a book from a library, or make a purchase with a credit card, we produce data. On the one hand, we are aware of this; it is not something completely hidden. On the other hand, we do not know exactly which data are collected and how they are processed and used. We are neither passive data-producing automatons nor fully in control of the profiles that emerge from what we do. The individualized insurance rate we get offered may result from algorithmic calculations based, at least in part, on records of the patio chairs we purchased from a merchant who then sold our data to an insurer.[32] Much of our profile identities eventually emerges from such processes that incorporate individual agency, but only as it is embedded in multiple social and "interactive" contexts.

Websites no longer look the same for everyone. Not only ads but also YouTube videos and news coverage are user-specific, tailored to each of us with the help of algorithms. Critics of surveillance society, like Frank Pasquale and David Lyon, use the term "reputation" to describe what emerges from data analyses of people's behavior.[33] Pasquale writes, "In ever more settings, reputation is determined by secret algorithms processing inaccessible data" (14). However, the term "reputation" is misleading. It connotes a sincerity context where an individual has a more or less coherent and stable reputation and is known in a similar way to all members of a community. In profilicity, however, specific contexts or "settings" produce very different profiles. There is little coherence between a scholar's H-index (measuring academic impact), taste in music, and number of steps walked on an average day. Very different profiles are needed to evaluate a person's academic standing, suggest YouTube videos, or offer a health insurance rate. Unlike in sincerity, algorithms are not at all interested in a person's overall "reputation" in their communities. What matters is only that which is considered relevant in a specific context. Rather than having one reputation, in profilicity an individual has numerous profiles, and these profiles change constantly within highly dynamic social validation feedback loops. Compared with sincerity, profilicity allows for a much more diverse and flexible approach toward identity, in which multiple profiles can operate relatively independently of one another.

Profilicity allows for a rather different understanding of privacy than authenticity. From an authenticity perspective, surveillance is aimed at peeping into the private sphere of an individual, or into the core self, in order to discipline or manipulate it. But algorithms are not interested in authentic individuals; they do not want to know who one *really* is, beneath what their actions reveal about them. They are interested in specific behavioral patterns, in preferences and performances in various areas. They do not want to know which videos most deeply connect with or enrich your soul, but rather which video you are most likely to click on next. And they do so not by understanding the person behind the click but instead by crunching the numbers on how people with similar profiles usually click. Algorithms and AI work through correlations. They do not predict behavior based on causal understanding and do not explain why these correlations exist or what they say about anyone's mind. They do not aim to judge your character from your video preferences but to predict and influence future choices. What people privately think or feel is of little importance to an algorithm. Privacy, in this sense, becomes irrelevant—you can keep it to yourself.

Profiles are transparent. This is what they are made for. Our academic publications can be looked up anytime and anywhere on our Google Scholar profiles. These profiles make transparent how others academically see us. However, by knowing the totality of our scholarly profile, you still do not know us privately. Profiles and profilic identity do not invade privacy; to the contrary, they establish a public identity beyond and largely detached from privacy. We identify with our public profiles and, where we can, curate them to establish and express images of ourselves, but these profiles do not, and are not meant to, represent all that we think and feel.[34] And there is no key to unlock a "core self" within them.

Surveillance complements exhibition—exhibition to the general peer. It is there for a purpose; namely, to facilitate identity assembly in the mode of profilicity. Profiles need to be observed, and surveillance technologies do this very well and on a massive scale. With their help, individuals can see how they are being seen. They get access to and insights into their observers and can enter into validation feedback loops with the general peer. They learn how to present themselves so that they are seen in ways they desire.

Profilicity and transparency go together quite well. Profiles must be shown and seen, including the profiles of those who oppose transparency. Under conditions of profilicity, the denunciation of surveillance and simultaneous practices of transparency enter into a paradoxical symbiosis, as demonstrated by none other than Byung-Chul Han, author of *Transparency Society*, himself. Han's Wikipedia entry, as accessed on June 10, 2019, is quite extensive. But Wikipedia warns: it "is written like a resume" and "may not meet Wikipedia's notability guidelines for academics." Still, someone took the trouble of putting it there. The entry highlights that "until recently," Han "refused to give radio and television interviews and rarely divulges any biographical or personal details, including his date of birth, in public." Thereby Han's penchant for privacy is paradoxically used as a form of public profile-building: he is publicly marketed as an authentically private person.[35]

In any case, Han has broken his silence and allowed some transparency of his personality. In a report on him by the leading Spanish newspaper *El País*, posted in English on the web on February 7, 2018, Han chastises the loss of authenticity: "People sell themselves as authentic," he laments, and are forced to "produce themselves." The article includes a staged picture of Han, showing him in rock-star style, wearing fashionable black clothing and a black scarf while gazing thoughtfully into the distance. When we accessed it, the article, along with the photo, was framed by large advertisements.[36] The staged photo and the ads forcefully contradicted the article's message of anticonsumerist authenticity.

Han reflects deeply on authenticity, but, it seems, he forgot to take into account his own advice on the matter: "When a paradigm has come to provide an object of reflection, it means that its demise is at hand."[37]

Democracy

"The other thing about me is that I give zero-fucks about anything, yet I have a strong opinion about everything. Even topics I am not informed on," says Hannah in season 6, episode 1, of *Girls*. Her frank statement sums up nicely the functioning of participatory democracy under conditions of profilicity and pervasive second-order observation. So many social spheres have become "democratic," inviting votes, comments, critiques, reviews, and ratings by almost anyone and of almost anything. *Everything is reviewed*: hosts and guests democratically evaluate one another on Airbnb or Uber—which translate into algorithm-dictated rankings. The constant "interactive" personal evaluation process shown so effectively in the *Black Mirror* episode "Nosedive" is increasingly real. In profilicity, you need to be opinionated.

Originally, Enlightenment thinkers in the eighteenth century, and especially Immanuel Kant, envisioned a future society where human reason would rule. Every intellectually "mature" person would make use of their critical capacity, judging and deciding for themselves. If only provided with a public forum for exchanging ideas and views, rational individuals would collectively figure out what is good and right, better and best, and thus a truly democratic and free society would emerge. What is good, democratic, and free are here all grounded in reasonable judgments and rational exchange. This pattern of belief was carried on well into the twenty-first century by thinkers, including Jürgen Habermas, who came close to being the unofficial state philosophers of modern liberal democracies. Initially, many who held on dearly to Enlightenment beliefs hailed the internet as the "domination-free" (*herrschaftsfrei*, to use Habermas's term) forum where collective human rationality could flourish and a direct democracy would manifest itself. Alas, it turned out that the real internet world in the twenty-first century was not as much populated by Kants as by Hannahs from *Girls*.

In a highly diversified society, there is neither an overarching ethos nor a foundational rationality. The radical multiplicity of perspectives generated by all-pervasive second-order observation makes it possible to judge almost anything from almost any perspective. No ultimately valid review can be found. Given the temporal characteristics of the information feed in mass and social media communication, critical participation must happen instantly and perpetually. One rating is immediately followed by the next, and rankings can change anytime. Everyone is constantly invited to give an opinion on everything, ranging from a cat photo to an academic paper to a politically charged video. There is not much time to reflect, and if there were, it would make little difference. The point of rating, raking, and reviewing is not to judge something based on the depths of universal reason. The point is to confirm a perspective and make it count by contributing it to the data feed.

Critical judgments and opinions contribute to a profile. They, too, can be considered as profilic memes meant to be spread as widely as possibly. As memes, they are made in consideration of the general peer. Publicly generated and displayed ratings and rankings are products of second-order observation par excellence. They manifest "public reason" and the "right to express one's individual opinion" in times of profilicity. Liking or not liking a social media post or an academic paper is not only an act of joining the general peer but also a profilic exhibition to the general peer. Liking and not liking is in turn liked or not liked. My ratings and opinions are not only evaluations of something but at the same time also self-presentations. When presenting an evaluation to the general peer, I simultaneously evaluate and am evaluated. Judgments are part of the "democratic" social validation feedback loops that constitute profilic performance and identity work. Profilicity is democratic, and democracy is profilic.

PROFILE ETHICS

Jussie Smollett's Profile

The real reality show involving American actor Jussie Smollett brought more attention to his profile than he probably intended. It was a good show, though, with quite a few unexpected changes of events.

Global media attention was brought to Smollett after he reported to Chicago police on January 29, 2019, that he was physically attacked by two men who subjected him to racist and homophobic slurs. Smollett said that the men had shouted, "This is MAGA country," referring to Donald Trump's slogan "Make America Great Again," and put a noose around his neck. At the time, Smollett had already been quite famous for his lead role in the Fox TV series *Empire*. There he played a gay black man, a character that supported his public persona as a liberal advocate of gay and black rights.

The attack appeared blatantly political. It seemed to have been a double hate crime expressing antigay and white supremacist sentiments plaguing America and sometimes associated with Trump supporters or the president himself. As would be expected, once the story had been run by media around the world, it caused widespread outrage and public condemnation by major political figures, including Democratic presidential candidates (at the time) Kamala Harris and Cory Booker. Comments by Harris and Booker that the incident constituted a "modern day lynching" were obviously triggered by the noose that the attackers allegedly put around Smollett's neck. The story perfectly connected with the narrative of the great ethical schism that seemed to divide America more or less in half: the rift between progressives committed to the causes of identity politics or civil rights and conservatives sympathetic to Trump's contempt for political correctness.

The case took a bizarre turn when police publicly accused Smollett of having intentionally orchestrated the attack. It was suggested that he had hired the two attackers in order to eventually demand a pay increase for his role in *Empire* on account of having gained more fame. To the consternation of those who supported the political and ethical causes he represented and had rushed to side with him, Smollett was charged with filing a false police report. In another surprising twist, however, prosecutors and defense attorneys agreed to a deal, and in return for a few hours of community service and forfeiting his bond, all charges against Smollett were suddenly dropped on March 26, 2019. At present, it is unclear if there will be any further episodes of the story. The FBI is still investigating the circumstances of the dismissal of the charges, and the city of Chicago has sued Smollett with regard to public expenses related to the making of false statements.

The Jussie Smollett case was perhaps one of the first globally displayed criminal investigations widely described in terms of identity work and with the vocabulary of profilicity. In a report on February 21, 2019, the British *Channel 4 News* introduced Smollett by pointing out that he "had used a profile he built on the show [*Empire*] as a young, gay, black man to speak out against racism and homophobia."[38] The choice of words of the news report mirrored, in this instance, the vocabulary used by Chicago police superintendent Eddie Johnson when explaining Smollett's alleged motive. During a press conference, Johnson said that the actor had intentionally used the morally and politically charged symbol of the noose around his neck because therein he saw an "opportunity to manipulate that symbol to further his own public profile."[39] By using this symbol, or, more precisely, this *meme*, Smollett apparently desired to become an icon of the fight against racism and homophobia.

The similar choice of words by the news outlet and the police superintendent reveals what this reality show was essentially about: the curation of personal identity in the form of casting oneself into a profilic persona. Smollett had already, long before his alleged crime, built his identity, and his career, on assembling a profile that made use of positively charged memes, promising both public attention and sympathy. Consequently, the allegedly staged attack was regarded as an amplification of this very profile, intended to make it even more dramatic, more popular, more visible, and more profitable. The presumed attack was regarded as boosting the identity value of Smollett's persona as actor and activist and raising the exhibition value of *Empire*, leading, hopefully, to a higher salary for Jussie himself.

The public reaction to the case has to be understood in the exact same profilic context. Politicians, journalists, and social media commentators all tagged on to the story by employing and proliferating it as a meme. In doing so, they produced, willingly or not, the same effect Jussie Smollett was accused of desiring, namely, the embellishment of their own public profiles—although of course through legal means. The frustration felt when the alleged attack was said to have had been staged ran deep in part because this seeming revelation pointed toward the Jussie Smollett in all of us. Personal identity and careers, in entertainment as much as in any other social sector, are increasingly dependent on self-casting and the curation of profiles in times of ubiquitous profilicity. All public profiles, no matter if curated through criminal means or not, are staged to a certain extent. And politically and morally charged memes are especially powerful staging tools. The outrage over Jussie Smollett's perceived moral hypocrisy includes a general suspicion about the profilic motives behind the use of such memes—a suspicion regarding not only others but also ourselves.

When the Chicago police announced that they could prove the attack on Smollett had been commissioned by Smollett himself, a colleague of ours with liberal leanings made a quite telling remark that probably voiced the feelings of many: "I so much wish it [Smollett's account of the event] had been true." She obviously did not realize the rather problematic logic of her statement. She meant, of course, that it would be so much better for the liberal cause if the public profile of a gay and black rights advocate would not be revealed as a fraud. But what she said was, in effect, that she would have preferred that Smollett had really been attacked by white supremacists. She would have preferred one more racist and homophobic attack in America over one less for the sake of protecting Jussie Smollett's profile and thereby maintaining the consistency of the moral and political profile she identified with. She was, as basically everyone else who sympathized with Smollett, thinking about the attack also in connection with her own profilic identity. She regarded it on the level of second-order observation, seeing it as it was being seen, and evaluated it from this perspective rather than from the "factual" perspective of first-order observation. The Jussie Smollett case demonstrates how moral identity functions under conditions of profilicity. Not only Smollett himself but also those who tagged onto his case were spreading memes that affirmed, promoted, and perhaps developed their own profilic identity.

Taylor Swift's Politics

Taylor Swift is one of the most successful musicians today. Her heavy media presence makes her a major celebrity, particularly in the United States. She began her career in country music and then steered toward (even) more mainstream pop. Her songs, as Wikipedia puts it, are typically "about her personal life," covering the usual spectrum from falling in love to breaking up, and from celebration to gripe and grouse.[40] She is definitely not a protest singer, or someone with a pronounced social cause or political message attached to her music.

But Swift's silence about social and political issues ended in the fall of 2018. In the runup to the U.S. midterm elections, she expressed her support of Democratic candidates in Tennessee, her home state at the time. It seems this had quite an effect. CNN reported that within a day of Swift encouraging her followers on Instagram to register to vote through the website Vote.org, sixty-five thousand people did exactly that.[41]

This somewhat surprising political turnout raised some eyebrows. Why did Taylor Swift suddenly side with the liberals and join the chorus of stars and starlets voicing, in one way or another, their opposition to President Trump? Was this a PR stunt? Swift's country music background and mainstream success associate her with the conservative American heartland that makes up Trump's electoral base. Furthermore, being a successful white American woman with a kind of cheerleader appeal, she could be perceived as representing "white privilege." This might not be a helpful profile for a mainstream artist given the seeming preference for progressive political views and a liberal stance on social issues of the general peer in entertainment, the culture industry, and large segments of both traditional and new media. In an article for the *Atlantic*, Reihan Salam suspects Swift's political move was intended to protect her public image. In his view, "in the culture industries, making a show of social liberalism is increasingly the only option." Salam then presented a quite robust reflection on the potential motives behind Taylor Swift's political turn:

> Swift has sought to broaden her artistic horizons and, as you might expect, to transcend her middlebrow origins. Having achieved unsurpassed celebrity, she now finds herself in the uppermost echelons of the culture industries, where woke liberalism is de rigueur and departures from it are stigmatized. Her reluctance to explicitly embrace left-of-center politics was, I imagine, somewhat costly to her reputation among tastemakers. Critics who delighted in the enlightened political interventions of her peers took note of Swift's reluctance to definitively affirm their view of the world, and it informed how they received her work. Politics aside, her seeming conventionality—her basicness— already made her suspect, and less interesting than performers who could more plausibly claim marginalized identities. At best, Swift could be an ally to those who, in the theology of woke liberalism, command the most sympathy.[42]

It is interesting to note how sensitive Salam's analysis is to second-order observation and profilic phenomena. The "tastemakers" of whom Salem speaks are unnamed critics—in both mass and social media forums, we can assume—functioning as opinion leaders. They represent the general peer, like the jury on *American Idol*. The taste of the general peer can be deduced from the attention and acclaim received by Swift's actual peers, fellow musicians and celebrities, when proclaiming progressive political views. Disadvantaged by an all-too white, all-too conservative, and all-too "basic" profile, as Salam implies, it was high time for Swift to shift into a more expedient and ingratiating public persona, unleashing a preemptive publicity strike and generating some excitement in doing so.

Salam's view on Taylor Swift's political intervention is not political itself, nor is it moral. It is, in a philosophical sense of the word, a *critical* reflection that tries to identify the "conditions of the possibility" of a celebrity's public political pronouncements. Salam outlines the social context within which these pronouncements function—the conditions of moral communication, public media, and economic factors. He uses an especially apt expression to sum up the complex social framework he depicts: a "culture of competitive wokeness." This expression is fitting because it points far beyond the political and moral surface of the phenomenon: "competitiveness" highlights its economic relevance, and "wokeness" brings an almost religious dimension to the fore. The now popular term "woke" indicates a (leftist or liberal) political consciousness. Since it alludes to "awakening," however, it also evokes religious connotations. Indeed, "competitive wokeness" can be understood, as Salam says, in the context of a "theology" of liberalism—although since this "theology" has no God and is therefore not literally a *theo*logy, it is best classified as a secular or *civil* religion.

Unsurprisingly, Salam's depiction of Taylor Swift's political debut as exemplifying "competitive wokeness" did not please everyone. It found disfavor especially among those with liberal persuasions. The response by one reader, Abby Sessions from Seattle, published on the website of the *Atlantic*, is representative of the reaction from this political spectrum. Presuming that Salam believes "the political convictions held by young people are not sincere," Sessions describes the article as "condescending."[43] This presumption is as correct as it is misleading—as will be explained.

Abby Sessions uses the term "sincere" in the sense of "honest," or, in the terminology we apply in this book, in the sense of "authentic." Sessions's point seems to be this: the (leftist) political convictions of many young people, probably including Taylor Swift, are real. What these young people say is based on what they actually think. Therefore public political statements by (young) celebrities should be understood as based in authenticity.

With his notion of "competitive wokeness," Reihan Salam, however, never really questions if Taylor Swift, or other celebrities making "politically correct" statements, actually believe what they say. Salam never implies that Taylor Swift lied when she asked people to vote for the Democrats and that in truth she might have wished them to vote Republican. Indeed, this would have been a rather absurd claim to make. The very point of Salam's analysis is that the whole phenomenon of public political and moral communication by celebrities does not function on the level of either sincerity or authenticity. We do not, and cannot, know what Taylor Swift or any other star in entertainment authentically believes or feels when they post on Instagram or make public announcements—and *it does not matter*. Instagram posts, and in particular those by celebrities, cannot be appropriately understood in the registers of sincerity or authenticity. Like virtue signaling, this "political signaling" is about curating a profile, not expressing one's inner self.

On her social media accounts, Taylor Swift does not speak as an authentic single individual to other authentic individuals, nor does she enact the role of a sincere community member who communicates with present, personally known peers. *Here, the curated profile of Taylor Swift speaks to the general peer.* If we want to properly understand what is being said in such a context, we must not wrongly assume conditions of sincerity or authenticity. Sessions is right: Salam did, correctly, imply that political convictions, when expressed on social media to the general peer, are *not sincere.* But this does not mean that they are *insincere,* as Sessions wrongly took Salam to say. In other words, the general peer—or anyone personally unfamiliar with Taylor Swift, like Reihan Salam or the authors of this book—has no substantive concern with whether Taylor Swift's posts on Instagram are insincere or inauthentic. Questioning their sincerity or authenticity is moot. But through critical analysis we can evaluate the profilic character of what Taylor Swift's profile says through social media and other accounts. Moreover, the same is the case for whatever Abby Sessions or Reihan Salam publicly say on the website of the *Atlantic.*

Jay-Z's Question

Jay-Z invited philosophical reflection in his song "No Church in the Wild," rapping, "Is pious cause God loves pious? Socrates asked whose bias do y'all seek." He refers here to Socrates's aporetic inquiry in Plato's dialogue *Euthyphro,* which poses the following question: Is something good because it pleases the Gods, or does it please the Gods because it is good? Neither Plato nor Jay-Z provides a final answer.

To match the conditions of profilicity, the *Euthyphro* dilemma needs to be modified. We can replace "the Gods" with "the general peer." This gets us closer to the matter in a secular society: Are moral statements good because they are approved by the general peer? Or does the general peer approve of moral statements because they are good? Alternatively, we can ask: Is a moral cause good because it boosts my profile, or does a moral cause boost my profile because it is good? Do I identify with a moral stance because it suits my profile, or do I identify with a profile because it suits my moral stance?

Or does it even matter?

Taking advice from Socrates, we can assume that there is a dialectic at work here. If I identify with a cause, then aspects of my identity and of the cause become increasingly intertwined and interdependent, so much so that eventually they can no longer be clearly distinguished from one another. In profilicity, as in sincerity or authenticity, identity and morality can merge. The more profilic credit, or identity value, I get from the general peer for a moral cause, the more important the cause will be to me. And the more important it is to me, the more enthusiastically I will present it to the general peer. However, a conflict of interest between my identity and the moral cause now inevitably arises. When I identify with a moral cause so much that it becomes part of my profile, then the cause and my profile are equally at stake in a presentation to the general peer. The more strongly one identifies with a cause, the more "selfish" is one's engagement with it. People who identify with gay and black rights activism may wish that Jussie Smollett really had been attacked because such an attack can make their moral profiles seem more relevant and valuable. Similarly, environmentalists may welcome confirmations that global warming really is happening, because such news generates more social opportunities for people with a "green" profile, for instance, in politics or in academics. It increases their chances of being elected or published. "Whose bias do y'all seek?" In profilicity, we seek the bias of the general peer. And seek we must.

Virtue Speech

In profilicity, just as with any other identity technology, moral approval is especially important for shaping identity value. It is the heroin(e) of identity. Nothing else can boost it to such heights, and nothing else can shatter it so irreparably. We are proud when we can regard ourselves as *good*. Identity pride typically goes along with moral pride. Under conditions of profilicity, we can regard ourselves as good when our profile is seen as being seen as good. As in Taylor Swift's case, a perceived lack of a moral dimension in her profilic identity appears quite detrimental. A profile without morality is hardly commendable, and moral memes increase its value and virulence.

Moral speech has always been highly important for achieving moral identity, but it can also rouse suspicion. Confucius already pointed this out more than two thousand years ago: "There was a time, when in my dealings with others, on hearing what they had to say, I believed they would live up to it. Nowadays in my dealings with others, on hearing what they have to say, I then watch what they do."[44] Under conditions of sincerity, virtuous speech was not regarded as good enough. To the contrary, on its own it tended to be seen as dubious. Others might easily doubt the sincerity of someone who continuously stressed her morality. Is this person just bragging? Moral speech and

virtue signaling needed validation by moral conduct. In profilicity, this is somewhat different.

Today, people are still expected to walk the walk, not just talk
the talk—but we often have no way to actually "watch what they
do," as Confucius did, Most of the people Confucius dealt with
were in one way or another present to him, so he could see how
they acted in daily life. Today, this is not always so. We are not
in a position to judge what Taylor Swift, the person, really thinks
when her profilic persona posts something on the internet. We
are also unable to judge what she really does—because *all* that
we know about her is what mass and social media tell us. We
know her profile, and we know that we only know the profile.
We have no hope, no need, and perhaps no wish to get to know
her privately.

To be sure, strictly distinguishing between speech and action
has always been difficult. When Taylor Swift's profile speaks, it
is also an act. The notion of the speech act indicates precisely
this: speaking is also acting. However, speech acts today tend to
be different from speech acts in traditional societies prior to the
mass and social media. Under conditions of first-order observation, a speech act is typically announced to a present peer. "Is
there any salt?" means "Please pass me the salt." Someone at the
table then actually passes me the salt, which is an act, but not a
speech act. This is how J. L. Austin conceived of speech acts in
the early stages of speech act theory. They were understood as a
specific kind of act in the context of interactions between
present peers. Under conditions of second-order observation,
however, this has changed. A speech act today, like posting on
Instagram, is addressed to the general peer and typically remains
on this level.

We often communicate with unknown people who are not
present, and since they are not physically around, we cannot

merely interact with them in the traditional sense of "acting." We can only "inter-speech-act" with them. We hear what they say or read what they write on the web, but we cannot pass them the salt. Due to a shift toward second-order observation and emerging profilicity, the ratio between acts and speech acts in everyday life experience has shifted toward the latter. We increasingly observe what happens in the world, or what others do, through "descriptions of descriptions."[45] In our "democratic" and "critical" world, we continuously look at ratings, rankings, reviews, comments, criticisms, and opinions. These are all new forms of speech acts. Unlike making someone present pass you the salt, they may, however, make multiple unknown others buy a product, cast a vote, or watch a video.

The shift from interactions with present peers toward speech-inter-actions with the general peer has had its effects on the practice of morality. We encounter good or bad speech acts much more frequently than good or bad speechless acts. Therefore Confucius's strategy "On hearing what they have to say, I then watch what they do" does not apply to the same extent anymore. To fit contemporary society, we have to abandon his sincerity-based approach to speech acts among present peers performed under first-order observation and instead adopt a profilicity-based approach in evaluating speech acts directed at the general peer under conditions of second-order observation. Confucius's wisdom is in need of an update: "On hearing what they have to say, I then watch what others have to say about it." We have no way to watch Taylor Swift in person, but we have ample opportunity to see how she is being seen by the general peer.

In a context of second-order observation, one cannot simply do good. Today, merely passing the salt to someone is not as good as posting a video of passing the salt in addition to it, because the former lacks profilic value. Merely posting the video, moreover, is not as good as the video being widely viewed and liked. The point is not just to be seen as virtuous but to be seen as being seen as virtuous. Value lies in the display of something that is regarded as right or good or virtuous. Personal virtue has to be visible in rankings, reviews, or comments for it to count. This is why moral communication is so crucial today. The general peer cannot observe that we actually act virtuously, because it is not present. It sees only that our speech acts are seen as virtuous or not. Virtue is displayed to the general peer in form of *virtue speech*. We display our virtue by making virtuous observations, by displaying moral speech, by communicating ethics. What is now often called "virtue signaling," or, more crudely, "political correctness," is a form of moral communication where, by making moral observations, we exhibit ourselves for further moral observation. We inscribe our own moral profile into profilic moral validation feedback loops.

Under conditions of second-order observation, speech acts, but not unspoken acts, are *accountable*—when thinking of an "account" in the profilic sense outlined earlier. Through an account we post virtuous observations to the general peer and thereby join the ethos of the general peer. Virtue speech is accountable as virtue once it is fed into a profile of an account. This is how profilic virtue is made.

Moral Profiling

Given the attention shift from the act toward the speech act in the morality of profilicity, the flourishing of "virtue signaling" and the attention to political correctness come as no surprise. Virtue speech is a very powerful, often indispensable tool for achieving or increasing profilicity. Not only celebrities but also common individuals practice virtue speech to shape their profiles on social media—as do companies and countries to adorn their projected profiles. The self-profiling of individual politicians and that of political parties, too, relies heavily on moral communication. Of course, moral argumentation has always been part of politics. In recent years, however, political parties, for instance in the United States, have tended to emphasize moral concerns over more traditional economic and political issues. The Democratic Party has increasingly emphasized "identity politics" and thereby modified its former identity as economic advocate of the middle and working classes. In some ways, this moralization of the party line did not really work out very well: it seems to have been a major factor in Donald Trump becoming president (despite losing the popular vote by a large margin). But Trump, too, resorted to moral rhetoric of an intensity, or crudeness ("crooked Hillary"), hardly seen in recent memory. He countered the virtue speech of "political correctness" with a very different kind of virtue speech.

In traditional mass media, also, virtue speech is increasingly pervasive. Contemporary political journalism on both the American left and right tends to highlight moral evaluation—although still sometimes casting itself as "objective" or "neutral" reporting. Broadcasting companies, news outlets, and individual reporters are busy shaping their own moral profiles in presenting the news. Even Oscar ceremonies and other major entertainment events do not shy away from displaying highly visible moral profiles. These are all instances of attempts to acquire or increase ethical identity value.

Rather recently, moral self-profiling has become part of the regular employment and promotion processes in the academic system as well. Many universities in the United States now require people applying for a job or for tenure to write a so-called diversity statement. In analogy to a "teaching statement," it is expected to outline an academic's views on how to professionally promote the morally charged value of diversity (regarding especially race, gender, and sexual orientation). As the office of Graduate Studies at the University of Nebraska states: "You can safely assume that any university that requests [a diversity statement] is very committed to inclusivity and supporting their diverse population so they are looking for someone who would be supportive of that mission."[46] This only states the obvious: academics are not expected here to question the value of diversity. They are expected, instead, to express their support of it. No candidate who is interested in getting or keeping a job at a university that demands such a statement would dare to disclose any potential disagreement with this value. Therefore the function of the statement cannot really be to find out how sincerely or authentically committed someone is to diversity.

Diversity statements need to be understood in the context of profilicity rather than sincerity or authenticity. The official requirement of such statements is itself an act of virtue speech. A university uses this requirement to signal very clearly—to the applicant, to itself (its employees, students, stake holders), and to the public—its moral stance on diversity. It thus feeds its moral profile. Job applicants, correspondingly, are forced to engage in a practical virtue speech exercise signaling profilic alignment with the institution they hope to join. While their sincere or authentic commitment to diversity cannot be tested, their competence in casting themselves as diversity supporters is indeed tested. Whether this fosters sincere dedication to or an authentic pursuit of diversity in the applicant or by the institution is irrelevant for the procedure. It is relevant only to see if those who write such statements are willing and able to produce virtue speech and incorporate it into their professional profiles. The diversity statements shape the profilic identity of candidates in the way desired by the university, and the profile of the institution is also shaped and affirmed therein. The whole process is a moral validation feedback loop within which the profilic identities of the applicants and of the institution are reciprocally curated through virtue speech acts.

PROFILE POLITICS

"One can only become the leader if he is capable of manipulating how he is observed," says Niklas Luhmann (2013, 119; translation modified) in explaining how politics work under conditions of second-order observation, especially in democracies where elections are political popularity contests.[47] Since the German word for "leader" is *Führer*, Luhmann's remark can easily be interpreted as an allusion to Hitler, who had come to power in free elections. In democratic politics, anyone can succeed as long as he or she is capable of establishing a public profile that the masses are keen to identify with. This was the case long before the times of Donald Trump and social media. Democratic politics rewards good profile management because it is good politics.

Luhmann presents a short and almost poetic description of the democratic political process as a profilicity competition— without using this concept, of course:

> Children, simply out of fear, always needed to observe if they are observed or not. . . . The same is true in politics. Politicians must dance on the screen in front of public opinion. In spite of all the polls, no politician knows for sure what people really think. At best, one knows, statistically calculated, what some people say

they think. It is unimaginable that politics or a politician could know, or merely take into consideration, what is going on in the heads of individuals. Public opinion . . . is a replacement for this. Politics thus essentially consists in arranging how one is seen by public opinion—so that one is more favorably observed than the competition. . . . The truly political (*das eigentlich Politische*) is the reflection of second-order observation. (115; translation modified)

The radicalism of this statement needs to be highlighted. That politics—left and right, blue and red, green and pink—can be understood in terms of a populist "dance on the screen" is nothing new. Even if the concept "populism" was not used in Luhmann's day in the way it is now, it was obvious then that democratic elections were typically decided at least as much by the popular appeal of the profiles of politicians or political parties as manifested in their looks, charisma, campaign strategies, and capacity to instill hope or fear in the electorate as by the electorate's rational consideration of its interests or its political will. All this has surely been the case in politics then and now, but Luhmann goes a step further in his analysis when he points out that modern politics consists "essentially" in this—that the "reflection of second-order observation" has now become *das eigentlich Politische* ("the truly political," or "politics proper," or "politics as such").

Because elections are run as profilicity contests, politics need to be highly attentive to perception in the mass and social media. When decisions are made and power is executed, a prime concern must be "arranging how one is seen by public opinion." The election is not an exceptional case of periodically consulting the will of the people. Like the anxious children of helicopter parents, politicians *never* get a break from observing if and how they are observed. Their dance marathon never ends. Like the contestants in Sydney Pollack's *They Shoot Horses, Don't They?*

(1969), everything a politician does—marrying, eating pizza, or drinking a beer, for instance—can potentially become part of a competitive performance to the general peer and thus "political." In this sense, the political is in essence "depoliticized" or "populist." It is not at all restricted to traditional political decision making. In contemporary liberal democracies (arguably unlike in authoritarian states), there is relatively little "pure" first-order observation politics left where politicians can afford to make decisions merely for the sake of governing the state without considering how this may be observed by the general peer. The art of politics, following Luhmann, lies in being good at "the reflection" and the "manipulation," of second-order observation—or in curating profiles.

National Profile Building: The German Culture of Remembrance

Politics is not only about the profile work of politicians and political parties. It is not only about shaping their political identities. On a larger scale, politics is also about shaping the brand—or better, the profile—of a nation.[48] The nation-state still constitutes the major framework for today's politics. Politics as a profilicity contest is as much about governing as it is about representing a nation. Politicians compete to be "the face of the nation," and the face of the nation in turn contributes deeply to shaping the profiles that politicians present of themselves. The profile of a politician typically inscribes itself into the profilic account of a nation.

Politics under conditions of second-order observation consist in profilicity work. This is to say that decisions are made not so much in the interest of the nation as in the interest of the nation's profile—or rather, that these two purposes have been largely conflated. What is good for the national profile is good for the nation. Nation building today is national profile work.

Traditionally, national identities were built on supposedly common characteristics of a people, such as race, language, religious belief, ideological persuasion, or historical experience. These are still powerful identity markers today. A nation can cast itself, for instance, as an Islamic Republic or a Jewish State, or as formed by a shared "manifest destiny." In one way or another, politicians within such a nation will have to curate and feed their own profiles in line with the curation and feeding of the national profile. They offer competing options for making a national profile "great again."

A highly curious but nevertheless surprisingly successful case of national reprofiling has taken place in recent German history. This case is an instructive illustration of how profilicity works in the larger context of shaping the identity of a nation and of how a nation's profile can be connected with the individual profiles of its citizens.

Germany emerged speedily out of the ashes of the Third Reich. Through the "economic miracle" of the 1950s, it soon achieved an astonishing level of wealth. Its national image, however, remained hopelessly stained by the Nazi past, or so it seemed. The attempts of postwar Germanys to simply define themselves as "antifascist" (in the East German case) or "postfascist" (in West Germany) had only limited success. Their antifascist past did not help the East German Communists improve their image of being a repressive, totalitarian regime. West Germany attempted to pay off its inherited sins with money so that eventually a *Schlussstrich*, a sort of finishing line, could be reached after which it would emerge free of guilt. This, too, did not quite bring about the intended result.

After reunification, however, a sort of "identity miracle" took place and complemented the German economic resurgence. In the past few decades, Germany has managed to curate a new national identity and new national pride. This was made possible by the practice of a new form of German civil religion at the center of public life: the so-called *Erinnerungskultur*, or "culture of remembrance." This reprofiling process is ongoing and generates a need for constant political attention.

Through their etymological connection with "mind," the English words "remembrance" and "reminiscence" depict memory as "bringing something back to mind." The German word *Erinnerung* for remembrance, however, has a remarkably different etymology and connotations. Unlike "re-," the prefix "*er-*" does not denote "bringing back" but rather a goal-oriented process or an intensification. What is more, "*innerung*" implies something deeper than a purely intellectual act—it suggests an encompassing internalization. *Erinnerung* does not simply mean to think of something again, but quite literally (especially for Hegel in the *Phenomenology of Spirit*) to make something that is external also internal, to make the objective also subjective, and thereby to make it one's own and to possess it. It means internalizing elements of history, thereby shaping one's identity.

When speaking of German Erinnerungskultur, the centrality of the identity-shaping aspect of *Erinnerung* must be recognized. The function of Erinnerungskultur is not merely to preserve knowledge of the past; it is also aimed at intensifying and thereby transforming this knowledge into a collective identity meant to be internalized by the nation and its citizens.

Such use of remembrance rituals to support, or give rise to, a collective identity is neither new nor rare. It has been common to communities both small and large, ancient and modern, east and west. The contemporary German Erinnerungskultur, symbolized most dramatically by the monumental Holocaust Memorial inaugurated in 2005 in the center of Berlin, is, however, rather special for two reasons. First, it focuses exclusively on the relatively short and recent period of the Third Reich and regards it as altogether atypical—so atypical that today's Germany defines its identity not as a continuation of this period but in opposition to it. Second, the core object of remembrance—the Holocaust—is neither a heroic expression of the nation's greatness nor a tragic hardship or injustice that it had to endure and withstand. To the contrary, it is understood as a most heinous crime of hardly fathomable dimensions.

Paradoxically, in this case identity work is based on generating pride not through the memory of glory and triumph, or of perseverance, but through accepting abject shame and admitting utmost guilt. This act of accepting almost unacceptable shame and admitting almost inadmissible guilt quite ingeniously recycles shame and guilt into a form of postheroic grandeur. Guilt is converted into guilt-pride. It is a moral pride that claims ethical exceptionality for having the strength to remember and thereby to take on responsibility for one of the greatest sins ever committed. This is the narrative of Erinnerungskultur: because we Germans dare to remember what others would not dare to remember, because we blame ourselves for what others would not dare to blame themselves for, we now deserve to be regarded as moral exemplars.

The German word *Erinnerung* expresses more correctly what memory is than the English word "remembrance." It is not primarily a process of bringing the past mentally back into presence but rather collective or personal identification with a story that "we," as individuals or as a group, have come to accept—and like to hear—about ourselves. Typically, such stories make us proud, support firm belief in the rightness of our values, and

imbue us with the urge to share them. They provide the framework for shaping identity profiles that can be projected to
others.

The successful cultivation of the new German identity profile, however, has led to some paradoxical consequences. A political effect of the German Erinnerungskultur was the opening
of the German borders during the refugee crisis in 2015. To
prove to the world and to itself that the Nazi hostility toward
foreigners had been completely overcome, Germany developed
yet another *Kultur* (culture), the *Willkommenskultur*, or welcoming culture, inviting migrants to Germany, specifically those
fleeing wars and poverty in the Middle East and Africa. While
this policy was, at least initially, enthusiastically embraced by a
large part of the political spectrum in Germany, and also by large
parts of the electorate, it produced frictions within the European Union. Brexit can in part be described as a result of the
doomed attempt to export the German Willkommenskultur
to other nations less suited to it. These other nations have been
unwelcoming of welcoming culture because they lack the
backdrop—and identity—of Erinnerungskultur.

In Germany, however, the opening of the borders could be
experienced as a huge profilic success: being German could eventually feel good again. From a perspective that understands
politics in terms of profilicity, this decision was made primarily
with regard neither to the immediate interests of the migrants
(many of whom died on their way to Germany) nor to the material interests of German citizens (it burdened them heavily,
financially and otherwise). It was instead an investment in Germany's profile. And since what is good for a nation's profile is
also good for the nation and its citizens, it was thereby also a
decision made in the long-term interest of the German people.
But this logic could not be replicated in countries with very

different national profiles, such as the UK—which explains why such countries refused to follow suit.

In the wake of the new immigration wave of the border opening in 2015 came an increasing realization that Germany was now a multiethnic country—which in effect it had already been, following the mass immigration from Turkey and other countries that began in the 1960s. A multicultural Germany was of course a welcome confirmation of the new national profile, but it also created problems for the underlying Erinnerungskultur.

The German Erinnerungskultur demands identification through the Holocaust. While someone born after 1945, as most Germans today are, is not assumed to admit personal guilt for this great crime, Erinnerungskultur implies a duty to internalize shame and take on "historical responsibility" for it. But how could this be demanded of all these newly welcomed Germans? Could they, or should they, too, be asked to embrace a national and personal identity shaped by Nazi crimes? This predicament was singled out as one of the greatest challenges for Erinnerungskultur. Aleida Assmann, an influential postwar German memory theoretician, has suggested immigrants to Germany ought to develop "an interest for the stories of the victims [of the Holocaust] and also identify with them."[49] As an alternative to self-identification with victims of German genocide, Assmann also recounts the case of a student of Turkish origin who criticized her own father for denying the genocide of the Armenians. Thus, according to Assmann, immigrants to Germany seem to have two options to identify with German Erinnerungskultur: either they identify by proxy with the victims of the Holocaust, or they take on historical responsibility for a substitute genocide in the history of the nation or culture they stem from. Erinnerungskultur turns out to be a rather complicated identity construct. It works well, we trust, for Aleida Assmann's profile. But it remains to be seen how enthusiastic migrants to Germany will be about making it part of their profiles as well.

THE LOGIC OF LOGOS: PROFILICITY AND CAPITALISM

"Don't sell me a product, sell me an identity," demands River Clegg in a satirical column in the *New Yorker*.[50] He also tells us what kind of identity he would prefer: "Cool Guy Who Plays by His Own Rules." He should get a Mac.

In 2006 Apple launched its iconic "Get a Mac" advertisement campaign "in order to raise sales and take out the biggest competitor they have, Microsoft."[51] It was a huge success—probably one of the greatest successes in the history of advertising, or more precisely in the history of branding, or even more precisely in the history of *profilic identity marketing*. The campaign consisted of sixty-six TV spots, aired all over North America and in many other parts of the developed world.[52] It helped generate "a time of tremendous growth in Mac sales" with "a 12% increase year after year after the start of this campaign, resulting in a 39% increase in overall sales by the end of the 2006-year."[53]

The spots were in-your-face profilic identity marketing—a Mac would give users a personal profile. They all followed the same structure, format, and style: a short dialogue between a young, clean, casual guy, introducing himself with "Hello, I am a Mac," and a slightly older looking man appearing rather stiff with his suit, glasses, and regular haircut, who responded "And I am a PC." While the dialogues typically revolved around supposed benefits of Apple's Macs over Microsoft's PCs, these product comparisons were a mere vehicle for the more important message: the Mac is "the young, better looking, easy going character," while the PC is "very dorky looking, up tight, with an overall boring appearance."[54]

Identity-based marketing can hardly be more pronounced than in the Get a Mac campaign. It succeeded by operating according to the logic of profilicity. Pulling out a Mac in a coffee shop, classroom, or airport means you are going to be judged, consciously or unconsciously, by those who see you. It can't be avoided. You could potentially try to disguise your device by putting all kinds of stickers on it—but this, in turn, would profile you as well. This being the case, the computer has become an important part of your projected profile. Many who desire to curate their profile in a certain way have no choice but to get a Mac.

That Apple is not so much selling computers as it is selling coolness was noted by Naomi Klein in her bestseller *No Logo*, first published in 1999. *No Logo* is now two decades old, and it did little to prevent the success of the Get a Mac campaign or to check the proliferation of branding through new media. This proliferation started to take off at about the same time as the Mac campaign, and on the very computers it was selling. Klein's book did, however, succeed in presenting a detailed and well-written critical case study of the capitalist commodification of coolness, or identity value, and a widely read analysis of the economy of branding. From a (somewhat) Marxist perspective, Klein shows how big corporations spent immense amounts of money not to inform potential customers about products but to attach themselves, like enormous parasites, to the personas of human beings. They exploit and alienate human identity and enrich themselves through the production and sale of profilicity.

The notion of branding is very old—thousands of years, in fact. Very early on, branding was used to mark livestock. A brand indicated to whom the animal belonged. In early modern capitalism, branding no longer indicated direct ownership. Rather, it identified producers and sellers, often by their surname, like Ford or Hoover. At this stage, there was still an obvious analogy between the old and new meanings of "brand." In both cases the brand identified something not in terms of its own characteristics (as cow, car, or vacuum cleaner) but in terms of those who profited from it.

When the capitalist economy developed in step with the evolution of second-order observation, the logic of branding changed once more. Increasingly, the brand no longer referenced a manufacturer of goods, but an "image" of the product. This happened mainly through advertising. Advertising is a paid and staged form of second-order observation for capitalist purposes. It is a thoroughly profilic activity. Something is not merely presented so that it is known but presented as known to be known by the general peer so that it can be sold with a higher profit margin. Advertising not only shows the thing that you can buy, but, more important, it establishes and shapes a profile of the thing—the thing as it is, supposedly, regarded in public. Apple still refers to a manufacturer, but "Mac" is a brand denoting the profile that you purchase along with the computer. In advanced capitalism and under conditions of pervasive second-order observation, a brand denotes the identity of a commodity, neither via its owner nor via its producer but via its profile. Commodities have become profilic—and their profilicity is imparted on those who buy them, whether or not they want it. The profile of what you buy and own becomes part of your own profile. You are accountable for it because it has become part of your account. Thereby the traditional logic of branding has been completely reversed. In the old days, a brand would confer the identity of the owner on what was owned: if you bought an animal, you could brand it and thereby put your name on it. In contemporary capitalism, a brand profile confers the identity of a commodity on its owner: the computer that you buy will not be named after you, but the purchase will let you be seen as a "Mac person" if you bought a Mac, or as "PC person" if you bought a PC.

Naomi Klein's quasi-Marxist description of twentieth-century branding mechanisms is relatively comprehensive and accurate, but *No Logo* does not yet have the notion of profilicity in its conceptual tool box. With it we can better appreciate the complexity of the issues she was tackling. She was, for example, bewildered upon discovering a development that became a core theme of the book: "the idea that corporations should produce brands, not products" (xvii).[55] For her, this seemed to be somehow worrying, even scandalous. In a reflection published ten years after the first publication of the book, she writes:

> Nike isn't a running shoe company, it is about the *idea of transcendence through sports*; Starbucks isn't a coffee shop chain, it's about the *idea of community*. Down on earth, these epiphanies meant that many companies that had manufactured their products in their own factories, and had maintained large, stable workforces, embraced the now ubiquitous Nike model: close your factories, produce your products through an intricate web of contractors and subcontractors, and pour your resources into the design and marketing required to fully project your big idea. Or they went for the Microsoft model: maintain a tight control center of shareholder-employees who perform the company's "core competency," and outsource everything else to temps, from running the mailroom to writing code. Some called these restructured companies "hollow corporations" because their goal seemed to transcend the corporeal world of things so they could be an utterly unencumbered brand. As corporate guru Tom Peters put it: "You are a damn fool if you own it!" (xviii)

If, in a society operating with second-order observation, the profile of a commodity is more valuable than the actual product, then it makes sense that companies focus only on curating that profile rather than on manufacturing and distributing "stuff." The "utterly unencumbered brand" represents a shift from the earlier meaning of "brand," indicating the identity of an owner or manufacturer, to today's reference to profilic identity. Klein seems to have a certain nostalgia for more "authentic" capitalism where corporations actually make goods rather than outsource the production process. In profilic capitalism, though, profiles rather than products have become the primary source of profit, and this is what capitalists care about most.

Klein rightly sees an analogy between "hollow corporations" and "hollow politics." She describes how politics are nowadays also all about branding. Barack Obama was, for her, "the first U.S. president who is also a superbrand" (xix). Here, just as in the economy, she laments this situation and hopes for a return to "the real thing" (xxvii). The real thing, presumably, would consist in more authentic politics. If Klein would have understood the concept of profilicity better, and the effects that it has not only in the economy and in politics but throughout all of society, she would have had to realize that "the real thing" now *is* the profile. Profiles are, in fact, very powerful instruments for achieving identity, making money, and exercising power. To regard them as somehow unreal or merely inauthentic is a serious underestimation of their very real power.

To Klein's credit, it should be noted that she is very much aware of and explicitly addresses the fact that the great public success of *No Logo* made it a logo, too. Moreover, it made Naomi Klein her "own brand," no matter how much she may have tried to reject it (xvii–xl). Given the depth of her analysis of branding, Klein would have recognized the inevitability of these developments. They follow the logic of logos, and profilicity. This, once more, shows how *real* profilicity is. Paradoxically, under conditions of profilicity, any "successful" attack against it will only result in more profilicity.

POWER TO THE PEERS: ON THE REVIEW PROCESS IN PROFILICITY

In the economy, profiles make money. In politics, they grant power. In academia, they establish "truth," or at least credibility. High-profile academics find it easy to publish. They get invited as keynote speakers to major conferences where hundreds or thousands listen to them. Afterward, these hundreds or thousands of lower-profile scholars split up into tiny panels listening to one another's exegeses of high-profile academics.

This is one of the major frustrations that come with profilicity: only a few can be high profile. The rest must remain low profile and find a way to cope with their situation. In sincerity, everyone can be sincere. You need only your immediate peers—your family members, for instance—to confirm your sincerity to you. In authenticity, one way of feeling especially unique is to self-identify as the genius unrecognized by the masses. One can feel content living authentically only if a few people realize authenticity; after all, everyone else is fake. These strategies don't really work in profilicity. Your family members' likes don't really count, and the unseen profile is all but worthless. Just as in the capitalist economy, the profilicity lottery only increases the gap between those who are really successful and those who are not.

Chances are that you are not the one drawing most of the attention and that your profile, all things considered, will remain unimpressive. You will not be the keynote speaker; you'll join the ranks of peers filling the hall. There is compensation, though. At least sort of. The all-pervasive social validation feedback loop is open to everyone. Even if you, as most of your peers, have to come to terms with a low-profile identity, you are still given the constant opportunity to validate others. On *American Idol* very few get to sing, but many get to vote. This is basically the same in academia, thanks to the peer review system whereby nearly all manuscripts submitted for publication are reviewed by several fellow researchers to filter out the few that get the nod.[56]

Having worked in academia for decades, the authors of the present book have come to the conclusion that double-blind (names of authors and reviewers are not revealed to one another) peer review can bring out the worst in people, including, sometimes, ourselves. Under the cover of anonymity, there are many good reasons why academics may feel on occasion enticed to write a condescending, destructive, and even ignorant review of a work with the intention to prevent its publication. Maybe the reviewer had a bad day. Maybe the reviewer can tell who the author is and hates her. Maybe he is, by nature, a pedantic, narrow-minded, evil-spirited nitpicker. Maybe he thinks rationally and does not see why he should provide a competitor with the opportunity to further her academic profile. Or maybe he is frustrated that many of his own previous submissions got rejected and now feels it is payback time. Of course, there is also the distinct possibility that the essay under review is actually horrible.

The second to last of these potential reasons for the sporadically encountered uncharitable peer review report may provide an inroad into the psychology of academics and anyone else who needs to do profile work. Statistically, one is much more likely to be at the low rather than at the high end of profilicity (and we are not sure how many reviews high-profile authors like Naomi Klein or Judith Butler write). This can become a source of major discontent. One diligently curates one's profile day by day, yet the decisive breakthrough never happens—which can get to one in the long run. Identity value steadily crumbles and feelings of hopelessness creep in. Most social spheres, however, provide a highly effective valve for frustration relief, a regular process injecting intervals of stimulating doses of empowerment to the masses that constitute the general peer. In *American Idol*, and elections, the people can make their voices heard and their vote counted. On YouTube they can comment, and on Amazon.com and in academia they can write reviews.

To keep the social validation feedback loop going, it is of crucial importance to regulate and channel the power flow. Yes, power is concentrated in high profiles, but all low profiles are, and must be, integrated into the ongoing circulation of power lest they drop out of the loop. Social validation feedback loops are social power generators and regenerators. Just as in the capitalist economy the poor need to be given the constant opportunity to spend the little money they have (so that this money can eventually make the rich richer), in profilicity the low profiles constantly need to be given the opportunity to spend their profilic power in evaluating the profiles of others. And the cycle is self-reinforcing. By citing Naomi Klein or Judith Butler, we further their high profiles. And if we don't cite people like them, we lower our profile even further by not being "in the discourse."

The feeling of being one with the general peer can be elating. It restores a much needed sense of dignity in low-profile peers. It shows everyone not only that they can make a difference but, actually, that they are needed, that their participation in the symbolic constitution of the general peer is an absolute necessity. High profiles are made possible only insofar as they are generously granted by the general peer. This is their exclusive source under conditions of profilicity—there is no God, no family member, and no inner self that can provide it instead. The masses need to be rewarded with feelings of pride and dignity, with feelings of relevance, with feelings of "agency," and with the feeling that their identity is, after all, accounted for. Since their own low profiles can never fulfill such desires, they are regularly allotted the salvific experience, the soteriological event of uniting with the omnipotent general peer.

NOTES ON THE HISTORY OF PROFILICITY

Profilicity is not new. It is not just a social media phenomenon. The history of profilicity, however, remains to be written. Here, we present a few notes on this history. We focus specifically on earlier theories that describe aspects of profilicity but used neither this term nor the conceptual framework attached to it.

The Picturesque: Profilicity in Times of Print and Photography

The University of Macau is located on Hengqin Island in the Pearl River delta. There's a wall around the campus separating it from the rest of the island, which belongs to mainland China, not Macau. The only access to the campus is through a tunnel underneath the Pearl River estuary that connects it with Macau proper. When you exit the tunnel and reach the campus, the first thing you see on your left is a welcoming board presenting a picture of the university as seen from above the tunnel exit. Your attention is thus drawn away from your actual view of the campus, which opens up to your right, and directed toward your left where the same campus, only from a higher angle, is shown on the welcoming board.

The picture on the welcoming board is nice. It was taken on a very clear sunny day, which you don't often get in Macau. It shows the university, quite literally, in its best light. But what is the purpose of such a picture on the left when you can see what's on it, at the same time, to your right? The answer: profilicity. Under conditions of profilicity, you do not simply see things, but you see things as they are seen, or ought to be seen, or would like to be seen.

The profilicity principle is applied frequently throughout Macau, particularly in the big casinos. The Macau Venetian is more or less a copy of the Las Vegas Venetian, which in turn is a re-creation of the actual Venice. It includes a reinvented St. Mark's Square, the Rialto Bridge, and an indoor version of the Grand Canal complete with Caucasian gondoliers singing gondoliers' songs. Right next to the Macau Venetian is the Parisian, where you can climb a mini Eiffel Tower or stroll through the Grand Boulevards.

Visitors from Italy or France may find the mass touristic "cultural appropriations" of major sights of their home countries slightly offensive. They may seem kitschy. They may be perceived if not as an insult then as an irreverent falsification of great architectonic and artistic inventions for purely commercial purposes. In other words, visitors might judge Macau casinos on the basis of an authenticity prejudice. Indeed, from the perspective of authenticity, the Macau Venetian and the Parisian are epitomes of inauthenticity—but they were never meant to be authentic. Just like the picture of the University of Macau on its welcoming board, they are meant to show a place in its best light—or more precisely, they are not supposed to show a place at all, but how a place is seen as being seen. They show profiles of places and do not pretend to do anything else.

From a semiotic perspective, profilic images or artifacts are not so much representations as presentations. They do not represent an actual object but present its profile. They can be understood in the tradition of the picturesque. Perceiving something as picturesque means not to perceive it as such but as it is seen by someone looking at a picture of it. The notion of the "picturesque," and its practice in art, became popular along with Romanticism in the eighteenth century and remained so for quite a while.[57] It manifests an earlier, pre–social media and pre–internet wave of profilicity.

When travelling through eastern Saxony in September 1800, the German writer Heinrich von Kleist was deeply impressed by the beauty of the rural scenery.[58] In a letter to his fiancée Wilhelmine von Zenge, he wrote: "Every farm is a landscape," alluding to their aesthetically perfect appearance. When enjoying a panoramic view from the top of a hill, the land below looked to him "just as a wholly framed painting."[59] Von Kleist's way of expressing his feelings was not uncommon at the time. It was around 1800 that the perception of a landscape, "as the most beautiful painting"—as picturesque—was, according to the contemporary writer Ludwig Tieck, a "stereotypical observation" among intellectuals associated with German Romanticism.[60]

When overlooking the fields of Saxony, Heinrich von Kleist did so, and not without enthusiasm, through the lens of the landscape paintings he had seen somewhere else. He saw the image in front of him in the form of a visual model that he had brought with him in his conceptual rucksack. This mode of observation indicates a reversal of what may be considered a "normal" order of perception. When looking at a painting—a portrait of a person that we know, for instance—we might exclaim: "Yes, it looks exactly like her," and thereby measure the quality of the image by the degree of its correspondence with the original. In the case of the picturesque, however, this order is reversed. Von Kleist measured the beauty of the landscape he saw by its degree of correspondence with a painting.

The picturesque made quite a career in the wake of its Romanticist inception. It had a significant influence on the practice of literature and the arts throughout the nineteenth century. This popularity was made possible by the development of the mass media and the increased availability of pictures to an increasing number of people. Journals and books included illustrations and, later on, photographic representations of artworks and "natural beauty." Museums, too, were founded and became accessible to many. Aesthetic perception was significantly shaped by the images seen in this way. They demonstrated to everyone how things needed to look to be seen as beautiful, interesting, or stylish, and worthy of being shown in public. Images impressed by being impressed onto paper and distributed to many.

In a study on Bram Stoker, the author of *Dracula*, Matthew Gibson shows in detail how paintings served as a major influence and inspiration for writing and staging theater plays in the nineteenth and early twentieth centuries. As Gibson points out, in his fiction Bram Stoker "frequently refers to paintings or the painter's art when trying to direct the reader's 'concretization' . . . of a scene" or draws "upon the reader's acquaintance with existing well-known . . . paintings of the Victorian era."[61] Plays and novels of the time employed the technique of the picturesque in order to appeal to the taste, and in particular to the profilic expectations, of an audience.[62] Today, bestselling novels often call up images and scenes from films. And when the 9/11 attacks were broadcast live on TV, many people felt that the news coverage looked like a Hollywood movie. The attacks, too, were "picturesque" and probably intended to be so. In Stoker's time, popular writers would make people think they were looking at a painting when reading a story or watching a play. Today, a novel (or terrorist attack) can be made more spectacular when evoking cinematic experiences. In both cases, the artwork does not attempt to represent reality but to attract attention and to be "liked" by presenting things, people, or events as they are seen as being seen.

The picturesque is somewhat paradoxical. Rather than making the landscape the standard by which a landscape painting is measured, the landscape painting becomes the standard for a landscape—or for a description of it in a novel. When describing a landscape in a novel, a picturesque writer will not be guided by what he may have seen "out there" but rather by what he has seen in a journal or a museum. And his success as a writer will depend on how well he is able to do this.

The paradox is especially noteworthy in the connection with Romanticism, the period when the picturesque gained traction. The Romanticists are typically associated with a quest for authenticity.[63] Von Kleist, when writing to his lover, can be expected to have intended to express himself most personally, most subjectively, and most intimately. In the letter to Wilhelmine, he presents himself as a true *connoisseur* of landscape. By depicting the landscape in terms of a painting, von Kleist not only elevates the scenery to the level of art by infusing it with aesthetic value. At the same time, he also elevates himself to the level of a cultured aesthete. He casts himself, paradoxically, in the stereotypical profile of the authentic romanticist that inspired his generation of intellectuals.

Von Kleist's powers of observation not only let the landscape shine in its best light, they also let him appear as a passionate, creative, and sensitive man. In the form of second-order observation, he wants Wilhelmine not only to imagine the landscape but also to observe the observer, namely, himself. He presumably intends her to see him how he likes to be seen—and who would not want this when communicating with one's lover? His letter not only presents the profile of a landscape, it also outlines von Kleist's profile as an authentic individual. Not merely a description of scenery, it also presents a portrait of the artist as a young man.

Exhibition Value: Profilicity in Times of Film

The picturesque bears all the hallmarks of second-order observation. It represents an earlier form of the practice of profilicity. It was not, however, understood as such. Rather, people understood this romanticist phenomenon first and foremost as an *aesthetic* idea, a way of being or making something beautiful and appealing. It was not understood in wider social and psychological contexts, and its connection with the "problem of identity" was hardly reflected on. Even its close relation with the emerging mass media seemed of little concern. Instead, alongside the blossoming of the "age of authenticity," the picturesque remained more or less a bourgeois nineteenth-century pastime, an available ornament for the paradoxical expression of individuality. The picturesque had little theory; it was all style.

In the twentieth century the bourgeois aesthetics of the picturesque receded further into the background and was eventually overtaken in relevance by newer and much more powerful forces of profilicity. Industrialization had taken hold of Europe and was spreading all over the globe. A new kind of people, the working class, was shaping itself into a political force and stirring up revolutions. New technologies profoundly changed not only ways of living—and of dying, as evidenced in World War I—but also mass media. Photography rapidly spread and changed the way reality was perceived, and out of it the new medium of film soon developed. These massive evolutions and accelerations also allowed profilicity to evolve and accelerate on a grand scale. And this was now theorized. If not in these exact terms then at least in substance, the (arguably) first theory of profilicity appeared in print in 1936: Walter Benjamin's famous essay on *The Work of Art in the Age of Mechanical Reproduction*.[64]

Benjamin's approach to art in this essay is not aesthetic, at least not in the traditional sense of an enquiry into what makes art artistic, beautiful, or appealing. It is an analysis of the revolutionary social function of an altogether new kind of art enabled by altogether new technologies. Benjamin reflects on the fact that photography and, especially, film have thoroughly transformed the mode of artistic production and fundamentally changed its sociopolitical potential. In the forms of film and photography, art had aligned itself with the mass media, and it has to be understood in this relation rather than in the old-fashioned manner of aesthetic contemplation. While Benjamin still uses the traditional notion of "art" when reflecting on the sociopolitical and cultural aspects of film and photography, he in fact already regards them as, in essence, mass media.

About seventy years prior to Charles Taylor's proclamation of the "age of authenticity" in *A Secular Age*,[65] Benjamin had already expressed an idea that is central for our understanding of profilicity: the peak time of authenticity is running out. Its demise has been not in the least due to the mass media and their social effects. According to Benjamin, before the era of technological reproduction, works of art had been original creations, housed at one special place, often a religious site. Due to their singularity and limited accessibility, these art works would acquire an "aura." Their aura made them objects of reverence and conferred them with "cult value." In religion, this cult value manifested itself in the ritual contexts within which art works had typically functioned. Still, even in secular times, under bourgeois conditions, the particular value of these works was attributed to their uniqueness. "Great" works of art retained their cultic value and were not normally displayed to the public. There was still only one original at only one place, and this place was more or less secluded.

A core insight informing Benjamin's theory is that "the whole sphere of authenticity is outside technical—and, of course, not only technical—reproducibility."[66] Concretely, this means for him that "from a photographic negative, for example, one can make any number of prints; to ask for the 'authentic' print makes no sense" (20). Photos and films have no originals, there is nothing authentic about them, they don't have an aura, and they lack the corresponding religious or bourgeois cult value.

For Benjamin, the shift from the authentic original to the reproduced copy is not only a shift in art; it is also, and primarily, a sociopolitical shift. Once art is shown to and consumed by the masses, it no longer functions in the context of religious ritual or aristocratic aesthetics. It becomes a mass media phenomenon, and thereby part of mass society and of proletarian life. The shift from art to mass media signals the shift from feudalism to capitalism—which may pave the way, as Benjamin seemed to hope, for a further shift to a future communist society.

For Benjamin, the development of art away from privileged social spheres to become a medium for the masses signals a change in perception. Although he does not use this expression, it is in essence a change toward second-order observation. When watching a theatrical play, the audience is present and sees the actors physically in front of them. This changes fundamentally in a movie. Here, the actor is filmed, and the audience sees the actor as being filmed. As Benjamin says, "the actor's performance is presented by means of a camera" so that "the actor is subjected to a series of optical tests" (27). He is shot from different angles, from different distances, and the shots are finally shown in a highly edited way. Benjamin concludes that unlike in traditional theater, in film "the audience's identification with the actor is really an identification with the camera. Consequently, the audience takes the position of the camera" (27). This is a decisive step. The audience no longer simply sees a character but sees a character as being seen—and this invites a different form of identification. We now can identify not only with the character but at the same time also with the "peer" who is observing him.

In Benjamin's analysis, the perceptional shift that goes along with the shift from theater to cinema "permits the audience to take the position of a critic, without experiencing any personal contact with the actor." In film, the aura is lost, and thus also reverence. Second-order observation is irreverent. It sees a performance *as a performance*, and it is put in a position to evaluate it from a critical distance. Benjamin writes: "It is inherent in the technique of the film as well as that of sports that everybody who witnesses its accomplishments is somewhat of an expert" (31). In film, the power of the observer over the observed becomes more pronounced.

Benjamin portrays film actors as almost trembling with fear in front of an invisible mass audience on whom their fates depend. This brings him very close to regarding the film audience as the emerging general peer. But, given his Marxist theoretical framework, he prefers to conceive of it in terms of a personification of the capitalist consumer market:

> While facing the camera [the actor] knows that ultimately he will face the public, the consumers who constitute the market. This

market, where he offers not only his labor but also his whole self, his heart and soul, is beyond his reach. During the shooting he has as little contact with it as any article made in a factory. . . . The film responds to the shriveling of the aura with an artificial build-up of the "personality" outside the studio. The cult of the movie star, fostered by the money of the film industry, preserves not the unique aura of the person but the "spell of the personality," the phony spell of a commodity. (31)

Here, Benjamin not only presents (a little naively, as we will explain in the next section) a Marxist portrait of the general peer as movie customers. He also, somewhat contradictory to his overall argumentation, seems to express some nostalgia for the "unique aura of the person." In any case, his depiction of the "personalities" of movie celebrities as a "phony spell of a commodity" is quite in line with our understanding of the profilic persona. Phony or not, in a capitalist context the "personalities" of movie celebrities represent the commodification of identity. The same is true of the profilic personas of the rest of us.

In film, there is no authenticity and no uniqueness, neither of artwork nor of artist. The new "cult" is no longer tied to the secrecy of religious ritual; it is out in the open, in front of the masses. The new value of art and artist, as Benjamin neatly calls it, is *exhibition value*. From our perspective, this analysis is not only correct with regard to the arts, the mass media, and the culture industry. Exhibition value is the value attached to the exhibition of all identity profiles throughout society. Under conditions of profilicity, not only actors and artists exhibit and market their profiles to the general peer; politicians and academics do so as well. In the economy, too, value is a variation of what Benjamin called exhibition value—as was shown by John Maynard Keynes in 1936.

The Beauty Contest

In his classic study *The General Theory of Employment, Interest and Money*, Keynes used the example of a peculiar beauty contest to explain how value is generated in the modern economy:

> Professional investment may be likened to those newspaper competitions in which the competitors have to pick out the six prettiest faces from a hundred photographs, the prize being awarded to the competitor whose choice most nearly corresponds to the average preferences of the competitors as a whole; so that each competitor has to pick, not those faces which he himself finds prettiest, but those which he thinks likeliest to catch the fancy of the other competitors, all of whom are looking at the problem from the same point of view. It is not a case of choosing those which, to the best of one's judgment, are really the prettiest, nor even those which average opinion genuinely thinks the prettiest. We have reached the third degree where we devote our intelligences to anticipating what average opinion expects the average opinion to be.[67]

This is, of course, how *American Idol* and many other shows function. As Elena Esposito points out, the Keynesian beauty contest not only is an excellent illustration of how prices are constructed in the economy, it is also a most pertinent illustration of second-order observation.[68] A traditional beauty contest is based on first-order observation. A number of people look at a number of faces and then choose the prettiest. The face that gets the most votes wins. All this changes, and becomes much more complex, when the contest switches to the level of second-order observation. Now not only those subjecting themselves to evaluation compete but also, and even primarily, the judges. The judges compete to guess which face will win the beauty contest, which shifts their evaluation to the level of second-order observations. They look not only at the faces but, at least imaginarily, at how the faces are being seen. This brings about a further and most decisive shift. Now *everybody is aware that everybody else is also observing and evaluating in the mode of second-order observation*, and what people "genuinely think"—that is, what they observe in the mode of first-order observation— *becomes irrelevant.* The exclusive object of observation and evaluation are other people's observations and evaluations. To be a competent participant in this contest, moreover, you need to realize that the observers you observe also observe in the mode of second-order observation. They, too, look not at the faces themselves but at how others look at the faces. Thus the faces themselves are at best secondary objects of evaluation. Rather, the judges scrutinize what other judges think about what other judges think. This form of competition calls on us to observe other people's observations of other people's observations.

The Keynesian beauty contest illustrates the dynamics of Instagram and other platforms, where the reality of second-order observation—that is, the reality of profilicity—is manifest. What people genuinely think about the prettiness of the faces in the beauty contest is just as irrelevant as what Taylor Swift (or anyone else for that matter) genuinely thinks about an Instagram post. The point is to devote your intelligence to anticipating what average opinion expects average opinion to be.

Keynes originally came up with the beauty contest example to show how investors think and act, and thereby how value in the finance industry is established. The beautiful faces correspond to stocks or bonds. Their market value is derived neither from inherent value (which does not exist) nor by first-order observation, that is, by what investors "genuinely think" about them. Market value is established by looking at how something is seen as being seen. To speak with Benjamin, we may call this exhibition value: value in the eyes not of a specific peer operating in the mode of first-order observation but of the nonpersonal general peer. In the economy, the general peer is the market. In film, it is the mass audience. And this also means that Walter Benjamin could have been more precise in his analysis of how celebrities and their personality value functions. They seem less like an "article made in a factory," as he wrote, and much more like stocks traded on Wall Street.

In the Keynesian beauty contest, the one who can guess average opinion most accurately—that is, the person who functions most efficiently in predicting second-order observation—wins. In real life today, everyone competes as a judge, observing in the mode of second-order observation and knowing that everyone else does so as well. This mode of observation is no longer merely a peculiar skill needed for winning odd newspaper games. It has become a general mode of observation throughout all society.

The Spectacle

Three decades after Benjamin and Keynes, in 1967, another theoretical account approximating a description of profilicity was published. This time it was written by a French author, and perhaps more passionate, more poetical, and more forceful than the previous German and British attempts: Guy Debord's *The Society of the Spectacle*.[69]

The book starts with a powerful proclamation, sounding like an implicit call to arms: "All that once was directly lived has become mere representation" (1). Instead of being a "direct" life experience, existence in modern capitalist society takes place in and through images. Here, we live life in a representational and

exhibitory way. In the society of the spectacle, all "social relationships between people" are "mediated by images" (4). This
shift from direct immediacy to indirect representation also
involves a "shift from having to appearing" (17). People not only
look at images, they also consume and project these images,
including their own self-images. They possess goods in the form
of images and act in the form of symbolic conduct. In the society of the spectacle, "the perceptible world is replaced by a set of
images that are superior to that world yet at the same time impose
themselves as eminently perceptible" (36).

The spectacle reverses hierarchies: The world has been "turned
on its head" (9). In the old days, there was a primacy of the
"direct" existence of people and things over representations of
this existence. Now, the image has gained the upper hand; it
becomes most valuable. Debord's depiction of this reversal follows, in effect, the Romanticist aesthetics of the picturesque
where paintings became the standard for perceiving the beauty
of a landscape. It parallels Naomi Klein's account of the logic of
logos where the value of the brand name determines the value
of the product, rather than the other way around. Debord speaks
of an "inversion of life" (2) where "signs" (8) are the ultimate "end-
product." At times, he decries these signs or images as mere
"illusions" or indicators of a "false consciousness" (3). Simultaneously, though, he stresses that "the spectacle is real." Poetically put, "reality erupts in the spectacle." Whenever Debord
highlights that the images and signs constituting the spectacle
are products "of real activity" (8), they resemble very closely
what we call "profiles." In the spectacle, authenticity has lost its
function—or rather, it only assumes a function when put into the
service of the spectacle (or in our terms, of profilicity): "What
has been passed off as authentic life turns out to be merely a life
more authentically spectacular" (153).

In the course of his argumentation, Debord subordinates his semiotic analysis to a Marxist critique. Dressed in Marxist vocabulary, the spectacle is eventually redefined as "capital accumulated to the point where it becomes image" (34). In this way, it is supposed to be understood as "one particular economic and social formation." It is a "world view transformed into an objective force," so that in the "material realm" it becomes the "dominant mode of production" (5–6). The spectacle becomes an economic and ideological concept. It is made responsible—not unlike the logic of logos for Klein—for making profit out of human alienation and exploitation. The spectacle becomes a huge commodity, the major resource for the accumulation of capital.

Like Benjamin before him, Debord sees a close connection between the political economy of capitalism and the technological reproduction of images. News, advertising, and entertainment are for him "specific manifestations" of the "real unreality" of the spectacle (6). The mass media accordingly turn out to be the "most stultifying superficial manifestation" of the spectacle (24).

Like Benjamin, Debord too reflects on how the mass media, as an omnipresent form of the spectacle, affect human identity. Mass media stars are denounced as being in the service of the spectacle and thus false individuals. Not only this, a celebrity is "the enemy of the individual in himself as of the individual in others" (61). Celebrities make themselves spectacular and seduce others to do the same. They sell out to the spectacle, commodify themselves, and lead others to buy into this and sell out, too. As Debord poetically laments, celebrities are "distilling the essence of the spectacle's banality into images of possible roles" (60). Apparently, he thinks that while life in the spectacle is banal, there once was a time before the spectacle took hold when it was not. If movie stars and others in the service of the spectacle had not tempted us into taking on banal roles, the nonbanal life, beyond role enactment, might still exist.

Guy Debord never really outlines what the nonbanal and non-role-based life of true individuality prior to the spectacle used to look like. We are not sure, to be frank, that it ever really did exist. Nevertheless, Debord's descriptions of the spectacle, of its predicaments, and of the social and individual pathologies that it produces are highly relevant—and bear striking resemblance to certain dimensions of profilicity. At times he seems almost to be presenting prescient analyses of today's online world—analyses that would make some contemporary critiques of the internet and social media look stale in comparison. At other times, however, he falls back on an all-too-standard Marxist insinuation of the possibility of perfect human life, of perfectly congruent identity, looming behind the menace of the spectacle. It seems very unlikely, however, that before the spectacle there was in fact an idyllic primitive society without class distinctions where all lived happily and content. If understood as the regime of profilicity, the spectacle did not replace "all that once was directly lived"; it replaced the regimes of sincerity and authenticity. A return to these modes of identity would not be a return to paradise. No paradise has been lost, and none is around the corner when the spectacle ends. In fact, these false utopias, no matter if capitalist or communist, are also spectacular images. They are signs easily appropriated and put in the service of the perpetuation of their own spectacles.

Further Debates on the Revolutionary Significance of a Toaster

Guy Debord was a Marxist who did not like the mass media, and particularly not television and film. He found them too spectacular. His negative attitude was representative of the political left at the time, which in the wake of Walter Benjamin and

Theodor W. Adorno and Max Horkheimer tended to denounce the "culture industry" as a manifestation of the "dialectic of enlightenment."[70] The mass media turned bourgeois freedom against itself; the new opium of the masses, mass media dumbed down and enslaved people by leading them to "amuse themselves to death" (in Neil Postman's phrase). Paradoxically, the mass media seemed all-too mass-oriented for many intellectuals taking sides with the working class.

There were exceptions, though. In 1970 the German writer Hans-Magnus Enzensberger published a short essay in *Kursbuch*, a trendy German leftist journal he edited. This essay, titled "Constituents of a Theory of the Media" in English translation, was meant to revolutionize the leftist approach to the mass media. Rather than merely looking at the media as an expression of capitalist domination, Enzensberger hoped to raise awareness of their "emancipatory potential" and "mobilizing power."[71] Once *these* means of production were taken out of the hands of the capitalists who owned the movie companies and TV and radio stations—once they were truly democratized, taken over by the people—everybody would be enabled to contribute to them. This was possible through their very technology, Enzensberger pointed out: "Every transistor radio is, by the nature of its construction, at the same time a potential transmitter: it can interact with other receivers by circuit reversal" (97). Unfortunately, due to capitalist monopolies, the media were not functioning the way they should. As of yet, there was only one-way communication from the big companies, or the state, down to the people. This allowed the capitalists to manipulate and exploit the masses for their own benefit. The people remained mere receivers. However, once the potential of the new technologies was liberated, everyone would both send and receive. Through the new technologies, technically, "every reader, as it were, should write his own book" (127)—or, more literally, every radio listener or TV viewer would produce their own broadcasts. In this way, a truly democratic and socialist society could emerge: the mass media would be owned in common and everyone would actively take part. Enzensberger put it poetically: we will become "as free as dancers, as aware as football players, as surprising as guerillas" (97).[72] Here, he sounds like an earlier Marxist incarnation of *Wired* magazine cofounder Nicholas Negroponte, who, like so many others, hailed the wonderful potential of the internet to make all of us happy, creative, and politically active.[73]

Enzensberger was soon rebutted by a major French cultural and media theorist of his time, Jean Baudrillard. Famous for developing core notions of virtuality, such as "simulation" and the "hyperreal," Baudrillard responded with a devastating critique, countering Enzensberger with a preprofilicity account of the mass media.[74] His main point was that even a liberated mass media would not bring about a free and equal society where everybody would interact productively with one another. To the contrary, in mass media everyone was taking part in a mass exercise of "speech without response" (169). For Baudrillard, "the mass media are anti-mediatory and intransitive" (169). That the media are "intransitive" is to say that they do not establish real relationships. They might allow everyone to say or to show something, but what you get in return is not intersubjective engagement. It is just another display. Mass media devices made life only more technological and thereby isolated us from one another rather than bringing us closer together. They lacked any personally liberating or politically subversive power: "As if owning a TV set or camera inaugurated a new possibility of relationship and exchange. Strictly speaking, such cases are no more significant than the possession of a refrigerator or a toaster. There is no response to a functional object" (171). Similar to what Sherry

Turkle and others wrote four decades later about social media technologies,[75] Baudrillard's point, put in slightly different words, was that TV and radio make us "alone together." And not only do they make us more rather than less alone, they also make us less rather than more original. They do not turn everyone into a creative writer, as Enzensberger believed, but instead produce hokey hacks. What Baudrillard says about the walkie-talkies of the early 1970s is often said, in slight variation, about smartphones today. He writes: "We know the results of such phenomena as mass ownership of walkie-talkies, or everyone making their own cinema: a kind of personalized amateurism, the equivalent of Sunday tinkering on the periphery of the system" (182). Just as Enzensberger's vision of the liberation of TV and radio bears a striking similarity to the later celebrations of the internet by Negroponte and others, Baudrillard and Debord sound like earlier incarnations of the Sherry Turkles and Roberto Simanowskis today, for whom the online world is a dystopian black hole where we "lose ourselves."[76] Explicitly or not, both Debord and Baudrillard saw the new media of TV and cinema as threats to authenticity. These media, they feared, destroyed the "true" subjectivity of direct life experience, of intersubjective exchange, and of individual creativity.

If, however, we disregard Baudrillard's and Debord's hidden or not so hidden authenticity bias and nostalgia, then important aspects of profilicity come to the fore. Profilicity is not inauthentic but nonauthentic. Baudrillard was right to dampen Enzensberger's enthusiasm about the mass media. They do not enhance authenticity and have no potential to do so. Today we can see more clearly than in the 1960s or 1970s that the mass and social media function not so much as a negative force destroying true authenticity—which never in fact existed—but as a platform for the proliferation of profilicity. They also do not make politics more truly democratic but do enhance the profilic performance possibilities of democracy. And while they do not actually further empower us as democratic agents, they do allow us to unite with the general peer and thus to *feel* more empowered than before. We do not all become original artists, but the rise of these social and technological conditions forces us to constantly curate our profiles, exhibiting what we do, make, eat, and buy. They do not make life altogether more intersubjective or interactive, but they establish social validation feedback loops tying us together and resulting in symbiotic relationships where we become interdependent peers, mutually affirming our identities.

The Semiotics of Profilicity: Making a Difference

When Guy Debord and Jean Baudrillard reflected on society, politics, and the mass media, they often employed semiotic concepts. This was fashionable at the time, particularly in France. In 1916 a quite revolutionary linguistic study had been published: Ferdinand De Saussure's *Course in General Linguistics.*[77] It made the point, among many other points, that the meaning of a word is not informed by the thing or the idea it designates but by its relation to other words. "Drizzle" is not an objective term for a specific type of precipitation, but gets its meaning by being different from "sprinkle," "downpour," and other such words. Thus we have to look at the structure of language— *at the differences within language that constitute its structure*, to be precise—in order to see how linguistic meaning works. We need to look at these differences within language, and not at something outside, such as, for instance, things or concepts, to make sense of it. De Saussure's ideas were foundational for the development of structuralism, and thereby also for poststructuralism— which gets us back to Debord and Baudrillard, who can both be associated with this intellectual scene. Which gets us back to semiotics.

The idea that meaning is based on making internal differences (that is, the differences between "signs" themselves) rather than on external representation (that is, the representation of something by a sign) was of great importance for Western intellectual history in the twentieth century. It has a lot to do not only with French poststructuralism but also with the linguistic turn in Anglo-American philosophy, with social constructivism in sociology, and with the rise and fall of semiotics. It also has something to do with this book and the notion of profilicity. Profilicity, too, is postrepresentational and concerned with such differences.

Traditionally, for instance in Aristotle's short treatise *On Interpretation*, written words were taken to represent spoken words, which in turn were taken to represent an idea in our mind representing a thing. This commonsense understanding remains pervasive today and tells us there is a real world of things and ideas that can be represented by words. The meanings of the words are thus grounded in an objective reality, although the words themselves may be arbitrary. I can call a dog "dog," or, in German, "*Hund.*" Words can also, of course, misrepresent. We can argue about whether a word or set of words correctly represents an idea. This, in turn, relates representation to sincerity and authenticity. Since we can ask if someone is actually a mother, we can thereby question if she sincerely corresponds to her role, or if her mother persona is a true expression of her inner self.

Profilicity, in contrast, functions "postrepresentationally." My academic profile neither indicates role commitment nor represents my inner self. My H-index citation score gains meaning, instead, in comparison with the H-index citation scores of other academic profiles. Brian Piñeyro has numerous personas. The

question of whether DJ Xanax represents him most authentically is rather moot. Instead, the significance of DJ Xanax, or
better, his artistic "meaning," is understood in relation to other
musical personas—of Brian Piñeyro and of other artists. A
brand's image cannot be understood as an authentic or sincere
representation of a company. The logo "Mac" does not represent
Apple's true self. "Mac" is a profilic logo that must be understood in relation to other such logos, such as that of Microsoft.
This is what the "Get a Mac" campaign was all about: making
everyone understand the meaning of the Mac profile through
establishing its difference from the Microsoft profile. With profilicity, identity consists not in representation of a role or a true
self but in having a profile that is different from other profiles.

3

SINCERITY

It is probably no mere historical accident that the word person, in its first meaning, is a mask. It is rather a recognition of the fact that everyone is always and everywhere, more or less consciously, playing a role. . . . It is in these roles that we know each other; it is in these roles that we know ourselves. . . . In a sense, and in so far as this mask represents the conception we have formed of ourselves—the role we are striving to live up to— this mask is our truer self, the self we would like to be. In the end, our conception of our role becomes second nature and an integral part of our personality.

—Robert Ezra Park, *Race and Culture*

We do not show ourselves to our children as to our club-companions, to our customers as to the laborers we employ, to our own masters and employers as to our intimate friends. From this there results what practically is a division of the man into several selves; and this may be a discordant splitting, as where one is afraid to let one set of his acquaintances know him as he is elsewhere; or it may be a perfectly harmonious division of labor, as where one tender to his children is stern to the soldiers or prisoners under his command.

—William James, *The Principles of Psychology*

FACEBOOK INTEGRITY

According to Mark Zuckerberg, Facebook has an ethics of integrity at its core. In *The Facebook Effect* (2010), David Kirkpatrick recounts Zuckerberg's musings on identity—which seem intended to diffuse the often heard critique that social media undermines human "authenticity" by giving users the opportunity to present multiple profiles of themselves:

> "You have one identity," he says emphatically three times in a single minute during a 2009 interview. He recalls that in Facebook's early days some argued the service ought to offer adult users both a work profile and a "fun social profile." Zuckerberg was opposed to that. "The days of you having a different image for your work friends or co-workers and for the other people you know are probably coming to an end pretty quickly," he says.
>
> He makes several arguments. "Having two identities for yourself is an example of a lack of integrity," Zuckerberg says moralistically. But he also makes a case he sees as pragmatic—that "the level of transparency the world now has won't support having two identities for a person." In other words, even if you want to segregate your personal from your professional information you won't be able to, as information about you proliferates on the Internet and elsewhere. He would say the same about any images one seeks to project—for example, a teenager who acts docile at home but is a drug-using reprobate with his friends.
>
> Zuckerberg, along with a key group of his colleagues, also believes that by openly acknowledging who we are and behaving consistently among all our friends, we will help create a healthier society.[1]

Zuckerberg's plea for integrity as the public display of a consistent personality can hardly escape accusations of hypocrisy. As duplicitous as the teenager in the example, the self-proclaimed "connector of the world" values openness while simultaneously living a rather reclusive life. He spent $30 million buying up the neighboring homes around his Palo Alto compound just to ensure his privacy.[2] And although boldly suggesting that "you have one identity," he is known as a bold and ruthless entrepreneur who can be self-assured and even condescending in front of Congress but also famously shy and unassuming during interviews. He uncomfortably fumbles his way through his own 2018–2019 video series titled "The Future of Technology and Society."[3] Despite his claim that human identity ought to be singular, Zuckerberg regularly presents himself through multiple personas.

So which identity is correct? Who is the real Mark Zuckerberg? Is he simply a hypocrite who asks others to do something he himself cannot or will not do? Is he a "fake," lacking the very integrity of identity he desires Facebook to enable? Maybe the actual problem is not Mark Zuckerberg himself but his simplistic philosophy of identity and, consequently, his flawed ethics of integrity. Instead of questioning Zuckerberg's personality, we should challenge his reasoning. Is it actually possible for someone to present the same character across all social settings?

Of course, people *do* act differently in different situations. They do not address their boss like they address their baby. A parent is not treated like a stranger, and vice versa. We do not act in a classroom as we would at a ball game, or in church—and would it really be better if we did? Different situations make different demands on us, as do particular people and the various roles we have.

Zuckerberg's sweeping claim that "you have one identity" has little to do with historical, sociological, or psychological evidence—and is flatly contradicted by social media practices. Identities are fragile and dynamic patch works. The common and, as in Zuckerberg's case, often unquestioned idea that everyone has a single underlying self that ought to be identified and publicly expressed in the form of a coherent individuality in order to have "integrity" rose to prominence only rather recently, in the modern "age of authenticity." The semantics of this age guide the semantics of Facebook's ethos. Prior to this age, however, identity was often understood differently. It was acknowledged that people had to assume numerous roles in society, and thus integrity did not lie in presenting the very same, "true" persona all the time. Rather, it rested in carrying out one's different roles properly and virtuously, as well as in fully committing to those roles, to the extent of truly identifying with them. This was the integrity of sincerity.

PEACHES AND ONIONS

The late American-Confucian philosopher Henry Rosemont, Jr., used the metaphor of peaches and onions to illustrate the difference between viewing people as having a core self versus being composed of social roles and relationships:

> People may be seen as peaches: an external skin that is public, the fruit itself which is our body as well as our personality and history. And then there is the peach pit, our self, that which endures, does not change from day to day, and is quite literally the seed of future life (biological and mental). . . . But think instead of an onion. I peel off successive layers; first son, then husband, father grandfather; I continue peeling away the layers of friends, students, teachers, colleagues, neighbors, etc. And what is left when there are no more layers? Nothing at all.[4]

Never shy about his own predilections, Rosemont pounced on anyone who opted for the peach view of themselves: If you claim to have a core immutable self, why is it that any description of that self can be readily explained through your social interactions? What meaning could your life possibly have outside of roles and relationships? We do not live our lives as abstract individuals with accidental relationships but become who we are through bonds with others. We live as fathers, daughters, brothers, teachers, and so forth. We are an aggregate of various dynamic personal connections. When they change, we change. Even a small variance can unsettle us, while big changes can completely alter our identity. A family member dies and our life is transformed. We get married or have children and our world dramatically shifts. Rosemont paraphrases David Hume, "replacing 'perception' with 'role,'" to make the point: "For my part, when I enter most intimately into what I call *myself*, I always stumble on some particular role or other, of son or father, friend or neighbor, teacher or student. I never can catch *myself* at any time apart from a role, and never can observe anything except from the viewpoint of a role" (49–50). The self, person, or I is simply the complex amalgamation of various roles and relationships. This is what "sincerity," as a method of achieving identity, refers to: recognizing that social role encumbrances make us who we are.

The position Rosemont advocated is clearly radical. For him, social roles and relationships do not simply contribute to a sense of self or one's identity; they constitute it entirely. He was a leftist communitarian who hoped to achieve social justice and overcome the evils of capitalism by promoting a fundamentally role-based conception of identity, cleansed of its oppressive aspects and adapted to contemporary contexts. Today people are likely to disagree with such an "extremist" conception. Authenticity (with its emphasis on creating or finding one's individual self) has become increasingly important over the past few hundred years. But in premodern times the onion view of personhood could easily be regarded as convincing. From a somewhat idealized reconstruction of the premodern role ethics of Confucianism, Rosemont drew inspiration for his attempt to root out the hyperindividualism he perceived to be the source of most sociopolitical problems in the modern world.

Rosemont's metaphor of the onion fits a premodern ethics and notion of identity. People were taken to be born—as onions, so to speak—into multiple roles and relationships that defined them and were more or less inescapable. They left little space for developing the idea of a unique and original core self. There was relatively little choice in life regarding one's occupation, where to live, whom to marry, with whom to be friends, and the like. A baker's son was not likely to become a king, a duke, or even a blacksmith—and a baker's daughter's life would largely depend on whom she married. People tended to be placeholders of their specific roles in society. A ten-year-old king was still king. Major role reversals were rare. Divorces were uncommon, as were changes to political ideas and religious beliefs. There were, of course, exceptions. Nevertheless, identity in premodern times by and large was tied to roles acquired by birth and fortune that would remain relatively stable over a lifetime. These roles determined one's relations to others, one's sense of self, and one's view of the world.

In his seminal *Sincerity and Authenticity*, Lionel Trilling refers to G. W. F. Hegel to explain the experience of sincere identity in premodern times:

> The historical process that Hegel undertakes to expound is the self-realization of Spirit through the changing relation of the

individual to the external power of society. . . . In an initial stage of the process that is being described the individual consciousness is said to be in a wholly harmonious relation to the external power of society, to the point of being identified with it. In this relation the individual consciousness renders what Hegel calls "obedient service" to the external power and feels for it an "inner reverence." Its service is not only obedient but also silent and unreasoned, taken for granted; Hegel calls this "the heroism of dumb service." This entire and inarticulate accord of the individual consciousness with the external power of society is said to have the attribute of "nobility."[5]

Under conditions of role-based sincerity, identity is achieved by conforming to "external powers" as manifested in pre-established relationships, norms, and customs. Identity value and moral credit ("nobility") is generated through "obedient service" in the form of compliance with social expectations and role-based interactions with others. "Inner reverence" refers to a commitment that aligns one's thoughts and feelings with one's roles, eventually resulting in a "heroism of dumb service" that finds glory in complete role submission.

Under conditions of sincerity, a "dual correspondence" is often required. One should not only act in accordance with one's roles but also endorse one's actions psychologically. In this way, one honestly identifies with one's roles. In this view, moreover, it is generally assumed that if everyone does so, harmonious interactions and social stability will follow.

Sincerity was a prime method of achieving identity in premodern times, and it is still applied today—for instance in the family, in religious communities, and in sports. In professional contexts, too, role commitment and identification with one's job, or position in a group or a team, is often celebrated. These can ground a person's sense of selfhood and become a major source of meaning and significance. Sincerity provides normative frameworks.

In *After Virtue*, Alasdair MacIntyre introduces the notion of "characters" to describe the identification of an individual personality with a social role.[6] His "characters" include, for example, Prussian officers, Social Democrats, and university professors of nineteenth- and twentieth-century Germany. They all represent examples of sincerity in an already modern society and demonstrate how this technology of identity has been able to coexist with an emerging age of authenticity. A professor, for instance, had to show up at the university to lecture, grade assignments, and attend department meetings—these are duties that MacIntyre would associate with modern "social roles in general." In addition to meeting such "general" role expectations, however, a true character had to do much more. The character extended to all sorts of non-university-related areas; in everything from shopping to riding the train, professors were expected to be dressed, behave, speak, think, and feel like professors.

MacIntyre's "characters" illustrate the continuation of role-based identity technology and its associated ethics into modernity. In a premodern society dominated by sincerity, people could be regarded as an onion and identified by their roles and relationships. In modernity, the individual could become a peach—with a unique personality pit as distinct from "general" social roles. The modern character, however, is a hybrid between peach and onion. As MacIntyre points out: "In the case of a *character* role and personality fuse in a more specific way than in general" because "*characters* merge what usually is thought to belong to the individual man or woman and what is usually thought to belong to social roles" (28). On the one hand, MacIntyre proposes, in a typical modern way, that social roles and "the individual man or woman" are separable—like a pit from a peach—but by introducing the "character," he almost transforms the peach back into an onion.

FACE AND HONOR

In tight-knit communities, social roles dominate, and one is expected to live as an onion. Where this happens, pressure to conform can become immense. Role-related beliefs about how one should behave, think, and feel are thick enough, sufficiently extensive in their reach, and held by enough of one's peers that people can drown in a sea of external expectations—a veritable regime of sincerity. Whenever sincerity becomes such a regime, for instance, in the form of an oppressive Confucian ideology or a strict Puritan ethos, social expectations rooted in role-based standards can easily become harmful to individuals and societies. Suicides in rural China provide a contemporary example of how the demands of sincerity can become unbearable.

Until about two decades ago, China had one of the highest suicide rates in the world, and suicide was particularly common in rural areas. Along with rapid modernization, economic growth, and urbanization, the suicide rate fell spectacularly. Still, China stands out in one respect: It "is one of the few countries in the world that has a higher suicide rate by women over men."[7] As empirical research suggests, both the prevalence of female over male suicide and the prevalence of rural over urban suicide can be related to a continued regime of sincerity in a pre-industrialized setting where women, given their subordinated status, suffer even more from role pressures than men.[8] Such factors seem to outweigh mental illness as a decisive suicide trigger. Introducing an extensive collection of case studies on suicide in China, Wu Fei points out:

> In [Chinese] stories of suicide, some psychological factors certainly play important roles, but we would be greatly oversimplifying them if we were to define them with current psychiatric terminologies. . . . Because people who suffer domestic injustice are likely to become depressed and commit suicide, of course psychiatry will play an important role in the control of suicide; but people do not merely want to be mentally healthy. They also want to be happy and lucky, and this is already beyond the reach of psychiatry. After a long period of fieldwork on suicide, I have come to understand suicide [in China] from the perspective of justice.[9]

Wu's notions of "justice" and "injustice" are directly tied to social roles and relationships, as the stories of suicide he recounts demonstrate. "Justice" indicates for Wu treatment in accordance with a role identity that enables a person to assume their proper social position and to be "happy." Those who suffer "injustice" feel that they have been treated in a way that fundamentally undermines their role identity and prevents them from engaging in proper relationships. They cannot be "happy."

Many of the suicide motives that Wu mentioned might astonish Western readers, but they make perfect sense in the context of a Confucianism-informed regime of sincerity:[10] "There was no egg in his soup while everyone else had it"; "His daughter-in-law hid steamed buns from him"; "His sons mistreated him"; "Her husband blamed her for the mistreatment of her grandmother"; "His father blamed him for not carrying water"; "As a prostitute she could not marry her lover."[11] In each case, a person has been denied recognition of their role identity within their

Hold crap

community. Not to receive one's proper food is considered expulsion from the family; to be mistreated by one's sons is considered the destruction of one's status as father. Blame for not having fulfilled one's role obligations (serving one's grandmother, carrying water) is perceived as de facto ejection from one's kinship group. The inability to marry prevents one from achieving central role-identity characteristics, and such a situation can be highly precarious, especially for those who are already at the bottom of the role hierarchy. If identity can be found only in successful role fulfillment and community relationships, then a denial of role recognition is perceived as catastrophic. Since the onion has no pit, there is no "personal core" that one can retreat to.

Under a harsh regime of sincerity, it is impossible to achieve identity if one's role enactment is thoroughly frustrated. In such cases the only way out, it may seem, is to let the onion, that is, one's network of relationships, crumble. Without a "pit," proactive agency is difficult to establish on one's own, so suicide, as a radical form of "passive aggression," becomes an option. By killing oneself, the subject who is denied personhood within the family brings severe disrepute to that family and thereby shames and socially punishes it. If someone feels that they have "lost face"—that is, their identity—at the hands of their family, they can in turn make the whole family lose face by committing suicide. The family is publicly exposed as dysfunctional and violating proper role enactment. The act of suicide serves as an act of revenge for the injustice received—the denial of role identity—and is intended to bring the perceived perpetrators to justice by harming their reputation and status within the local community.

In European contexts, the pathologies of a regime of sincerity could manifest themselves in violence committed in pursuit of role-based honor. In his *History of My Life*, Giacomo Casanova details his duel with the Polish Colonel Franciszek Ksawery Branicki. Casanova was relatively poor when he went to Warsaw in 1766 but dressed and acted like a rich traveler.[12] At the local theater one night, Colonel Branicki ran into Casanova as he was leaving the changing room of an Italian actress. Casanova knew the woman well and had surprised her with a visit. Unfortunately, she was the mistress of the jealous colonel, who made a snide remark to Casanova as the two passed each other. After brooding for an evening, Casanova came to the conclusion that he needed to challenge Colonel Branicki to a duel. Although the insult was not great, given the position he was masquerading and the fact that other people had been present, he had no choice but to avenge himself. Both Casanova and Colonel Branicki survived the pistol shots, but while Casanova's hand was wounded, Branicki was seriously injured. As the colonel's friends and the authorities scoured the land to finish off the Venetian troublemaker, Casanova made his way to the only safe haven he could find—a monastery. When doctors were finally allowed to visit, they unanimously agreed that Casanova's hand was gangrenous and needed to be amputated. The stubborn playboy didn't believe them, rightly guessing that they only wanted to amputate to help the colonel recoup some of the honor he lost in the duel.

This example, like Wu's work on Chinese suicides, shows the overwhelming power of sincerity. From the insult, to the duel, to the malevolent misdiagnosis, everything that happened between Casanova and Colonel Branicki was a function of their social roles and the expectations tied to them. Sincerity can provide meaning and identity. But it can also outweigh the desire to live and make those whose roles are violated feel bereft enough to commit suicide or kill others just to prove a point. In guiding how to live, sincerity also informs decisions about how to die.

Importantly, even when people do not commit suicide or challenge others to combat, the regime of sincerity can prove a crushing demand. The helicopter parent who stifles their own personal life, and their son's childhood, feels an overwhelming duty to "be there" for the child. On the other extreme, parents who obsess over work and providing for their children might find themselves living some version of Harry Chapin's *Cats in the Cradle*: "When you comin' home dad? I don't know when, but we'll get together then. You know we'll have a good time then." Anyone can feel the pressure to continually perform, to meet goals, and to otherwise live according to certain expectations. But the most glaring difficulty with sincerity is its internal paradox. At the heart of all these issues, from suicides and duels to obsession with family life or professional achievement, is the impossible demand for a person's inner psychology to become fully congruent with external social expectations. As with any other method of achieving identity, sincerity has as much potential to enrich as to oppress, especially when obsessively overidentifying with one's roles so that any other aspects or potentials of selfhood seem false or wrong, or even evil.

THE PARADOX OF SINCERITY

Greek, Shakespearean, and real-life tragedies often involve conflict between the different roles held by a single person. Incompatible demands pull the protagonists in opposing directions. The tragedy is that no matter what they do, nothing will resolve the contending values of their disparate duties.

A paradigmatic example of the problems that can arise when roles conflict is presented in Sophocles's play *Antigone*. Here the major characters include the four children of Oedipus's incestuous relationship with his mother—Antigone, Ismene, Polyneices, and Eteocles—along with Oedipus's brother-in-law Creon and Creon's son Haemon, who is betrothed to his cousin Antigone. After the brothers Polyneices and Eteocles slay each other during the civil war in Thebes, the ruler of Thebes, Creon, decrees that Eteocles will be honored and buried while Polyneices is to be decried as a traitor whose corpse will rot on the battlefield. Antigone, as a citizen of Thebes, feels an obligation to follow the law, but she is also burdened with familial responsibility toward her brother Polyneices. She meets with her sister Ismene outside the city gates to tell her that she, Antigone, has decided to martyr herself in order to fulfill her sisterly duty to bury Polyneices. When she is eventually discovered to have buried her rebellious brother, Creon sentences Antigone to death. Ultimately, Antigone and Haemon end up taking their own lives, and Creon realizes that he brought about their deaths.

Judith Butler has argued that *Antigone* is philosophically provocative for its progressive feminism and sexual politics, and Slavoj Žižek praises its depiction of rebellion against an oppressive social order.[13] These interpretations, although justified, deemphasize the obvious clash between roles at the center of the plot. The play involves a complex reflection on a thoroughly tragic sincerity conflict, internally for the characters involved, and socially through their interactions.

Antigone is torn between being a good sister and a loyal citizen. Doing what is right in one area ignores and conflicts with the other. Creon's own situation is no less difficult. He promised to take care of his niece Antigone, but his duty as ruler leads him to condemn her to death. Whichever decision each figure makes cannot be wholly right, and their relationship to each other makes things even worse. Hegel concisely conveys the dilemma Antigone and Creon find themselves in: "Both are in the wrong because they are one-sided, but both are also in the right."[14] This dilemma, like many others both on stage and in real life, reflects a foundational paradox in the regime of sincerity: the plural demands of different roles are incommensurable and often at odds with one another.

Traditional roles in the family or the community, of course, did cohere with one another to some extent. Women, for example, were typically in the inferior position, as daughter, sister, and wife no less than as citizen or politician. In all these roles, females were generally (but not always) expected to defer to their male counterparts. Nevertheless, this sort of role coherence is limited, as the complicated case of Antigone demonstrates. Eventually, the various roles of most individuals turn out to be, at least to some degree, incompatible. Such incompatibilities, as in Antigone's case, have to do with differences among the groups that one belongs to—familial, political, religious, professional. Each of these systems has particular social structures and ethical expectations that do not fully converge with those of the others. Despite what the image of the onion suggests, the network of social roles is in reality not an organic whole consisting of multiple parallel and neatly fitting layers. It is not the case that multiple social roles harmoniously enclose one another and naturally converge.

Systemic role incompatibilities under a regime of sincerity are the norm, not the exception—and they reveal the underlying paradox of sincerity. Typically, a sincerity ethos will claim that roles within social organizations—the family is the prime example—are not "socially constructed" but grounded in natural or divine law. The Catholic Church, for instance, maintains that marriage can mean a lifelong partnership only between one man and one woman and considers any alternative to this both unnatural and against God's will. Similarly, Confucians will emphasize that lifelong affectionate submission to one's parents has little to do with social conventions but is an inborn human trait as exemplified by semidivine role models. Any deviation from such submission can be considered wrong and "perverse." In addition to family structures, both the Christian and the Confucian traditions also justified various feudal political structures as reflecting the same natural or divine order.

The counterfactual logic of sincerity suggests that one can build a coherent personality through various social roles because they are manifestations of an overarching divine plan, a moral order, or (human) nature. This is precisely why "living roles rather than playing them" (as Confucians such as Henry Rosemont insist on) is supposed to secure identity.[15] Social order is deemed to result from an identification with roles, and actual incompatibilities, conflicts, and incoherencies, particularly with respect to different social spheres, are then seen as the result of a failure to live one's roles. If we cannot emotionally internalize, rationally justify, and practically exemplify our conflicting social roles, then this is our fault—or exceptionally bad luck that can be aestheticized as "tragedy." It is not, and cannot be, the fault of the roles.

The "commandment" of sincerity is paradigmatically expressed in chapter 22 of the Confucian classic the *Doctrine of the Mean*: "Sincerity is the way of nature/heaven; making it sincere is the way of humankind." The contemporary Confucian philosopher Roger T. Ames explains quite aptly what this means: "One becomes human by cultivating those thick, intrinsic relations that constitute one's initial conditions and that locate the trajectory of one's life force within family, community, and cosmos."[16] The problem is, however, that actual social roles, like those in the family (or "community and cosmos"), do not mirror any "initial conditions" or "the way of heaven." Relational identity, like motherhood or fatherhood, is in fact not at all as "thick, intrinsic," as Ames claims. Yes, there is a natural relation between parents and children through birth, but none of the concrete moral values and social norms attached to this relation, from a Confucian ethos of "filial piety" to a Christian insistence that true marriage can exist only between one man and one woman, stem directly from any mystical "trajectory" of a "life force." Instead, they are all embedded in social structures, conventions, practices, beliefs, etc. Everything that's "thick" about family roles is not intrinsic, but extrinsic, that is, "cultural" or social; and everything intrinsic (natural or biological) about them is extremely thin—it does not necessitate specific norms or values. In other words, there is no more one "thick" and "intrinsic" way to be a daughter or mother than there is to be a woman.

The weakness of the claim that ties a Confucian role ethics to a supposed "way of heaven" was already pointed out (satirically) in a story in the early Daoist text *Zhuangzi* (29.1). Here a social outcast, the notorious Robber Zhi, instructs a hypocritically moralistic Confucius (who tries to bribe the robber into an alliance) that in the early days of humankind, prior to a corruption by Confucian "civilization," people lived a perfectly simple, happy, and peaceful life along with other animals and only "knew their mothers, but not their fathers." In other words: There is nothing "intrinsic" in human procreation that would privilege Confucian family values over any other way of life. They are not more in accordance with "human nature" than "free sex." Human history is rich with a wide variety of lifestyles, ranging from the absence of marriage to highly elaborated kinship organizations. Any of them could be morally adorned and, counterfactually, presented as reflecting supposed "initial conditions" and therefore as the social formation that defines the right way to "become human."

The paradox of sincerity is grounded in the implied claim that social roles have some "intrinsic" coherence that gives rise to identity. An ethos of sincerity tends to depict the relational tiers that make up identity as an integrated, organic unit—like an onion. However, the more we develop our identity and the more role relations we engage in, the more role conflicts tend to evolve, some of them perhaps quite tragic. The bigger the "onion-self" gets, the more difficult it becomes to conceive of it as an onion rather than as a basket of apples and oranges and other somewhat incompatible items within a complex society where not everything matches up. Eventually we may realize that the regime of sincerity itself—its norms and laws, social institutions (the "family") and belief systems (ideologies and religions)—is a major factor making life, and our identity, more complex, more difficult to integrate, and more "unnatural." Rather than connecting us with a presumed state of nature, this regime is, as Robber Zhi in the *Zhuangzi* suggests, a social and psychological tool that forces us into all kinds of contrived social institutions, thereby generating—rather than resolving—often conflicting demands.

POLITICAL NEW SINCERITY

The transition from sincerity to authenticity is linked with modernization. Francis Fukuyama, in his book *Identity: The Demand for Dignity and the Politics of Resentment*, makes up a simple story to show how someone who grows up under the conditions of sincerity might shift to value authenticity:

> Consider the situation of a young peasant, Hans, who grows up in a small village in Saxony. Hans's life in the little village is fixed:

he is living in the same house as his parents and grandparents; he is engaged to a girl whom his parents found acceptable; he was baptized by the local priest; and he plans to continue working the same plot of land as his father. It doesn't occur to Hans to ask "Who am I?" . . . However, he hears that big opportunities are opening up in the rapidly industrializing Ruhr valley, so he travels to Düsseldorf to get a job in a steel factory there. . . . He is no longer under the thumb of his parents and local priest and finds people with different religious affiliations than those in his village. He is still committed to marrying his fiancée but tempted by some of the local women he has met, and he feels a bracing sense of freedom in his personal life. . . . For the first time in his life, Hans can make choices about how to live his life, but he wonders who he really is and what he would like to be. The question of identity, which would never have been a problem back in his village, now becomes central.[17]

The predictability of Hans's life in his village was so encompassing that he never thought about his own identity. In Düsseldorf everything changes. Fukuyama says that Hans "can" make choices. More accurately, Hans *has to make choices.* And he does not just "wonder" about who he is. The question of identity demands an answer. (Just remember your own teenage struggles to figure out who you are.) Identity as authenticity came to characterize modern life in a way previously unknown. The old sincerity has survived in certain areas of life, but its dominance is gone. Only on the fringes of society, such as among the Amish perhaps, does it still strongly pervade entire communities.

When authenticity grew out from philosophical inquiry, past religious and artistic experiences, and beyond Hans's basic question of identity, it contributed to reshaping the political landscape, uprooting hierarchies, overturning monarchs, and developing democracies. The individual's claim to be recognized as such gained more and more currency. Although early attempts to grant individual rights were not greatly inclusive, over time people of color, women, and homosexuals fought for and acquired many of the same rights as straight white men. In the wake of these developments, a new sociopolitical attitude became increasingly popular. More nuanced characteristics of individual personality were announced inherently important and in need of sociopolitical recognition. Identity politics was born, eventually also inspiring a revival of the sincerity ethos, but in a new form. This development left what may be called a postauthentic "political new sincerity" in its wake.[18]

According to Fukuyama, identity politics arose out of the modern idea that there is an "authentic self buried deep inside us" and the fear that "society doesn't give it adequate recognition."[19] Thus "the problem is not how do you bring the individual into compliance with society, the problem becomes how do you change the society. Society is wrong and the inner self is right" (*Ezra Klein Show*). This view, in turn, can foster the divisive feeling that "the authentic people in my group are the good people and everyone else is bad" (Commonwealth Club). Fukuyama suggests that the social divisions created by identity politics may be addressed by revitalizing the conception of a "national identity"—which is supposed to replace the primacy of the authentic identity paradigm. In a public lecture he states, "National identity is one of my solutions because I do think we need to get back to the idea of an overarching identity" (Commonwealth Club). To be sure, for Fukuyama equal rights for marginalized groups are an integral part of the American national identity (or civil religion). He fully endorses these values. But we also need, he argues, to rely on another dimension of national identity within which we properly fulfill our roles as citizens and community members. In other words, we need a political new sincerity. Only in this way can the problematic consequences of an obsession with authentic identity be avoided.

Fukuyama is not the only prominent voice in a growing political new sincerity camp emerging out of opposition to identity politics. Another major monograph in support of political new sincerity is Mark Lilla's *The Once and Future Liberal: After Identity Politics*.[20] Identity politics is nothing more, Lilla says, than a "pseudo-politics" which only serves to unravel the state. With it, "citizenship dropped out of the picture" and "the only meaningful question became a deeply personal one: what does my country owe me by virtue of my identity?" (67). This "turn toward the self" (111) and the devaluation of the "democratic *we*" (133) are a result, Lilla argues, of a "hyperindividualistic culture in which personal choice and self-definition have become idols" (136). Kwame Appiah's book *The Lies That Bind: Rethinking Identity* joined the choir soon after. Appiah acknowledges that gender, religion, race, nationality, class, and culture are identity markers foundational for our being-in-the-world. But what brings people together, what really binds them as members of a community, he suggests, has more to do with their shared communal *praxis* than with the specific content of their self-identification.[21] Michael Sandel, too, can be regarded as a major popular representative of a political new sincerity for whom an inflated individualism is the culprit for income inequality, meritocratic hubris, dedignifying work, and a lack of national community in America today. In his works, from *Liberalism and the Limits of Justice* through *Encountering China* and *The Tyranny of Merit*, Sandel has argued for an encumbered conception of the person, that is, one where individual identity is constituted by shared common ends.[22]

Given their anti-individualist leanings, along with their emphasis on the value of communal duties and roles, current critics of identity politics such as Fukuyama, Lilla, Appiah, and

Sandel align themselves with older sincerity ideals. All four, however, seek to integrate personal choice, plurality of ways of life, and individual rights into their models of identity and citizenship. The explicit inclusion of such authenticity-related values makes their political sincerity *new*.

The advocates of political new sincerity typically decry contemporary social ills in terms of an excess of authenticity or "hyperindividualism." Implicitly or explicitly, they operate with a dualistic pattern of thought that sees some form of sincerity, for instance, in the form of a new civil nationalism, as the only available alternative to such excesses. However, to avoid an altogether conservative call to turn the social clock backward, and to preserve the merits of authenticity, their new sincerity is supposed to maintain and preserve uniqueness and agency under the umbrella of a commitment to community values.

The limits of a sincerity-hyperindividualism binary lead to misinterpretations of some signs of the times. What, from the perspective of political new sincerity, is described as an excess of authenticity can also be seen as quite the opposite: the gradual dissolution of authenticity and its replacement by profilicity. One case in point is Francis Fukuyama's rather striking (mis-)assessment of Donald Trump. Here profilicity is mistaken as authenticity.

Fukuyama writes: "Trump was the perfect practitioner of the ethics of authenticity that defines our age: he may be mendacious, malicious, bigoted, and unpresidential, but at least he says what he thinks."[23] Trump's Twitter posts are cited as illustrative examples of his "authenticity." They suggest, according to Fukuyama, that Trump is saying what he really thinks and feels. Unlike the tweets of George Bush or Barack Obama, which were obviously vetted for political incorrectness and intended to garner appeal, Trump is harsh, offensive, and downright nasty, but precisely therein he is judged to be authentic.

However, this so-called perfect practitioner of the ethics of authenticity is actually a self-made mass media project through and through. He is well-known for his prior successes and failures in branding, in projects ranging from steaks to hotels. And, as is widely acknowledged, his electoral victory was to a large extent due to his and his team's social media savvy. The obviously curated nature of Trump's public image and persona is hardly an expression of a core inner self, and thus it is difficult to consider the former host of *The Apprentice* a model of authenticity. Trump's "inauthenticity" is, moreover, not masked. The president is, as *Vox* put it, "weirdly honest about his lying."[24] His account of the creation of his core electoral catchphrase "Drain the swamp" is a paradigmatic example: "Funny how that term caught on, isn't it? I tell everyone: I hated it! Somebody said, 'Drain the swamp.' I said, 'Oh, that's so hokey. That is so terrible.' I said, 'All right. I'll try it.' So like a month ago, I said, 'Drain the swamp.' The place went crazy. I said, 'Whoa. Watch this.' Then I said it again. Then I started saying it like I meant it, right? And then I said it, I started loving it." Trump represents neither the sincere statesman-like father of the nation nor the rugged individual whose every utterance reveals his authentic inner self and convictions. Instead, he embodies a political triumph of profilicity. He says what he says because it furthers his profilicity-based popularity, not because it is authentic. His audience doesn't care that he uses phrases only to please them—they are still pleased! Many of his followers do not take him as authentic but love his staged public persona and the way he mocks his political opponents' increasingly unconvincing attempts to be authentic. While profilicity appears from the perspective of authenticity as a "weirdly honest" lie, authenticity appears from the perspective of profilicity as a weirdly dishonest truthfulness.

Ironically, the authors advocating political new sincerity reviewed previously do not notice the profilic qualities of

Donald Trump, even as they themselves operate under very similar conditions. What they say and write about new sincerity simultaneously contributes to strengthening and proliferating their own profilicity. Mark Lilla, Francis Fukuyama, Kwame Appiah, and Michael Sandel are all *high-profile* authors and professors at elite U.S. universities. Lilla is a frequent contributor to the *New York Times* and the *New York Review of Books*. Fukuyama lectures at all sorts of forums, many of which are uploaded to YouTube. Appiah writes regularly for the *New York Review of Books* and lectures to public audiences on television and the radio; many of his talks and interviews are on YouTube as well. And Sandel is, with the help of the BBC, "The Global Philosopher"—hosting a TV program cum philosophy class by that name where students from around the world interact.

These pioneers of political new sincerity have mastered profilicity to a degree very few academics—and hardly any philosophers today—have. This is by no means to suggest that they are insincere. They are, to the contrary, caring fathers, dedicated teachers, committed colleagues, and honest shoppers (at least the one of them we know personally). But in attempts to appeal to readers of the *New York Times*, YouTube audiences, and critical thinkers the world over, they exhibit their expertise in profilicity. Here they may be sincere too, but sincere under the conditions of profilicity. And how could it be otherwise in a society where profilicity has become the reigning identity paradigm?

SINCERITY AND PROFILICITY

There are similarities between sincerity and profilicity. The two overlap with each other sometimes more than either does with authenticity. Some of the very dimensions in which they seem similar, however, are also sites of critical differences. Three similarities in which we find important differences are: (1) both sincerity and profilicity derive self-validation from presentation for an audience, but in sincerity the audience is usually copresent (e.g., family members), whereas profilicity appeals to the general peer; (2) both sincerity and profilicity submit to external expectations, but in sincerity these are rather stable, while in profilicity they are highly fluid and dynamic; (3) sincerity and profilicity both value the public persona, but in sincerity public reputation is expected to be tied to personal virtue or charisma, whereas in profilicity excellence is often metrically generated by algorithms or other mechanisms.

Using the theater as a model, Erving Goffman described the intricacies of social interactions as performances, ranging from the setting of the stage to front-stage cooperative role play to back-stage personal downtime. *The Presentation of Self in Everyday Life* (1956, 1) opens with an observation: "When an individual enters the presence of others, they commonly seek to acquire information about him or to bring into play information about him already possessed. . . . Information about the individual helps to define the situation, enabling others to know in advance what he will expect of them and what they may expect of him." This is how self-presentation to an immediate audience works. When people are actually present, all sorts of information can be gained through anything from clothing and accent to gestures and demeanor. The situation is shaped by how those who are present present themselves. Everyone involved operates under similar assumptions about how things should go. Presentations reoccur over time, and as people come to know one another, reputations develop.

Profilicity also requires presentation to an audience. This audience, the general peer, is much more abstract though. The review of a stay I post on Airbnb—or my reflections on it in a book addressed to unknown, more or less intellectual readers—might differ drastically in tone and content from the funny stories about it that I am telling my friends. In these different contexts I am asked to comment on the same event, but the nature of the audience radically influences what is said. The former relies on second-order observation and all that this entails, while the latter is based on comparatively simple first-order observation.

Sincerity standards are more or less stable; people are interested in what someone else wears because it indicates a fixed role and dimension of their persona. In profilicity, showing that one wears clothing of a certain brand might stress the degree of one's coolness rather than conforming to a role. But then, in profilicity one also has to consider that coolness is subject to rapid and unpredictable fluctuations—and can itself become uncool at any moment; it can be no longer a thing. What is confirmed by a social validation feedback loop one day might very well be rejected the next.

When someone is known, a reputation is established. Where sincerity dominates, that reputation is supposed to be trustworthy, especially if it is grounded in personal interaction. In contemporary contexts, algorithm-generated profiles have come to overshadow such personal knowing. In her book *Weapons of Math Destruction* (2016), Cathy O'Neill shows how mathematical models increasingly determine everything from how much we pay for a car or health insurance, to credit card rates, to schools we can go to. Such data are considered more reliable, more transparent, and less biased than personal evaluations.[25] As *Forbes* reports, these calculations may be as astonishing as they are accurate:

> Based on a single person's purchases of, for instance, cocoa-butter lotion, zinc and magnesium supplements, the retailer Target

thought it could figure out which of their customers are likely pregnant and sent out coupons for potential items of interest to them. A man whose teenage daughter was receiving the coupons complained to a manager: "My daughter got this in the mail!" he said. "She's still in high school, and you're sending her coupons for baby clothes and cribs? Are you trying to encourage her to get pregnant?" The manager apologized and then called a few days later to apologize again. On the phone, the father was somewhat abashed. "I had a talk with my daughter," he said. "It turns out there's been some activities in my house I haven't been completely aware of. She's due in August. I owe you an apology."[26]

4

AUTHENTICITY

Life isn't about finding yourself, or finding anything. Life is about creating yourself.

—Bob Dylan (pioneer of profilicity), *Rolling Thunder Revue: A Bob Dylan Story*

AUTHENTICITY, INDIVIDUALISM, AND MODERNIZATION

When Hans moved from the small village embedded in sincerity to the authenticity-laden city of Düsseldorf, his transition was more than physical. Smacked with the question of identity, he began to think of himself, others, and the world differently. This same move was made by millions of real-life Hanses the world over. Authenticity and the question of identity has been thrust into the face of basically everyone living in developed, "liberal" countries, and especially so if they are familiar with Protestant doctrines or Romanticism, have seen Shakespeare's plays, or have read Friedrich Nietzsche.

But not everyone is content with authenticity—with its jargon that alternatively, but also sometimes simultaneously, emphasizes the contradictory demands to discover or create an original self, with its stereotypical image that implies that genuine human identity lies, or ought to lie, behind the "masks" taken on in society, and with the ideology of individualism that accompanies it and values personal autonomy over collective bonds. From Henry Rosemont and Roger Ames, who want to reinvent a traditional sincerity, to David Foster Wallace and Michael Sandel, who recommend various types of a new sincerity, nostalgia for thick social roles, for shared norms and expectations, and, in short, for a robust notion of community beyond individualism is not in short supply.

America, which has often been at the forefront of parading authenticity and individualism, got off to a rough start in its attempts to develop non-sincerity-based values in its inhabitants. Willingness to give up the comforts of modernity for a life in tight-knit Native American tribes was common in the New World during the seventeenth and eighteenth centuries. Benjamin Franklin observed:

> When an Indian child has been brought up among us, taught our language and habituated to our Customs, yet if he goes to see his relations and make one Indian Ramble with them, there is no persuading him ever to return, and that this is not natural to them merely as Indians, but as men, is plain from this, that when white persons of either sex have been taken prisoners young by the Indians, and lived a while among them, tho' ransomed by their Friends, and treated with all imaginable tenderness to prevail with them to stay among the English, yet in a Short time they become disgusted with our manner of life . . . and take the first good Opportunity of escaping again into the woods, from whence there is no reclaiming them.[1]

Hectoer de Crèvecoeur, a French emigrant, made a similar observation: "Thousands of Europeans are Indians, and we have no examples of even one of those Aborigines having from choice become European."[2] Drawing on Franklin and Crèvecoeur, Sebastian Junger argues that the desire to live interrelatedly with others in small communities—that is, a sincerity-based life—was the main reason early Europeans in America preferred to be among the Native Americans.[3] A largely independent, atomic, "individualized" life might be convenient, but it takes its toll:

> As society modernized, people found themselves able to live more independently from communal groups. A person in a modern city or a suburb can go through an entire day—or an entire life—mostly encountering strangers. They can be surrounded by others and yet feel deeply, and dangerously alone. The evidence that this can be hard on us is overwhelming. Although happiness is notoriously subjective and difficult to measure, mental illness is not. Numerous cross-cultural studies have shown that modern society—despite its nearly miraculous advances in medicine, science, and technology—is afflicted with some of the highest rates of depression, schizophrenia, poor health, anxiety, and chronic loneliness in human history. As affluence and urbanization rise, rates of depression and suicide tend to go up rather than down.[4]

Still, the desire to move back from, or beyond, authenticity and individualism is rather limited today. Jordan Peterson, whose quasi-commonsensical, anti-PC, no-bs commentary on current issues has gained even more fame than the "man-up" self-help philosophy on which it is founded, audaciously states:

> The fundamental assumptions of Western civilization are valid! How about that? You think it's an accident? Here's how you find out, ok. Which countries do people want to move away from?

Hey, not ours! Which countries do people want to move to? Ours! Guess what, they work better. And it's not because we went around the world stealing everything we could get our hands on. It's because we got certain fundamental assumptions right, thank God for that! After thousands and thousands of years of trying. And because of that we've managed to establish a set of civilizations that are shining lights in the world. . . . [We aren't that great] but nonetheless, you know, we're as good as it's got. And unless we can come up with something better, we should be very careful about messing around with that. So why don't we start with the assumption that we are doing something right? One of the things we are doing right, for example, is that we actually value the individual, right? The individual has intrinsic value in Western societies. Do you know how long it took for people to formulate that as an idea? And how unlikely that idea is that poor you, you know, useless powerless you, with all your damn faults, you're actually worth something! You're worth something to the point that the law has to respect you. God! We don't want to abandon that for some half-witted collectivism, which we're doing as rapidly as possible. Because one of the things that characterizes the radical Left types is, they don't give a damn about you as an individual, or about individuals at all. You're black or you're white, you're Latino, or you're transsexual or you're homosexual, whatever. You're a group, you're a member of a group, and the only thing that matters is the group. Well I can tell you, if the only thing that matters is the group, you bloody well don't matter very much![5]

The "group" Peterson criticizes is not the premodern tribe Junger idealizes. But still, Peterson's defense of individualism, and his general attitude in his lectures and texts, gives little credence to old-fashioned sincerity (despite his own personal life).[6] It took thousands of years for Western societies to shed themselves of stringent collectivist, role-based identity, and Peterson hopes we never go back. Although many thinkers are less enthusiastic about this development, most share Peterson's historical depiction of progress.

We can, of course, find traces of authenticity and individualism almost as far back as we want. Plato, for example, is often taken to have believed in antecedent selfhood—a defining feature of individualism. His notion of an unchanging soul and theory of knowledge as memory set the stage for the search for one's inner self to become a guiding motif in Western conceptions of identity. But the real explosion of authenticity happened only later. Whether through Niccolò Machiavelli, Martin Luther, William Shakespeare, Immanuel Kant, the French Revolution, Romanticism, or some other spark, most agree that authenticity and individualism as we know them today arose with "modern societies" or "modernization" in some form.

While the connection between modernization and authenticity is widely agreed on, what exactly defines modern society and precisely which factors contributed to developing authenticity and individualism are highly contested issues. Numerous theories have been developed to answer these question. Marxists pointed to the accumulation of private property in the hands of a few, Max Weber to the rise of Protestantism, and Émile Durkheim thought that a new "cult of the individual" prioritized the rational agency of the person. Later, Niklas Luhmann claimed that functional differentiation characterizes modern society and opened up a quest for individual identity.[7]

THE JARGON OF AUTHENTICITY

Modernity is an "age of authenticity," Charles Taylor has argued. We agree, except that we think it is coming to an end. Finding examples of the "jargon of authenticity" that embellish self-discovery or self-creation is not a difficult task.[8] Not limited to art, literature, and philosophy, everything from beer commercials to political debates to textbooks—and the nooks and crannies in between—is so jam-packed with authenticity speech that we found it impossible to pick a best representative. Whenever one of us chose a quote, a screenshot, or an advertisement, the other would find something better. A photo of the Nike slogan "Make Yourself" was one-upped by lyrics from Mike Posner's hit song "Be as You Are," which was challenged by the quote from Bob Dylan introducing this chapter.

Western societies are completely permeated by the language and imagery of authenticity and individualism. In their respective styles, they also pervade the writings of both the Continental existentialist and Anglo-American political philosophy traditions; in daily language they dominate advertising, self-help manuals, and pop songs.

Historically speaking, authenticity is a "facet" of "modern individualism," according to Charles Taylor.[9] For us, it may perhaps be the other way around—individualism may be a facet of modern authenticity—but in any case we agree with Taylor's depiction of modernity as a break from a regime of sincerity: "People were often locked into a given place, a role and station that was properly theirs and from which it was almost unthinkable to deviate. Modern freedom came about through the discrediting of such orders" (3). Modern authenticity and individualism blossomed when personal autonomy and creativity became identity ideals. For Taylor, it all began with the Romantics: "[By 'authenticity'] I mean the understanding of life which emerges with the Romantic expressivism of the late eighteenth century, that each one of us has his/her own way of realizing our humanity, and that it is important to find and live out one's own, as against surrendering to conformity with a model imposed on us from outside, by society, or the previous generation, or religious or political authority" (475). "Freedom" is freedom from the "external power of society." Authenticity is then marked by the demand that everyone ought to develop their own uniqueness, regardless of social powers or conventions that may obstruct such an endeavor. Following the Romantics, one needed to "express" one's own identity. Or one could choose who to be. Taylor further defines the notion:

> Authenticity (A) involves (i) creation and construction as well as discovery, (ii) originality, and frequently (iii) opposition to the rules of society and even potentially to what we recognize as morality. But it is also true, as we saw, that it (B) requires (i) openness to horizons of significance (for otherwise the creating loses the background that can save it from insignificance) and (ii) a self-definition in dialogue. That these demands may be in tension has to be allowed. But what must be wrong is a simple privileging of one over the other, of (A), say, at the expense of (B), of vice versa.[10]

While the term "authenticity" became widely popular in philosophy through the translation of Martin Heidegger's *Eigentlichkeit*, Taylor's outline speaks past Heidegger and cuts through the murkiness of the German philosopher's works. Most readers will recognize the astuteness of Taylor's analysis of authenticity from watching commercials, listening to TED Talks, conversing with coworkers, friends, and family, or, for that matter, just thinking.

Interestingly enough, both elaborated and restricted usages of the authenticity semantics often mix, somewhat paradoxically, the demands to "find" or "discover" oneself with the demand to "create" oneself. Taylor does exactly this in his definition (A) (i) just quoted.

From a sociological perspective, Ulrich Beck and Elisabeth Gernsheim-Beck define the individualism attached to the pursuit of authenticity as "disembedding without reembedding." In other words, the person is uprooted from "solidly established traditions," social roles, and thick expectations and never really replanted. Pulled from these well-nested niches, and without recourse to long-lasting alternatives, the individual can seem condemned to a "nomadic" life, in Zygmunt Bauman's terms; holding up only temporarily in barren rest spots, there is no alternative: "individualism is a fate, not a choice."[11]

Alternatively, authenticity and individualism may also be credited with allowing humans to take on "the God-like role of being the originator of their own selves."[12] Authorship, creativity, and whatever "being true to yourself" means are then all thrown into the mix because the "external power of society" will not and, as Bauman says, *cannot* be determining for identity.[13] So go out and "become what you are"—to refer to an iconic demand by Nietzsche as well as a book title by Alan Watts.[14] (This slogan is another good candidate for one-upmanship in finding catchy expressions of the jargon of authenticity.)

THE PARADOXES OF AUTHENTICITY

The Iranian American journalist and Catholic convert Sohrab Ahmari describes his own childhood difficulties with the inward turn of authenticity. Growing up in Iran, he was, like his parents, rebelling against institutionalized Islam. Ahmari did, however, feel a strong need for some type of guidance: "I longed for some cosmic and moral absolutes. Yet the only absolute command that my father handed down to me was: 'Be yourself.' It was maddening. Who was this 'self' dwelling inside

me, to whom I owed such fidelity? My father wouldn't say."[15]
More than simply difficult, however, this dictum is fundamentally paradoxical. Ahmari's father wasn't *letting* his son "be
himself," he was *commanding* it. Ahmari first had to learn that
he should "be himself" and then figure out, through the examples of others, what "being yourself" meant: "Hadn't my father
urged me to be myself to cut my own path across life's thicket of
choices? Well, I would do just that. It didn't occur to me at the
time that, in the name of independence and originality, I was,
in fact, adopting someone else's persona, a prefabricated cultural type" (64). Idealizing comic book heroes, writers, artists,
and film directors, Ahmari chronicles his early teenage
attempts at "being himself." As with anyone else, his authenticity was all about trying on other people's costumes and seeing which ones were comfortable for a time. He could only
"discover" himself by imitating models, and his models were,
predictably enough, Nietzsche, then French "Existentialists,"
then Marxism, and finally Christianity.

Ahmari's search for "cosmic and moral absolutes" was a search
for external regulatory guides such as those readily given under
the conditions of sincerity. Ahmari was confused, as many are,
because of the internal paradox the command to be himself presents: looking outward for guidance, he finds the external standard of authenticity, which tells him not to look outside oneself
for guidance. As a teenager and young adult, Ahmari was ear-
nestly trying to "be himself" but had to imitate others in order
to develop the creativity and originality that "being yourself"
requires.

Mike Posner, whose songs have over eighty million views on
YouTube, describes his experience of the impossibility of becoming authentic by trying to define oneself in opposition to other
people's "likes":

I would try to prove my autonomy by doing the opposite of what I know you like. So there was a point in my career like two to three years ago where I thought everyone knows me [in] this one way, I'm gonna do the opposite. So I feel like I'm still my own guy, I make my own decisions I'm not pandering to other people's. I remember I stopped [eating], like I was eating every other day, I lost like 30 pounds and I was already a healthy weight when I started, so I was really skinny and I dyed my hair green, I had a green mullet. And I was doing photo shoots where I was wearing makeup and women's clothes—and there's nothing wrong with that—they actually look pretty cool. But it wasn't . . . the reason was messed up, that I was doing it. Not the actual thing, some of the photos are very beautiful. The reason was: I was doing the opposite to prove to myself "Hey I'm not attached to your opinion." But if you really think about it, I'm still very much attached to your opinion. Your opinion is still dictating what I'm doing even though it's the opposite of it. Instead of me just being me.[16]

Posner tries to be unique by rejecting other people's expectations of him. But he eventually realizes that the rejection of other people's expectations is, paradoxically, also a reaction to their expectations—it is not doing simply one's own thing and being authentic. Under a regime of authenticity, everyone feels obliged to be authentic. Individuality is a demand enforced by a crowd. By countering the expectations of society and trying to be special, I fulfill society's expectation to be special. Or, as Elena Esposito puts it, "nothing is as unoriginal as the desire to be original."[17]

Today, the discovery of the inauthenticity of authenticity, as in Posner's case, is a common experience. Suspicion hangs like a dark cloud over authenticity. It is increasingly railed against by those who see the promise of pure, stark, awe-inspiring, and unconquerable authenticity as not only paradoxical but ultimately unfulfillable. Before authenticity became the norm, however, in the transitional period from sincerity to authenticity, its discovery could still be perceived as a marvelous revelation, full of promises of grandeur and originality. One prime example is Jean Jacques Rousseau's (1813/1953) autobiographical celebration of his own authenticity in the *Confessions*. He sees himself in opposition to convention and brazenly claims to be completely one-of-a-kind: "I know my own heart and understand my fellow man. But I am made unlike any one I have ever met; I will even venture to say that I am like no one in the whole world. I may be no better, but at least I am different. Whether Nature did well or ill in breaking the mold in which she formed me, is a question which can only be resolved after the reading of my book" (17). The conflict between sincerity-based role conformity and an emerging demand to be authentic is present in many novels and dramas of the eighteenth and nineteenth centuries. Jane Austen's works often represent a new kind of tragic situation which, unlike in *Antigone*, does not emerge from the incompatibilities between different roles but from the incompatibility between a role-based identity and the simultaneous desire to be authentic. The protagonists Marianne Dashwood in *Sense and Sensibility* and Elizabeth Bennet in *Pride and Prejudice* both illustrate the experience of conflict between sincerity and authenticity. Their challenges to social expectations and institutions of sincerity are, like Rousseau's, largely perplexing for their peers. Rousseau's strange insistence that no one else, not even Montaigne, was as unique or truthful as himself, like Elizabeth's stubborn love for Mr. Darcy, offered tantalizing new descriptions of an identity problem just starting to bubble up.[18] We can easily imagine Hans and his relationship to his bride back in the village at the center of another *Northanger Abbey.*

The difficulties with authenticity expressed by Rousseau and Austen point to another paradoxical aspect of authenticity: to be fully authenticated as authentic, one needs to be seen by others as authentic. Authenticity wants to be observed as authentic. The concept of "recognition," stemming back to Hegel and of great importance for much Continental and Anglo-American philosophy, implies that one's authenticity relies on acknowledgment by other authentic individuals. In authenticity, it's all about being an independent original individual—but one's status as such an individual is still utterly dependent on recognition. It craves identity validation.

In authenticity, the way people dress and what they eat, believe, and do can all be taken as expressions of the self. However, clothing, dishes, and faiths are already found in society. The best one can do is chose among and perhaps modify these; they can hardly be created from scratch. Accordingly, although in authenticity we do not follow norms, we do follow trends or fashions—and whether a fashion is fashionable is not up to the individual but to society. Others thus need to approve one's "originality" in such matters. As Elena Esposito has shown, nothing highlights the paradoxical dialectics of modern authenticity better than fashion:

> Fashion—as is well-known, and not by chance—is started with modernity. An inherently social phenomenon, no one is fashionable alone. You do not just imitate models, as people once [did] in traditional societies. . . . In fashion the simple reproduction [of models] is not good. . . . Looking at fashion we follow others, but not in order to do the same as the others . . . but in order to do something different. . . . It is a very curious form of imitation that

leads all of us to do more or less the same, but each trying to be different. . . . We follow the model of fashion in order to distinguish ourselves.[19]

The need for recognition then brings about yet another paradox of authenticity. Since authenticity needs to be recognizable, authentic individuals need to be authentic in more or less the same "fashion." In this way, too, fashion exemplifies the mechanisms of authenticity. In the following quote from Esposito, we replace the word "fashion" with "authenticity":

> This is another really peculiar strange feature of modern culture: We all, as individuals, would like to achieve and express our individuality, our originality—that what makes us unique and special. And we want, we would like, the others to accept it. And we do it with a detail, with a combination of colors, with a variation of [authentic] forms that must be at the same time recognizable as [authentic], and original as our own. The same and the different at the same time. For example we wear the same shoes that the other is wearing but of a different color, or combined with something else. We all know the subtle devices we use in following [authenticity], so that diversity in [authenticity] must be somewhat the same in order to be appreciated. The new, in a sense, must be a little bit old otherwise we wouldn't recognize it, we wouldn't appreciate its novelty. A perfect original would be incomprehensible.

Esposito goes on to note that the character of the nephew in Diderot's *Rameau's Nephew* (1805) is taken as a crazy person because his originality has no familiar correlates. Anyone who is too authentic risks not being appreciated as such.

The paradoxical character of authenticity is threefold: (1) authenticity is learned from others; (2) authenticity has to be recognized by others in order to count; and (3) everyone is expected to be authentic in recognizable and thus necessarily similar ways.

AUTHENTICITY NOSTALGIA

Given its paradoxes, "true" authenticity is impossible. But this does not mean that this identity technology does not work. Like sincerity, authenticity allows people, including the authors of this book and probably most of its readers, to form a sense of selfhood, to internalize a set of most cherished and commonly held values having to do with independence, individual rights, and freedom, and to functioning socially. Following Niklas Luhmann, we can note that social structures emerge and evolve not despite the paradoxes they involve but with their help. Paradoxes provide endless opportunities for "unfolding" (*Paradoxieentfaltung*), they stimulate not only thought but also communication, and thereby human society. As contradictions, they can be the engine of history, as Hegel and Marx already explained.

Now that authenticity is on the wane, two closely related reactions are common, particularly among older generations: First, we find it hard to let go. It hurts seeing the values of authenticity recede—values we have cherished and that have guided us throughout our lives. Second, given our nostalgia and our bias in authenticity's favor, we intuitively reject profilicity. We generally do so, however, only by regarding it as what it is not. Profilicity seems merely inauthentic. We get upset about it, complain, and rebel. However, as much as we, the present authors, can sympathize with these attitudes—and empathize with them as well—we find such reactions unhelpful, from both theoretical and practical perspectives. As difficult as it may be, it is time to acknowledge that authenticity is losing its hold because it increasingly lacks efficiency and credibility in a society becoming daily better suited to profilicity.

Sherry Turkle is the Abby Rockefeller Mauzé Professor of the Social Studies of Science and Technology at the Massachusetts Institute of Technology. She is also the founding director of the Initiative on Technology and Self, part of MIT's Program in Science, Technology, and Society. Her books are bestsellers in the quasi-academic genre "human-computer relations," perhaps second only to those of Nicholas Carr, author of *The Shallows* and "Is Google Making Us Stupid." Amazon's author page on Turkle describes one of her most popular books: "Her 2011 *Alone Together*, argues that we are at a point of decision and opportunity. Technology now invites us to lose ourselves in always-in mobile connections and even in relationships with inanimate creatures that offer to 'stand in' for the real. In the face of all this, technology offers us the occasion to reconsider our human values, and reaffirm what they are."[20] Turkle's empirical work on new media is rich, and her descriptions of the digital age are full of most interesting details. Her conceptual narrative, however, is simple and slimmed down to a moralistic binary: the digital world and the social media are fostering inauthenticity left and right, and we need to safeguard ourselves against the imminent threat they pose to our authenticity. The Amazon description of Turkle's book appropriately highlights a catchphrase: the new media are allowing us to "lose ourselves," thereby implying that reading Sherry Turkle will help us find or keep track of ourselves. As its subtitle indicates, Roberto Simanowski's *Facebook Society: Losing Ourselves in Sharing Ourselves* tells more or less the same story as *Alone Together*—and also promises to be a similar safeguard against threats to authenticity.[21]

Turkle's message finds much resonance because it neatly corresponds to the feelings many of us have toward the digital world as the prime platform of profilicity's proliferation: Technology changes us, often for the worse. Communicating over a phone, especially via text, rather than in person alters not just the how but the what. As Marshall McLuhan said: "The medium is the message."[22] A "thank you" text pales in comparison to looking someone in the eye and expressing gratitude. A father who used to spend hours talking to his baby daughter confesses to Turkle that he now mindlessly rocks his second child while checking his email and scrolling through Instagram. We are all interested in what is going on, amazed at how captivated infants and young children are by iPads, puzzled by how teenagers seem to lose empathy, worried about the smart dolls that mimic siblings, and welcoming the screen-free camps being set up to counter a new media addiction growing all around the world.

Once more: we (the writers of this book) share the general apprehension in the face of the new media revolution expressed by authors like Turkle, Carr, and Simanowski. The phenomena they describe are real and worrisome. However, we do not think that the authenticity nostalgia that informs their work is helpful. Theoretically, it prevents rather than enables a conceptual, or philosophical, critique of the social and psychological factors at work. What is unfolding is not merely a "lack." Quite to the contrary, we see a whole new identity type fulfilling functions that sincerity and authenticity did in the past. Profilicity curates identity in a complex world where technology has drastically changed the environment within which people must exist, in both body and mind. To understand and cope with this new type of identity curation a new and more complex conceptual framework is needed. We cannot merely copy or carry forward the semantics of authenticity in a dualistic struggle between losing and finding identity. Most importantly Turkle, Carr, and

Simanowski are wrong: people can find "themselves" in the new media and in profilicity. They might lose their authenticity, but they find their profilicity. While the way in which identity is assembled may be novel, it is no less a form of identity. We need to work toward a vocabulary that can adequately address rather than just dismiss this fact. We also must be open to the possibility that profilicity offers a timely way of seeing ourselves and one another.

A critique of the new media and new identity technologies is both justified and useful. However, an uncritical celebration of authenticity is neither. When reading authors like Turkle, Carr, or Simanowski, we cannot but think of them in parallel to intellectuals like Edmund Burke in the eighteenth century, who fought against emerging authenticity and individualism and wished to preserve a sincerity-based way of living and thinking. They, too, wanted "in the face of all this," to put it in the language of the Amazon description of Turkle's book, to "reconsider our human values, and reaffirm what they are." It is just as problematic now to react to the emergence of profilicity with idealized reaffirmations of authenticity as it was problematic in the eighteenth century to react to the emergence of authenticity with idealized reaffirmations of sincerity.

Much of the recent literature on new media is characterized by the semantics of authenticity and tends to express a certain nostalgia for it. Ironically, precisely this nostalgia, along with a moral and political scandalization of aspects of new media usage, has worked to improve the profilicity of the profilicity foes. Turkle and Carr can be easily added to the long list of *New Yorker* journalists, political new sincerity advocates, and cultural critics who are paradoxically putting out the fire with gasoline— propelling their own profilicity in the fight against it.

BOHO BEAUTIFUL: AUTHENTICITY IN
THE SERVICE OF PROFILICITY

Two young adults sit on the ground in front of a camera. Both are handsome, sporting sun-bleached hair and skin, slim, fit bodies, and cool rustic clothing. They sigh in a practiced near unison, look at each other, and perfectly project a feeling of unease. The video cuts out and comes back. They are not trying to pretend that the shot was not edited. Far from it, the obviously edited nature of the material is an important part of its presentation.

These two good-looking people are masters of home videos—professionals in fact. The couple, known simply as "Juliana" and "Mark," are "Boho Beautiful." They wrote the book *The Happy Healthy Plant Based Eating Guide*, make fitness and yoga videos shot around the world, sell memberships through their website to all kinds of exclusive content and coaching, and promote products. But mainly they are YouTube stars. This video is not, however, a new yoga session on a beach in some exotic Southeast Asian island. It is not a meditation video shot on a mountain, nor is it "Best Ab Workout in 10 min ♥ Tummy & Muffin Top" or the famed "Brazilian Butt Lift Challenge ♥ The Perfect Butt Workout." On March 17, 2019, Boho Beautiful told over one million subscribers they were experiencing "Creator Burn Out." (It was the same video, by the way, that announced they had reached one million subscribers.) After two years of success—traveling the world on no other income then what they make from uploading their videos—the couple needed a break.[23]

There are now, many months after the video was uploaded, a mere 227,415 views. It is part of a "diary" series, where Boho Beautiful document their travels, life philosophy, eating habits, and romance. Their diary series gets significantly less views than their workout videos (some boasting millions of views). But that's okay.

"Burnt Out: Milestones & Big Changes for Boho Beautiful" is ten minutes and thirty-six seconds long. Importantly, YouTube pays more for videos over ten minutes long.[24] These longer videos often get more views and can carry more ads. So even if it only averages 1,700 or so views a day, "Burnt Out" will still be profitable. This means the few extra seconds of getting ready in the beginning not only give an authentic feel to the video but also fatten the paycheck.

Mark discusses the one million subscriber landmark in terms of what we call social validation feedback loops:

> To us it's kinda like, it's just like, it's a sign that things, things they're going the right way and that what we are doing, and, and that what we are doing is connecting with people. But what's even more valuable to us is that you guys are connecting back to us. And when it comes down to it, that's the beauty of the internet and that's the beauty of YouTube, is this reciprocal, like, give and take of energy, through videos, through comments, through texts.

As Mark highlights, the reciprocal "give" from the viewers, mainly through comments, liking, and subscribing, is the most *valuable* thing to them. Consequently, they invite ever more second-order observation-based feedback—feedback that is publicly seen as being seen, so as to improve their profilic appeal:

> [Mark:] So if there is any kind of content that we have done in the past that isn't class-based content [i.e., fitness, meditation, nutrition]—cuz we know we are going to keep doing that—but if there is stuff that we have touched on that has affected you or that you'd love to see more of, that's been of value to you please

let us know. . . . Or if there is stuff that we haven't done that you'd love to see us do, like a direction to take Boho Beautiful, we are taking this intermission right now [because we are burned out] to just figure out where to grow.

Juliana and Mark want to grow spiritually, and continue their creative life journey, albeit in a way that the general peer will like.

In their diary videos, Boho Beautiful display their authenticity through profilicity-based means. They put (staged) authenticity in the service of profilicity—as Byung-Chul Han and Jiayang Fan know to do as well. Unlike the latter, though, Juliana and Mark cannot help but explicitly worry about their profilicity even when baring their souls. The knowledge that the world—actually the general peer—is watching and judging is a constant concern for them. Just as democratic politicians must always be aware of the polls, YouTubers vigilantly track viewer analytics. After getting negative comments on an emotionally charged video shot in Nepal about abused and neglected dogs,[25] Boho Beautiful provide immediate feedback (within forty-eight hours!) in their June 24, 2019, video "I Love Your Yoga Videos, but . . . Subscribers Keep Leaving Our Channel?!":

[Mark:] We thought it was really important to do a quick response video. [Juliana:] That's the right way to call it, a response. [Mark:] Yesterday, actually, we posted a really important video. Probably one of the most. [Juliana:] Challenging I'd say, it was one of the hardest videos we've ever had to put together because it was just so emotionally deep—for us. [Mark:] And it was just . . . I dunno . . . it was a really special video. And um . . . when we looked at the analytics after we posted it, this morning, we saw this common pattern raising its head. [Juliana:] When we first started doing our diaries, when we sold everything and left and started documenting, kind of, our experiences and putting it through Boho Diaries, we noticed that there is, like Mark is saying, this pattern of people unsubscribing or leaving our channel and so we did a response video about it. And it's interesting how, what is it a year, [Mark:] two years, [Juliana:] we are still seeing this kinds of patterns. [Mark:] Which is ya, everyone is fleeing our channel the minute that we strive to provide something deeper and more authentic to ourselves. And it's interesting, the word "authentic," um, it's something that is really important to the two of us. And I think that's because when we started this journey into yoga, into Boho Beautiful, there was a huge part of us that felt that we were not living our authentic lives. And so we wanted to journey towards the truth in ourselves, and then on top of that I think the diaries were a huge challenge for [us]: is it even possible to express an authentic truth as soon as you press record on a camera because all of a sudden you know the world is watching and you are being judged and you are in your head and all these things.[26]

On this journey of authenticity, the analytics must be constantly monitored. Juliana and Mark superimpose a graph of subscribers over their own faces for their viewers to see (fig. 4.1), perhaps indicating what's really important.

Once again, Boho Beautiful made sure that the documentation of their emotional depth is over ten minutes long: as the bottom left of the image indicates, we have a 10:07-long video. Mark goes on to say, "It may not be the best thing for our business to continue [these diaries], because people leave. But, it's the best thing for our soul." We might note in parallel, however, that these diary videos, although not viewed as often as their other stuff, are good for adding authenticity to their profile. And

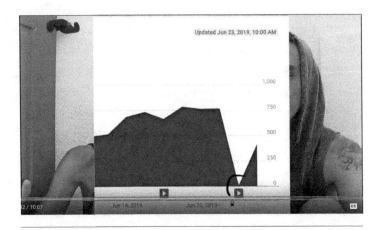

FIGURE 4.1 Boho Beautiful graph of subscriber statistics.
Screenshot from https://www.youtube.com/watch?v=-RAyPCbMYno,
July 31, 2019. Reproduced by permission of Boho Beautiful.

this is a very valuable investment. The diary videos help curate a profile of authenticity that is finely tuned to viewers and sponsors of the next trip. So of course they won't quit: "[Mark:] So really, we are not going to stop, because of the ones who are still here, because of you guys that are watching this."

Juliana and Mark took bold steps to exhibit their authenticity. In 2016, they say, they sold all their belongings to adventure around the world, and we do not doubt that they actually did so. We equally trust, simply by looking at them, that they never stray from their vegan diet. They are not inauthentic. Similarly, Michael Sandel, Francis Fukuyama, and Mark Lilla are, by most accounts, not insincere. They really do care about their roles and take steps to strengthen solidarity in their respective communities. But once on the stage, they do what they do and cannot but do so in the service of profilicity. The successes of Boho Beautiful's videos, Sandel's *Justice*, Fukuyama's lectures, and

Lilla's articles are to a large extent due to profilic presentation of authenticity or sincerity. Just like sincerity, authenticity is easily put in the service of profilicity. Precisely, therefore, when analyzing these phenomena, we need a conceptual framework that goes beyond the authenticity/inauthenticity binary. We need a vocabulary of profilicity.

PERSONAL PROFILE MANAGEMENT

When Donald Trump changed his mind and started liking the phrase "drain the swamp," he operated according to profilicity. His success as a political brander reflects his profilicity savvy. Whether he consciously knows this, or to what extent he understands the theoretical basis of what he does, is obviously another story. Similarly, despite their YouTube success, we do not take Julianna and Mark to be forerunners in developing a philosophy of profilicity; but they certainly have some degree of intuition about second-order observation, social validation feedback loops, and the general peer. They are practitioners who apply the logic of profilicity very well. As profilicity calmly surges into all areas of society, the Boho Beautiful duo show how authenticity can be transformed into a powerful profile asset. The result of this transformation is neither authenticity nor inauthenticity but profilicity.

Eva Illouz has shown that in current "emotional capitalism," the public exhibition of feelings and personal preferences can make the self a valuable commodity. For her, this results in a tension: "The technology of the Internet thus positions the self in a contradictory way: it makes one take a deep turn inward, that is, it requires that one focus on one's self in order to capture and communicate its unique essence, in the form of tastes, opinions, fantasies, and emotional compatibility. On the other hand, the Internet also makes the self a commodity on public display."[27] Public self-display, as Illouz points out most accurately, is directed toward an "abstract and anonymous audience," a "general audience of unknown, abstract candidates" or the "generalized and abstract audience" (80–90). We fully agree and call this audience the "general peer."

Illouz, however, does not seem to acknowledge that the focus on self-presentation to the general peer fundamentally alters identity. Sticking, for instance, to the idea of a "unique essence," Illouz's authenticity-based assumptions get in the way of fully appreciating the shift toward profilicity. She still assumes that self-presentation through social media–based profiles "presupposes a movement inward toward one's most solid sense of self (who am I and what do I want?)" (76). Illouz thinks, as many did in the early days of the internet, that the web can enable the communication of individuality, and she agrees with those "who argue that people can and do form meaningful bonds on the net because it enables the expression of what they call the 'authentic self'" (107). She thinks that multiple profiles not merely reflect a multiple and playful "postmodern self" but are rooted in the good old Cartesian *cogito*:

> Whereas the postmodern self implies there is no core self, only a multiplicity of roles to be played, the self that is posited by the conjunction of psychology and the Internet technology is "ontic" in the sense that it assumes there is a core self which is permanent and which can be captured through a multiplicity of representations (questionnaire, photo, emailing) and so on. The Internet revives with a vengeance the old Cartesian dualism between mind and body, with the only real locus for thought and identity being in the mind. To have an Internet self is to have a Cartesian

cogito, and to be involved in the world by looking at it from within the walls of one's consciousness. (80–81)

Unlike Illouz, we do not see any unsurmountable tension or Cartesian dualism in profilicity between, on the one hand, a publicly displayed profilic self that is commodified and appears in all its multiplicity in the new media and, on the other hand, a "unique essence" and authentic "core self." In profilicity, authenticity and the "unique essence" are thoroughly *aufgehoben* or sublated, to speak with Hegel. When put in the service of profilicity, authenticity ceases to be what it was. Instead of being an innermost core, it becomes a highly powerful and almost priceless profilic meme.

Today sensitivity to different contexts and a high degree of reflexivity on the web are the norm. All kinds of profiles, from Instagram and Snapchat to dating accounts and résumés, are carefully curated to appeal to the general peer. Nothing is posted without a concern for how one is seen as being seen. Nevertheless, as Illouz's reflections and Boho Beautiful's videos show, the idea lives on that underneath all these performative selves there must be the "Me, that poor old ultimate actuality, who, when all the roles have been played, would like to murmur 'Off, off, you lendings.'"[28] Despite increasingly obvious contradictions, the authenticity discourse not only stubbornly persists but even flourishes in profilicity. It thrives particularly well in the popular literature and professional marketing of "personal branding" or "self-branding."

"Personal branding" or "self-branding" are terms used to describe profile management—and often related to internet platforms. Following examples like Michael Jordan, Oprah Winfrey, and Beyoncé, many celebrities seek to become more than simply basketball players, talk show hosts, or singers. They seek to become their own brand. Or, more accurately, they curate an encompassing profile persona to be marketed and sold.

To help guide celebrities and noncelebrities in curating their profiles, *Forbes* magazine published "10 Golden Rules of Personal Branding." They are: "1. Have a focus. 2. Be genuine. 3. Tell a story. 4. Be consistent. 5. Be ready to fail. 6. Create a positive impact. 7. Follow a successful example. 8. Live your brand. 9. Let other people tell your story. 10. Leave a legacy."[29] Many of these rules simply vary the paradoxical demand, "Be your true self in a way that others will buy." Number 2, for example, is expounded: "There's an easy way to have an original personal brand—and that is to be genuine and authentic. Millennial influencer and head of marketing at Popular Demand, Monica Lin, says 'People can see right through a disingenuous act.'" In number 8 we find: "Tim Salau, community builder and founder of Mentors & Mentees, who works with college students to help them build brands that will get them hired, believes in this idea as well. 'Your personal brand should follow you everywhere you go. It needs to be an authentic manifestation of who you are and amplify what you believe.'" Of course, the maintenance of the authenticity profile requires frequent updates, modifications, and adjustments.

When teaching part of the course "Project You: Building and Extending Your Personal Brand" at Stanford University, American celeb Tyra Banks made sure to stress the importance of "figuring out when to pivot and evolve." Pivoting, Banks thinks, is critical. Commenting on her own ever-evolving personal profile, she says, "[My pivots] were necessary so I did not become obsolete. I couldn't model forever. I needed a plan and I needed to change." That doesn't mean overthinking things, since when "your brand and personality align harmoniously then your brand doesn't require strenuous maintenance because it will come naturally figuring out when shifts are needed." In other words, making sure to bring about "pivots" of your profile is essential, and you can do the necessary maintenance work most effortlessly if you manage to "authentically" identify with your profile. Then the curation activity will become less painful. Just find the general peer that you like best, and you'll pivot naturally, and sell yourself above par. For instance, instead of being on every social media platform, "a person should only focus on the ones that they are interested in because otherwise there's no authenticity to it and therefore it will be a subpar endeavor."[30]

Zhang Dayi does not need to enroll in Tyra Banks's class at Stanford. She is a major Chinese "key opinion leader," or influencer, and made over forty-six million U.S. dollars in 2016.[31] Her popularity comes from posting photos and short videos and doing live streams where she talks about "her own" fashion. That is, she is a master personal brander who is famous for nothing other than profiling.

Zhang's motto is *ganyu zuo ziji* 敢于做自己, which translated literally into English means "dare to be yourself." This seems to be a slogan brazenly and glaringly endorsing authenticity, but the literal English rendering is misleading. In Chinese, this now common catchphrase is normally understood in a different sense: it is more of an appeal to profilicity than anything else. In its actual usage, *ganyu zuo ziji* refers to daring to display oneself publicly, daring to "get on the scene."

Zhang makes no qualms about the entire process of developing a personal brand beyond the value of authenticity. She says: "Because [being an internet star] is itself something that happens through someone liking a photo or a video, this process will very quickly [influence] your life. Even in real life it's hard to expect something sincere [or genuine or authentic], how could you expect people on the internet to be sincere to you for a lifetime, it's totally impossible."[32]

She also understands her internet persona beyond the confines of authenticity: "My personality is the kind that you look at and think I'm totally easygoing, but actually I'm a very difficult person."[33] In effect, "daring to be yourself" means, paradoxically, dare to be different from how you have been so far. It does not, however, mean "dare to be inauthentic." It means dare to be profilic. *Profilare aude.*

5

IDENTITY

I hazard the guess that man will be ultimately known for a mere polity of multifarious, incongruous, and independent denizens.

—Robert Louis Stevenson, *Strange Case of Dr. Jekyll and Mr. Hyde*

PROUD TO BE ME

We are both proud to be the authors of this book. And we are proud that it is published by Columbia University Press. Paul is proud to be American. Georg is proud of not being proud to be German. What are you proud of? Are you proud to be a woman? Or are you a proud father? Perhaps you are proud of being a Muslim? Do you have gay pride? Are you proud of your business or job? Of having graduated from Stanford? Are you proud of your Tesla, and for not having voted for Trump? Are you proud that you quit smoking? Finished the Boston Marathon? Of your Airbnb rating? Are you a proud supporter of your local community? A proud fan of the New England Patriots? Have you proudly tweeted about your recent podcast? Proudly bragged about your recent trip to Nepal? Or are you simply "proud to be me"?

Pride is an emotion that indicates comfort with oneself. It celebrates successful identification. As a manner of enjoying who we think we are, pride allows us to feel, in one way or another, "at home" with ourselves. At the same time, pride is also a public expression; it can be displayed on one's face and in the streets, in an advertisement and in a political campaign. Pride touches others; it is marketed and sells—but it can also deeply offend those with a conflicting source of pride. Just as identity, to which it is tied, pride both unites and divides.

The two dimensions of pride, as a psychological experience and as a social signal, correspond to two poles of identity: the inner self and the outer persona. The dynamics of pride mirror the struggle for identity. In a moment of personal pride or at the occasion of its public performance, as in a parade, identity is, it seems, actualized: the inner and outer happily coincide. These very moments, however, once they are "reified," frozen in time, singled out, abstracted from the situation, and projected toward others and ourselves, lend themselves to suspicion. They appeal to us because they signal that an identity destination has been reached. But the very fact of loudly proclaiming this achievement can also prompt further questions. Is the woman that I am today all I am and ever will be? Is this really me? When the word "proudly" is used in advertising, as in Budweiser's "proudly a macro beer" commercial, isn't this insistence, after all, primarily intended to attract paying customers?[1] When I publicly signal pride in my identity, do I have ulterior motives—financial or political, for example? Am I trying to convince others of something—or perhaps myself? And for what reason? Are such identity assertions trustworthy? Do they promise more than they can hold?

DARLING, JUST FUCKING OWN IT:
IDENTITY VALUE

To identify as something is claiming to be it, and a claim flags ownership. Ownership, in turn, indicates possession, and a possession has value: ideal value, material value, or both. That I identify as a New England Patriots fan means something to me—and precisely therefore I am happy to spend thirty dollars for a hat proudly displaying my identification, although I could buy essentially the same hat, just without the Patriot's logo, for less than half the money. Identity value can add quite significantly to use value.

What people proudly identify with gains value, not only psychologically but also politically and, importantly, economically. Gay pride, for instance, once successfully established not only allows people to feel better about themselves and to become a political force to be reckoned with; it also fuels what has been described as "pink capitalism."

The capitalist economy sustains itself through growth, or, to speak with Hartmut Rosa, through "dynamic stabilization."[2] It maintains itself by expansion. A key avenue for growth, beyond mere geographic extension or increase in production, is the commodification of what has not yet been an object of commerce. Land, for instance, or other natural resources that in a precapitalist society belonged to no one in particular or to everyone in common were eventually turned into private property and assigned monetary value. Increasingly, less tangible goods were commodified as well, such as safety or security by the insurance industry, or knowledge and education through the privatization of schools or universities, and perhaps most generally, time. Along with such transformations of abstract entities into monetary worth, identity, too, became a marketable asset. This is most visible in advertising, where celebrities are paid large amounts of money to transfer the value of their identity to the value of a product. The same is true the other way around: the purchase and display of such products can increase an individual's identity value.

Psychological, political, and economic identity value—and pride—can be mutually enforcing or mutually destructive. Once Lance Armstrong was found out to be a major cheater, people were much less proud of him, and as a consequence he lost most of his financial identity value—his business partners no longer appreciated him. In capitalism, "appreciation" means not only that something is esteemed but also the accumulation of financial value. When Armstrong was depreciated as a person, his economic brand depreciated as well.

Since identity has a value, it can be bought and sold. When it's yours, you own it.

FIGURE 5.1 "Darling Just f*cking own it" bag. Photo by Paul D'Ambrosio.

THE PERSONAL IS POLITICAL: IDENTITY POLITICS

Personal identification with a belief or an ideology, with a nation or a people, or with a group or a class can feed political movements, form political consciousness, and inform political action. People often fight for their identities in revolutions, counterrevolutions, and wars. Identity value has immense political force. Often, political struggles strive to increase the identity value of, for instance a race, a gender, or a sexual orientation.

A gay pride parade is a political performance grounded in the desire to socially revalue homosexual identity. It struggles to display pride in an identity that others regard as shameful. Under conditions of systematic homophobia—in the form of legal, religious, moral, and cultural suppression of homosexuality—it is almost impossible to openly affirm and express a gay identity. A gay pride movement intends to reverse such a situation and to allow individuals to publicly and happily identify as gay. This identification operates, on the one hand, on a personal and emotional level, but also, and powerfully, on a public and political level. It is about changing attitudes toward homosexuality, both those of others and one's own, and it is also about overturning the institutionalized discrimination of homosexuality that serves as the sociopolitical foundation of "gay shame." To transform gay shame into gay pride is both a psychological effort and, arguably more fundamentally, a political act. "The personal is political."

"The personal is political" is a slogan associated with the emergence of contemporary "identity politics" half a century ago. The proper term "identity politics" was coined in the 1970s alongside various movements demanding the political emancipation of groups that were marginalized or suppressed on the basis of ethnicity, gender, sexual orientation, or religious views. Of

FIGURE 5.2 Gay Pride parade. Photo from Pixabay website,
https://pixabay.com/photos/gay-pride-gay-parade-lgbt-pride-5008124/,
accessed May 29, 2020.

course, such political movements already existed long before. The
African American civil rights movement, for instance, gained
momentum in the 1950s, but is easily traced back to the nineteenth century. "First-wave feminism," too, began in the nineteenth century when suffrage movements first demanded the
right to vote for women. The overarching consciousness and conceptual framework that have tied such diverse, and sometimes
even competing or contradictory, movements together under the
umbrella of "identity politics," however, developed more recently,
in the 1960s and 1970s.

The slogan "the personal is political" expresses the common
ground of the various strands of "identity politics." It rose to

popularity as the title of a short radical feminist statement by Carol Hanisch, first published in 1970 and republished with an introduction by the author in 2006. In that essay, Hanisch points out that many of the problems that women experience in their daily lives—"especially 'all those body issues' like sex, appearance, and abortion"—are typically framed as personal problems that ought to be dealt with in the form of "therapy."[3] However, Hanisch argues, these problems are in fact caused by social and political circumstances that place women in inferior positions and preclude them from acquiring equal status in personal and economic relationships. In her words, "women are messed over, not messed up" (3). The point Hanisch tries to get across is "the need to fight male supremacy as a movement instead of blaming the individual woman for her oppression" (1). In this context, "the personal is political" asserted that many supposedly personal problems of women are not actually personal but rather political problems. In this way, Hanisch's original essay implies that once the political problem of male supremacy is redressed—once a feminist revolution has succeeded—supposedly personal issues of female subjects will disappear. In short, what appears personal *is not truly personal* but political.

Hanisch emphasized that what are generally regarded as personal failures typical of a particular category of people are often only secondary effects of underlying problems with economic and political structures. She implied that feminism should not be primarily concerned with fixing these problems on an individual level but rather with reforming the social conditions that give rise to them in the first place. Somewhat paradoxically, the original meaning of "the personal is political" is therefore not really in line with the meaning this same phrase has taken on in the more recent identity politics discourse—which is perhaps why

Hanisch later complained that "these ideas have been revised or ripped off or even stood on their head and used against their original, radical intent" (3).[4]

The radical type of feminism represented by Hanisch is, because of its deemphasis of the personal, an early or weak form of identity politics. In a stronger conception of identity politics, identity itself becomes the primary concern of political action and is no longer regarded as a mere side effect of underlying sociopolitical structures. Here, the slogan "the personal is political" means that politics is in essence personal, which is to say: it is about personal *identity*.

A paradigmatic expression of a stronger identity politics interpretation of the slogan "the personal is political" is included in "The Combahee River Collective Statement" published by a group of Black feminists in 1977.[5] Here, the authors intend to give voice to "a shared awareness of how their sexual identity combined with their racial identity" and has made "their whole life situation and the focus of their political struggles unique." They stress that their African American and feminine identity is "inherently valuable" and gives rise to their "concept of identity politics": "We believe that the most profound and potentially most radical politics come directly out of our own identity, as opposed to working to end somebody else's oppression." From this perspective, political action is grounded in and properly emerges from the firsthand experience of identity: "Our politics evolve from a healthy love for ourselves, our sisters and our community which allows us to continue our struggle and work." Here, politics is explicitly defined in terms of an emotionally felt and physically embodied individual identity that is collectively enacted with others who share the same identity. Thus identity is political, and the political *is truly personal*.

A strong identity politics demands that political movements should evolve out of the experience of personal identity and be put in its service. The prime function of politics, according to this approach, is to empower and protect diverse forms of identity, especially racial, religious, gender, or sexual identity. The point, then, in contrast to Carol Hanisch's argument, is not to reform a problematic conception of "female" (or other) identity established in patriarchal or otherwise oppressive sociopolitical structures but rather to create sociopolitical structures that will enable, for instance, Black feminine identity to flourish. A consequence of strong identity politics can be the demand for an identity-based and identity-oriented state. Precisely this suggestion was made by Garrett Graham, whose book *The Gay State* was written for the purpose of initiating, as part of the subtitle reads, *The Quest for an Independent Gay Nation-State.*[6]

AGAINST IDENTITY POLITICS:
THE RADICAL LEFT AND
POLITICAL NEW SINCERITY

The strong version of identity politics developed out of the (North American) political left but, somewhat paradoxically, can easily be regarded as an aberration from earlier (European) leftist thinking, or, more precisely, from Marxist materialism. From a Marxist materialist perspective, the political economy constitutes the base structure of society. It determines cultural and ideological phenomena such as family organization along with gender divisions and sexual ethics, race relations, religious beliefs, and moral regimes, all of which belong to the superstructure of society. This is to say, quite in line with Hanisch's original understanding of "the personal is political": the current experiences

of, for instance, African American women living under capitalism are not ultimately rooted in certain characteristics unique to
subjects of particular racial and gender groups but rather are
shaped by socioeconomic conditions. Therefore a strong version
of identity politics can be criticized from a Marxist position for
sidelining the political-economic class struggle and focusing far
too much on a perhaps not-so-healthy "love for ourselves."

From a Marxist perspective, the strong emphasis on "identity politics" by the Democratic Party under Barack Obama
could be seen as a populist rebranding of the left that abandoned
the working class and its economic struggle. In fact, it seems that
in the post-Trump-election era some of the Democratic Party,
as represented by support for politicians like Bernie Sanders, is
steering back toward a more traditional socialist orientation. For
a traditional Marxist, identity politics can seem problematic precisely because it focuses too much on personal identity at the
expense of revolutionary socioeconomic politics.

The more mainstream liberal critique of identity politics comes
from a different angle. As early as 1991, Pulitzer Prize–winning
historian Arthur Schlesinger, Jr., published *The Disuniting of
America*, where he criticizes identity politics for splitting American society into different gender or racial groups. He accuses it
of betraying the common American identity grounded in a liberal political and moral consensus. Specifically, after Trump's
election victory in 2016—which was in part perceived as a triumph of antiliberalism—this kind of critique of identity politics has experienced a strong revival. Unlike the radical leftist
critique, it does not fault identity politics for focusing too much
on identity but rather for getting the idea of identity wrong: we
should not primarily identify ourselves on the basis of particular
racial, gender, or other categories but rather identify ourselves on the basis of what unites us, namely, a commitment to

American—or cosmopolitan—liberal values. This is the position we call "political new sincerity."[7]

The view of political new sincerity is paradigmatically summarized in Michael Sandel's plea to find identity "as members of this family or community or nation of people, as bearers of this history, as sons or daughters of that revolution, as citizens of this republic."[8] As discussed earlier, Kwame Appiah, Mark Lilla, and Francis Fukuyama have all published books making compatible points: strong identity politics needs to be replaced with a communitarian ethos.[9] Identity should be derived from a primary commitment to the larger community and one's place in it rather than from a priority given to the respective, and potentially divisive, unique identity of each individual.

SHARED PRACTICES AND SHARED SENTIMENTS: IDENTITY AS (POST-) NATIONAL CHARACTER

While strong identity politics conceives of identity typically in terms of an individual's ethnicity, gender, or sexual orientation, political new sincerity critics want to derive identity from a sense of belonging to a community bound together by shared values. The ensuing communal identity tends to be reminiscent of Robert Bellah's classic outline of "Civil Religion in America" defined as "a strong moral consensus."[10] In the same vein, Kwame Appiah envisions identification with the American melting pot through "shared sentiment" as the foundation of a new postnationalist nation-state:

> And so, if you want to build states around nations, you're going to have to do more than simply summon an existing people and

make a constitution. You're going to have to *make* a nation: you will take a population most of whom wish, for some reason, to live under a shared government, and then, after wresting them from whatever states they currently live in, you will need to build in them the shared sentiments that will make it possible for them to live productively together.[11]

Appiah further explains that a cosmopolitan nation-state that includes people with all kinds of different origins, races, genders, and sexual orientations must also be grounded in "shared practices" similar to those binding religious groups together. These practices, however, are not to be derived from transcendent beliefs (such as a belief in the same God), but from moral values—which is precisely what makes them *civil* religions and not religious per se:

> The trouble is that we've tended to emphasize the details of belief over the shared practices and the moral communities that buttress religious life. Our English word "orthodoxy" comes from a Greek word that means "correct belief." But there's a less familiar word, "orthopraxy," that comes from another Greek word, πράξης (*praxis*), which means "action." Orthopraxy is a matter not of *believing* right but of *acting* right. (12)

A "shared sentiment" about "*acting* right" will result, as Appiah implies, in a collective ethics and way of life: an "orthopraxy." This "orthoprax" way of life is supposed to be at the heart of a new civil religious identity. A larger common identity can bind individuals with their various personal identities together into a joint political community.

Appiah and his fellow new political sincerity post–identity politics thinkers conceive of identity as a collective *ethos* very much in line with the original meaning of this Greek term. *Ethos* indicated the character of a group, community, or society manifested (a) in a general consensus on basic moral values, (b) in shared customs ("practices" in Appiah's terms) in accordance with that consensus, and (c) in shared emotional experience or feelings ("sentiments" in Appiah's terms) arising from a shared morality and behavior. The concept of an "overarching identity" to be found in a (post-)national character, ethos, or orthopraxy is not new. Given its emphasis on collective character and the individual's roles within a group, it echoes older sincerity models. In contrast, a strong identity politics with its focus on individual experience and originality can be associated with an ethos, and perhaps a regime, of authenticity.

THE COMPLEXITY OF IDENTITY

The various conceptions of identity used in today's academic and political discussions can be clarified with a definition of different meanings of "identity" given in a paper by Sheldon Stryker and Peter J. Burke on "The Past, Present, and Future of an Identity Theory":

> Three relatively distinct usages exist. Some use *identity* to refer essentially to the culture of a people; indeed they draw no distinction between identity and, for example, ethnicity (see the collected papers in Calhoun 1994). . . . Others use identity to refer to common identification with a collectivity or social category, as in social identity theory (Tajfel 1982), or in contemporary work on social movements, thus creating a common culture among participants (Snow and Oliver 1995). Finally, some use the term . . . with reference to parts of a self composed of the meanings that

persons attach to the multiple roles they typically play in highly differentiated contemporary society.[12]

Clearly, the focus on race, gender, and sexual orientation that characterizes the strong identity politics discourse corresponds largely to the first usage of "identity" described by Stryker and Burke, if we shift that category slightly to include the broader range of group identities and categorizations into which one is (arguably) born. Here, race, gender, and sexual orientation *constitute* identity. Current critics of identity politics, however, almost exclusively draw on a notion of identity that corresponds to the second type listed by Stryker and Burke, again revised slightly to denote those group identities and categorizations that cohere through adopting a set of shared values. (Note that these two notions of identity are conceptually distinct but do not conflict.) Here, identity is derived from a "common identification with a collectivity or social category" of subjects that share common morals, which creates a "common culture among participants."

However, the third dimension of identity that Stryker and Burke list also needs to be taken into account when trying to understand how identity operates—and when reflecting on identity politics. The critics of identity politics are justified to point out that race, gender, or sexual orientation do not completely determine identity. However, shared values or a (post-)national character also fail to exhaust the phenomenon of identity. Identity can be limited to neither "genealogical" categories such as race or gender nor shared ethical practices. In addition to these levels of identity, there is the sociopsychological dimension that Stryker and Burke describe. It emerges from the sense of "meanings that persons attach to the multiple roles they typically play in highly differentiated contemporary society." Identity as

"self-identity" is the notion of selfhood that individuals develop—
who we think and feel we are—through the different personas
or social roles we take on in society.

To address and analyze the various ways of achieving identity is essential to avoiding some of the oversimplifications that
limit identity politics debates. The genealogical, community-
based, and sociopsychological dimensions of identity are not
incompatible. They cooperate in the constant patching together
of identity, and they can all be enacted in the modes of sincerity,
authenticity, or profilicity. All forms of identity technology
involve all three dimensions of identity.

Stryker and Burke rightly highlight the importance of the
sociopsychological dimension of identity. Identity is achieved as
the integrated individual psychological experience of selfhood
and its social performance. The formation of identity is situated
within larger contexts. People do have bodies. They are, for
instance, physically varied in their sex organs, skin color, and
sexual inclinations. At the same time, there are social structures
and systems framing the individual experience of identity. Politics, economics, religion, language, and culture contribute significantly to the experience of identity.

Identity is constituted, felt, and performed in complex ways,
and the various dimensions of identity do not always coexist in
perfect harmony. They constantly challenge one another—as the
identity politics debate illustrates. Racial or gender identity may
not perfectly coincide with communal commitments, and not
always be backed up by one's personal feelings and thoughts. And
identifications are subject to change. To be black or white, or gay
or straight, or American or German, does not mean the same
today as fifty years ago and is not the same here as it is there. How
we feel about our own selfhood and how we identify ourselves
can change from day to day. Identity is constantly negotiated

and renegotiated on both a personal and a social level. While, by definition, identity is that which is regarded as constant about us as particular subjects, it turns out to be subject to ongoing transformations. Identity is, somewhat absurdly, non-identical to itself. It is, nevertheless, necessary.

Identity is needed: psychologically for individuals to be able to function but also politically for shaping communities and forming social organizations. Yet there is no core dimension of identity that can firmly ground it; one's particular race or ethical commitments do not fully identify that person. Therefore technologies of identity are needed to make identity, against all odds, plausible. This is what sincerity, authenticity, and profilicity do. None of them is perfect, or necessarily better than the others; all serve the purpose of integrating various incongruent levels and dimensions of identity.

The main function of identity is to establish and uphold stability of personhood; identity merges the different aspects of a person into a whole. It promises reliability and recognizability on which trust and (self-)confidence can be built, and to which pride and value, including economic and political value, can be attached. From time to time, however, cracks between different dimensions of personhood come to the fore, and what we normally must take to be a coherent and congruent identity falls apart. Identity is a counterfactual but necessary postulate that allows us to reduce overwhelming human complexity to manageable simplicity—so that human complexity can further evolve.

HERMENEUTIC DESPAIR AND LOVE

In her introduction to Niklas Luhmann's book *Social Systems*, Eva M. Knodt refers to a dialogue from the nineteenth-century drama *Danton's Death* by Georg Büchner as "the primal scene of hermeneutic despair." Here, the protagonist, in frustration about the inability to achieve complete understanding between herself and her lover, points to her forehead and exclaims: "There, there, what lies behind this? Go on, we have crude senses. To understand one another? We would have to break open each other's skulls and pull the thoughts out of the fibers of our brains!"[13] Of course, such drastic action would not help much either, since thoughts are not actually imprinted in our brain matter. The theatrical scene quoted by Knodt illustrates a foundational insight informing Luhmann's systems theory: the systemic difference between biological, mental, and social operations makes it impossible for them to operationally connect. Brains neither think nor talk but operate biologically as living systems. Our minds think and feel, but unlike the brain they do not live biologically, nor do they actually talk. In society, all we can do is communicate, but the communications never literally *enter* either our brains or minds. We have to *mentally interpret* and *physiologically process* what we hear someone else say, but there is no *immediate connectivity* between communication, which happens in society, and brains or minds. Seen in this way, we are hopelessly disconnected from another person's thoughts and feelings, and even communication does not bridge the gap.

However, the three systemic realms of body, mind, and society are for sure, as Luhmann says, "structurally coupled." This is to say, they are in a symbiotic and "coevolutionary" relation and mutually dependent on one another in order to exist, function, and develop. Without bodies and minds, society could not have evolved as it did, and this is also true for minds and bodies, each of which requires the other two. Society, bodies, and minds are operationally distinct and need to remain so in order to continue their *autopoiesis*, that is, their self-generation and self-reproduction. But they also need the coexistence of other systems in their environment—they need a larger "ecosystem" that produces constant resonance between all the subsystems constituting it.

What we think matters when we communicate, even though spoken or written words are never a complete and perfectly accurate account of a person's mental contents. And while language is a common medium shared by minds and social systems, society cannot literally think or feel, and thoughts and feelings cannot literally speak. The "hermeneutic despair" Knodt writes about concerns the mutual understanding between two people. Even the most intimate couple can never fully understand each other. A distance between people's minds always remains. As much as we'd might like to convince ourselves of the contrary, it remains a fact that even two lovers are psychologically distinct from each other and do not meld into one.

The systemic fissure between minds, bodies, and society does not only separate different people from one another. It also separates the bodily, mental, and social spheres of a single human being. To highlight this point, Luhmann ends his programmatic essay "How Can the Mind Participate in Communication" with the perhaps counterintuitive but nevertheless factually correct statement: "I do not know if I mean what I say, and if I knew, I would have to keep it to myself."[14] The complete psychological intention, motivation, and significance of whatever I say, the full range of my inner mental operations, remains opaque *also to me*. And even if it wouldn't, there is never a complete and exact correspondence between what I know and what I say and what is understood once I have said it.

Social persona, inner self, and one's body do not form one coherent and synchronized whole where each part fully expresses or corresponds to the others. These dimensions of being human—mental states and operations, social personas, and a living body—are never, in the strict sense of the word, *identical*. The sociopsychological formation of identity is needed in order to be able to conceive of humans beings as "one" despite their fracturedness. It is needed to cover up our underlying incongruent multifariousness—to magically transform this nonidentity into makeshift or apparent identity.

Unlike what Knodt's expression "hermeneutic despair" might suggest, however, the gaps between the systemic dimensions body, mind, and social persona are by no means a depressing flaw of the human condition. Quite to the contrary, these gaps open up space for evolving complexity and development. They make possible biological, mental, and social flexibility, productivity, creativity, diversity, and "freedom." Humans are different from artificial intelligence precisely because the human body (including the brain) does not mechanically program what exactly we think and how we feel. Our thoughts and feelings take shape within a highly dynamic environment, most crucially constituted by our body and our social surroundings. Because of this systemic multiplicity, each systemic realm—mind, society, and body—can emerge in its own autopoietic way. Yes, we cannot really be sure what someone, including ourselves, *really* means when they say something. But precisely because of the systemic separation between communication and minds, the need for interpretation ensues, and thus we can have, for instance, psychology, philosophy, and literature. And, probably more important, precisely therefore we can also have love as we know it, namely, as a very complex and dynamic form of human interrelationship involving all kinds of social, psychological, and bodily bonds, exchanges, and interpretations. If, indeed, we would fully understand one another, like two connected computers having complete access to each other's data, love might not make sense.

ONE IS NOT BORN, BUT RATHER BECOMES, A WOMAN

"*On ne naît pas femme: on le deviant:* One is not born, but rather becomes, a woman."[15] When Simone de Beauvoir wrote this most famous of her sentences in the 1940s, it could still cause controversy, consternation, and even outrage. About a lifetime later, this is hardly the case. Today's broad acceptance of this classic feminist proposition is evident in a pervasive linguistic shift that took place in its wake. In English, and in many other languages, the distinction between "sex" and "gender" is now widely used. This distinction constitutes a thorough conceptual revolution brought about, at least in part, by de Beauvoir's book *The Second Sex*, from which the quotation is drawn. Here, de Beauvoir showed in great detail (often by analyzing passages from contemporary literature) how female identity, as performed in society, is not anchored in biological nature. Instead, it is produced by sociopsychological practices exercised, for instance, in ethics, religion, the law, mass media, the economy, politics, art, and education. She thereby countered the "conservative" claim of a biologically grounded "womanhood" that once and for all determines how women ought to think and live.

Of course, de Beauvoir's point is not to say that there are no biological differences between the sexes, but rather that such differences do not determine certain social or psychological differences. Social differences are, in fact, socially produced, and psychological differences are psychologically produced. De Beauvoir's quote emphasizes that femininity as it is commonly referred to is not a *natural* category. It does not genetically indicate what is so by virtue of *birth*. Therefore the notion of womanhood needs to be conceptually freed from biological connotations. For political, religious, and other social reasons—or, in short, for patriarchal purposes—it had been most convenient to maintain that womanhood is biologically determined, and to thereby suggest that the sociopsychological characteristics of female identity are somehow decreed by natural or divine law. This set up a pretext to morally and legally dismiss or sanction unwanted female behavior. As a consequence, the radical separation of sociopsychological features of femininity from their supposed biological roots, as pursued by de Beauvoir and others, was of utmost political importance. Only in this way could the claims to a foundational masculine superiority over women be subverted and debunked.

The by now common (at least in English) use of the lexical distinction between sex and gender speaks to the profound transformation that has taken place after de Beauvoir's famous pronouncement more than half a century ago. Similar political transformations followed regarding race, along with similar conceptual and linguistic changes. Arguments based on racial determinism, too, are no longer convincing to most and are thoroughly out of favor in the academic, legal, and political spheres.

To be able to easily distinguish between sex and gender means to deny neither the existence of biological distinctions nor the influence of biological features on social or psychological phenomena. To the contrary: of course it is immensely relevant that women give birth and men do not. While this biological fact certainly causes "motherhood" to come into existence, it does not determine any specific family structures to be "right" or necessitate any specific ethical or religious interpretation of what it is to be a good mother. Psychological and social features of motherhood are *contingent* on the biological fact that women, unlike men, are capable of giving birth—and "contingent" means both that one has something to do with the other and that the relation between the two sides is not one of strict causal necessity. There are coincidences and further circumstances to be taken into account. Things could have also come out otherwise. The fact that women give birth allows for a wide variety of psychological and social phenomena of motherhood to emerge, but none of them is causally grounded in any biological feature as its determining "root cause."

FROM NECESSITY TO CONTINGENCY

Under patriarchal social conditions, a firm congruence between the biological, psychological, and social aspects of sex/gender identity had been asserted. This assertion was typically supported by religious, ethical, or (pseudo-)scientific "master-narratives," Such master-narratives, as they are found, for instance, in the Abrahamic religions or in Confucianism, did not only provide rationalizations, and thus legitimizations, of gender inequality. What is more, they also facilitated the internalization of gender roles. The message could be: the Holy Father is male, and the Virgin Mary is female—now follow their paths! In this way, gender roles were perceived not as mere roles but on a deeper level, as the inescapable and invariable core of one's being. The more congruent and naturally or divinely linked the bodily and sociopsychological aspects of identity appear, the more binding and restricting they will become. Each aspect then tends to confirm and "prove" the other. Sociopsychological feedback mechanisms evolve and tie social and psychological practices ever closer together. If a sociopolitical, moral, or religious regime defines certain characteristics of womanhood as natural, then the woman who does not feel and behave in accordance with them must be taken to be—and must take herself to be—unnatural, and this is to say perverted, crazy, or neurotic. Enormous sociopsychological pressures of identification can build up. Through collective internalization they can become almost totalitarian and permeate all aspects of social life and mental experience.

The conceptual distinction between sex and gender made it possible to undermine traditional narratives about a congruent sex/gender identity. It brought the actual incongruity between these spheres into focus, and thus into consciousness. The emancipatory effect of the feminist redescription of womanhood lies precisely in its switch from a congruity-based to an incongruity-based understanding of identity. The move from necessity to contingency is at the heart of the philosophical revolution in which de Beauvoir and many others participated. Theologians, philosophers, moralists, and scientists—from Aristotle to Kant—had tried to identify the unchanging and necessitating causes behind social, psychological, and physiological phenomena. Thereby they intended to transform an apparently contingent world into a world of foundational necessities. Later thinkers, from Nietzsche to de Beauvoir to Richard Rorty, showed to the contrary how that which had been deemed to be a foundational necessity by traditional master-narratives was in fact contingent—contingent in the sense of due to a host of complex coincidences and circumstances and therefore open to continuous change.

A similar theoretical paradigm shift from necessity to contingency was most famously introduced into biology by Charles Darwin in the nineteenth century. Darwin replaced the previous dogma of divine creation, and thus of the biological necessitation of humankind, with a theory of contingent evolution.

This paradigm shift was then extended to the sociological and psychological dimensions of "human identity," not only by Herbert Spencer but later on also by distinctly different thinkers like de Beauvoir and others. It is possible to trace theories of contingency much further back than Darwin, certainly to Hegel and Marx, and quite possibly also to Western and non-Western antiquity.[16] Despite this trajectory reaching far back into the past, it is nevertheless hardly dubitable that dogmatic insistence on the congruity of biological, psychological, and social aspects of human identity was quite prevalent in premodern European and Asian societies and proved to be particularly useful to sustaining patriarchal structures and gender roles. After all, the terminological distinction between sex and gender did not really occur prior to the twentieth century. Until then, "gender" had been primarily a linguistic term classifying nouns.

The case of the feminist revolution that brought about the sex/gender distinction demonstrates well that the philosophical switch from necessity to contingency, along with the subversion of the dogma of congruent human identity, is nothing to be feared. It constituted neither a nihilistic destruction of human integrity nor a depressing dissolution of sane personhood. In fact, it brought about much-needed social and psychological liberation from stifling gender prejudices. That our body does not determine our mind and social persona is by no means a terrifying insight, and particularly not so if this body happens to be female or black. Modifying Hegel's famous dictum that freedom consists in the insight into necessity, it could be said (in line with Hegel's intentions, as we believe) that, more precisely speaking, freedom actually consists in the insight into the contingency of what was presumed to be necessary.[17] In other words, identity is free once we realize that there is no need to overinternalize it.

THE PROBLEM OF IDENTITY

Such freedom is a lot of work—and that this is so is another insight we can derive from Hegel. The toilsome nature of freedom also comes to the fore in identity. It certainly took a lot of effort and courage to make the once highly controversial claim that feminine identity is nothing natural. Moreover, if we do not regard identity as given by birth, then we are posed with the potentially arduous task of somehow achieving it. An advantage of premodern necessity- and congruity-based models of identity, manifesting themselves in regimes of sincerity, is that one does not have to question who one is. If this question does not arise, there is no need for a concept of "identity" in the contemporary sense to begin with. Douglas Kellner somewhat nonchalantly describes the corresponding assumption that there was no quest for identity in premodernity as "anthropological folklore":

According to anthropological folklore, in traditional societies, one's identity was fixed, solid, and stable. Identity was a function of predefined social roles and a traditional system of myths which provided orientation and religious sanctions to one's place in the world, while rigorously circumscribing the realm of thought and behaviour. One was born and died a member of one's clan, a member of a fixed kinship system, and a member of one's tribe or group with one's life trajectory fixed in advance. In pre-modern societies identity was unproblematical and not subject to reflection or discussion. Individuals did not undergo identity crises, or radically modify their identity. One was a hunter and a member of the tribe and that was that.[18]

In line with an ethos of sincerity, identity in premodern society tended to be socially fixed. Many social theorists, including

Anthony Giddens, Zygmunt Bauman, and Hartmut Rosa, to name a few, have said as much. Niklas Luhmann, too, shared this view and connected it with his definition of modern society as characterized by "functional differentiation"—social division into different systems (i.e., economic, political, religious, educational), which each function in accordance with their own respective structures. As individuals, modern humans need to operate within a wide variety of such systems and find it increasingly difficult to settle on an understanding of who they "really" are, and to describe their "true" selves to others. Luhmann says: "More typical of today are situations in which we have to explain who we are. . . . 'Identity' and 'self-realization' become problems."[19] We experience a gap between our inner self and our social personas, so that the "distance between the individual and society induces the individual to reflect, to ask about the 'I' of I, to search for an identity of its own" (51). We may feel that we are split into a number of social personas which are all somehow expressions of our identity. But what exactly is this identity? This is the paradigmatic situation of an "authentic" identity crisis facing the "problem of identity": "The individual becomes defined by divisibility. It is in need of a musical self for the opera, an ambitious self for the job, a patient self for the family. What remains for itself is the problem of identity" (223). The problem of identity is an ongoing one and not easily resolved. We are constantly busy with finding, elaborating, presenting, or improving our identity. Paradoxically, the "identity crisis" seems to have become a permanent state of affairs. The author Timothy Mo depicts the modern individual's quest for identity in terms of a constant preoccupation with drawing one's self-portrait: "Men will not act by grand plans or formulations of a scheme of ideas, or even by the impulsion of a vested interest, but in the very first instance by the notion they entertain of themselves—and this picture they draw of their private characters is one to which they will address themselves with assiduity of purpose over many years: no portrait is more intensely drawn, Gideon, than the self-portrait."[20] Luhmann, a sociologist, uses language that is similar to Mo's when he describes the concern with one's self-portrait in terms of the "projection" of an image: "A person can therefore not really know who he is, but has to find out whether his own projections find recognition."[21] The quest for identity is not only an issue for teenagers who have yet to "find themselves"; it is a lifelong task. Under conditions of profilicity, our actions in society are geared toward shaping and reshaping a self-portrait—or better, a series of self-portraits—that we can present publicly, hoping for acceptance and validation.

TOWARD A THEORY OF IDENTITY

Identity compensates for the systemic division between different spheres of human existence: bodily life, mental activity (thoughts and feelings), and social relations and communication. It transforms the incongruity between these spheres into seeming congruity.[22] Through identity, "selfhood" is achieved: we appear to ourselves and others as a coherent unit (although, of course, how I see myself may not at all coincide with how others see me—the way my identity looks to me might not be the same way it looks to others). My body, my mind, and my social persona are regarded as the various extensions of *my self.* Modern theories of identity were thus typically formulated as theories of the self. They first tended to focus on the relation between the mental and the social aspects of selfhood and to somewhat neglect the bodily sphere. Only the more recent discourse on identity politics, due to its focus on sex, gender, and race, has brought the bodily dimension more to the fore. Prior to this political turn, identity theory was often housed in sociology, psychology, and the interdisciplinary conjunction of these two fields. It thus centered on analyzing selfhood as a sociopsychological phenomenon—as programmatically expressed in the title of George Herbert Mead's study *Mind, Self, and Society*.[23] This book, first published three years after Mead's death and largely based on lecture notes taken by his students, comprehensively outlines a theory of selfhood as a mental notion that arises out of social interaction.

Mead distinguishes between two types of theories of the self, social theories and individualistic theories. A social theory of the self, as represented by Mead's own approach, "derives the selves of individuals from the social process in which they are implicated and in which they empirically interact with one another." Conversely, the other type "derives that process from the selves of the individuals involved in it" (222). The two types of theories thus relate to one another in a chicken-and-egg way. The first sees society as a flock of chickens that produces selves as its eggs. The other thinks that a number of eggs—that is, individual selves—eventually bring about a flock of chickens (society).

Importantly, Mead regards not only the individual self but also the individual mind that forms an idea of and identifies itself with the self as socially generated. According to him, gestures by which humans communicate with one another eventually become meaningful symbols out of which language develops. Language in turn allows for minds to evolve, and these minds can then give rise to notions of selfhood. In particular, Mead suggests, minds and selves take shape through seeing oneself as an object in the eyes of the other. This happens concretely in (child) play and in more organized forms, such as in games. The self consists of the two phases of the Me and the I. The Me is the representation of the social persona within the self, whereas the I is one's own agency that arises in reaction to this.

Mead's distinction between the Me and the I as two phases of selfhood that relate to its inner (psychological) and outer (social) dimensions is vaguely reminiscent of Sigmund Freud's famous tripartite theory of mental selfhood, which distinguishes between the id, the ego, and the superego, where the superego represents the internalization of social expectations that have to be mediated by the ego. Despite some significant differences between these two theories of selfhood, both regard selfhood to a large extent as a matter of sociopsychological dynamics (although Freud, because of his focus on sexuality and the related notion of the id, ascribes more importance to the bodily dimension of selfhood than Mead).

Mead also discusses, although not in these precise terms, the "problem of identity" that emerges in modernity. Reflecting Kellner's so-called anthropological folklore, Mead outlines a shift toward a more individual and complex form of identity in what he calls "civilized society." Identity in civilized society departs from the conventionally prescribed role-identity that prevailed in "primitive society":

> In primitive society, to a far greater extent than in civilized society, individuality is constituted by the more or less perfect achievement of a given social type[24]—a type already given, indicated, or exemplified in the organized pattern of social conduct, in the integrated relational structure of the social process of experience and behavior which the given social group exhibits and is carrying on; in civilized society individuality is constituted rather by the individual's departure from, or modified realization of, any given social type than by his conformity, and tends to be something

much more distinctive and singular and peculiar than it is in primitive human society. (221)

Here, Mead distinguishes between an earlier and later form of individuality, or identity, very much along the lines of Lionel Trilling's distinction between sincerity (as identity constituted by conformity to socially given roles) and authenticity (as identity built on a departure from social conformity, on distinctiveness, singularity, and peculiarity)—the notions of sincerity and authenticity adopted in this book.

A little more than twenty years after *Mind, Self, and Society*, another classic study associated with a social theory of the self, or of identity, appeared: Erving Goffman's *The Presentation of Self in Everyday Life* (1956). This study is of major relevance for our theoretical endeavor. Based on his fieldwork as a sociological observer in a remote community on the Scottish Shetland Islands between 1949 and 1951, Goffman developed a theory of society as a theatric performance. According to Goffman, individuals present themselves in society like actors on a stage. They cooperate with one another, coordinate their behavior, and organize their community like a troupe enacting a play together—and watching it at the same time. For Goffman, too, the self eventually emerges primarily through the consideration and mediation of how one is seen by others, or of how one's persona appears in front of an "audience"—that is, in society. The self-identity that results from this scenario is socially generated and formed through *presentation*. Nevertheless, just as for Mead, there is also an important inner or mental component of the self that is constitutive of identity. Goffman distinguishes between the social persona that appears publicly on the "front stage" and the private realm into which everyone withdraws when "back stage."

This private realm allows the individual to reflect on and prepare their "front stage" self-presentation. The private and public realms as the inner and outer dimensions of personal identity are mutually supportive and in constant negotiation with each another.

The theatrical vocabulary that Goffman uses is developed out of the notion of social *roles*. His role-based understanding of society leads to a role-based concept of identity. And Goffman clearly intended the ensuing theory of society and selfhood to be applicable not only to small, traditional communities like those of the Shetland Islanders. What he saw in rural Scotland, he implied, is in principle transferrable to any form of social interaction and formation of selfhood, both traditional and modern. Nevertheless, its central focus on role-play makes Goffman's theory specifically relevant for our concept of sincerity-based, and thus role-based, identity. Perhaps more significant, however, is that Goffman's theory, given its emphasis on presentation to an audience as an essential moment of the performance of identity, also allows for segueing smoothly to the postauthentic concept of profilicity.

Both Mead and Goffman conceived of selfhood, and thus of personal identity, as a phenomenon that is socially generated but maintained as a mental idea. The mental aspect of identity is inseparable from the social sphere and constantly concerned with and informed by the social persona. Despite the inseparability of the social and psychological dimensions of selfhood, Mead and Goffman both still attest to their respective distinctiveness. Mead's "I" and "Me" and Goffman's "front stage" and "back stage" selves are elements of one self, and thus of identity, but they are never totally congruent with each other. There remains a distinction between the inner and outer sides of identity, and a tension between them that calls for permanent mutual concern of each side for the other. That they are inseparable does not mean that they are the same.

A description of the dynamic relations between the inner and outer, or the psychological and social, dimensions of selfhood is typically the centerpiece of sociopsychological theories of identity. In essence, the chicken versus egg alternatives—that is, the "social" and "individualistic" theories of selfhood as outlined by Mead in the 1930s—are still in competition with one another today. Sheldon Stryker, for instance, is representative of a modified and updated version of the social argument, whereas Peter J. Burke leans more toward the individualistic side. However, in their joint publication on "The Past, Present, and Future of Identity Theory," they attempted to combine their two approaches. Summarizing their intentions of achieving a future unified theory, they state:

> Among the many traditions of research on "identity," two somewhat different yet strongly related strands of identity theory have developed. The first, reflected in the work of Stryker and colleagues, focuses on the linkages of social structures with identities. The second, reflected in the work of Burke and colleagues, focuses on the internal process of self-verification. . . . Each provides a context for the other: the relation of social structures to identities influences the process of self-verification, while the process of self-verification creates and sustains social structures.[25]

For Stryker and Burke, the notion of selfhood arises from mentally connecting one's various social personas. It is the idea we develop of who we are, and that society projects back to us, based on the different social roles we take on. Using Luhmann's language, we can conceive of identity more widely as a sense of selfhood that emerges in the context of the structural coupling between psychic, social, and living (bodily) systems. Identity is a concept of selfhood that minds and society need to establish so that they can cope with their incongruity, or operational division. There are a number of options by which this can be done.

In addition to self-identity in an individual sense, there are also collective senses of identity. The sociopsychological identity of an individual emerges in the context of larger collective identities that the identity politics debate refers to: gender identity, ethnic identity, sexual identity, national identity, and so forth. In addition to the individual and collective senses of identity, moreover, there are also institutional and organizational claims to identity. Companies claim an identity for themselves. Political parties present an identity, and even football clubs are nowadays concerned with their identity. This, too, has to be considered when trying to understand identity.

THE DIALECTICS OF IDENTITY

Although Mead and Goffman both touched on the historical aspects of identity, they were more interested in outlining a basic universal structure of identity formation, maintenance, and performance. More recent sociopsychological identity theorists, like Stryker and Burke, are even less concerned with how identity may vary over time and in different cultural environments. From a sociopsychological perspective, the dynamics between the social and psychological elements of selfhood matter, but not so much sociopolitical evolution. To be able to look at identity from a broader perspective that takes historical aspects into account, we return to Hegel once more.

One way of characterizing the grand project of Hegel's *Phenomenology of Spirit* is as a conceptual history of human consciousness, or of *Weltgeist*, the "world spirit." This book reconstructs the maturation of the world spirit through an analysis of its manifestations in society—in politics, ethics, religion, art, science, and so forth. Each historical epoch has its specific *Zeitgeist*, a "spirit of the times." History moves ahead and becomes more complex and more advanced once a *Zeitgeist* is no longer sustainable or once its contradictions become evident. Religious narratives, like the traditional Christian worldview, may lose their credibility when this happens. Along with this loss of credibility, ethical regimes are undermined, and traditional legal and political structures are stripped of their legitimacy. This, in turn, brings about new developments in art, science, education, and other areas of society.

Importantly, for Hegel, the evolution of the world spirit is not merely an "objective" development; crucially, it is a process of increasing subjective awareness. Over time, human consciousness (*Bewusstsein*) becomes increasingly self-conscious (*selbstbewusst*). This does not mean that it loses self-confidence, as the colloquial English usage of the term "self-conscious" suggests, but quite to the contrary, that it becomes increasingly self-aware, increasingly conscious of its own agency, and thus increasingly free and powerful. The move from one stage of history to another is transformative not only on the external sociopolitical and cultural level but equally on the internal level of individual consciousness.

According to our understanding of Hegel, the evolution of the world spirit does not mean that humans will ever reach perfect self-determination and achieve an ideal final stage of history where society eventually becomes perfectly just, rational, and free. Hegel is not a utopian thinker and does not intend to predict the future. Precisely because consciousness is living and because self-consciousness is multiple—there is more than one thinking mind in the world—it is dynamic and prone to conflict, contradiction, and self-subversion. Development and maturation are not oriented toward an entropic goal but produce more and more possibilities, more and more diversity, and more and more incongruity. This is to say that when self-consciousness reaches a higher level, it becomes more aware of its multifariousness and better equipped to enact it. For both society and individuals, maturation does not mean to become simpler or more single-minded. It rather means to become more complex and to open up more contingency.

From a philosophical perspective, we conceive of identity not merely as a sociopsychological phenomenon but, in line with Hegel's concept of self-consciousness, as a highly dynamic, evolving, and open-ended evolutionary process. This process allows both individuals and society to develop various and increasingly complex and contingent forms of sense-making. Crucially, there is a dialectical core to identity: it never achieves equilibrium but grows by challenging and eventually "sublating" (*aufheben*) itself. It maintains itself by negating and thereby elevating itself to a more complex stage. Paradoxically, identity develops by making itself increasingly different, or nonidentical.

Identity must be understood historically; its structure and content evolve. This also means—and this is what we take from Hegel—that both as a mental concept and as a social practice, identity challenges itself, negates itself, and sublates itself. The contradictions and paradoxes of an identity paradigm can become obvious and lead to the formation of new ones. Thereby identity increases in complexity and contingency. New modes of identity do not simply replace older ones but coexist with them. When, at a certain time in history, one mode, such as sincerity, loses its

credibility and ceases to work well together with new sociopolitical formations, it can appear old-fashioned and may no longer be
of central relevance in many social contexts. But it can still continue to function in other contexts or perhaps be reshaped and
"recycled." It can also be put into the service of newer identity
paradigms, such as authenticity and profilicity. Rather than simply vanishing into irrelevance, modes of identity can continue to
play their parts in an increasingly multifarious identity tool case.
We can wake up authentically in the morning, do our job sincerely
during the day, and curate our public profiles at night.

WHAT WE DIE FOR: IDENTITY CRISES

Identity matters. Seriously. It fuels the personal and public
outrage stirred by identity politics. It enrages antimigration or
separatist protests. It inspires those who seek martyrdom for
their religious beliefs. People die and kill for it. Pride and
honor, hate and love, are tied to it. It divides or unites me and
you, us and them. In the economy, brand identity decides success and failure and creates wealth. Huge amounts are spent on
campaigns to establish it, disseminate it, and impress it on
everyone.

Here's a story about a teenager who once experienced an
identity crisis. He noticed that he acted differently toward his
parents than toward his friends. And not only this: he seemed
to be a different person when with his father than when with his
mother or sister. When with his male friends he behaved decid-
edly differently than when around girls. And he talked in a different way to his high school teachers than to his teammates in
the soccer club. As these observations took hold of him, he
became increasingly worried. He started watching himself

constantly, questioning what he said and how he said it, what he felt, and what he thought. What was real and what was fake? What was his true way of thinking, of speaking, of acting? With whom was he most comfortable and thus, perhaps, most like himself? Slowly but surely, these reflections turned into an obsession. Instead of making progress, his search for his true self became ever more difficult. Everything he said could be scrutinized, every thought seemed contrived, and every gesture eventually appeared somehow forced and unnatural. Did he have multiple selves, every single one slightly, or not so slightly, different from the other? Or worse: Did he have no self at all? Was he a complete fraud? Smoking pot did not help, of course. In fact, it made matters much worse. He became weirder and weirder, unable to connect with others. He started panicking, falling apart, verging toward schizophrenia, considering suicide. Without identity one cannot live. But, as is luckily often the case with teenagers, he soon was distracted from himself. Stuff happened. He met people, dated girls, went places, and grew up. Things smoothened out, shifted toward a different normal, and he was saved.

Speaking precisely, this perhaps rather common teenage experience should be called an *authenticity* crisis. Our teenager was looking for an *authentic* identity, a unique self, an original and creative I that would inform all his different roles, all his social personas. Like Sohrab Ahmari he was looking for such an authentic self because of the books he had read, the music he had listened to, the movies he had seen—or, more generally, because of the "age of authenticity" in which he happened to live. In this age, to achieve identity meant to be an authentic individual. Under these conditions, failure to be authentic meant identity failure. And, taken to its extreme, identity failure can lead to madness and self-destruction.

Authenticity is by no means a universal identity mode. Had our teenager grown up in a society where a regime of sincerity was in place—such as, for instance, in traditional China—it would not have appeared suspicious at all to behave differently when with your friends than when with your parents. To the contrary, in order to develop personal excellence it would have been required to cultivate just such behavioral differences in accordance with the respective social settings one participates in. Under such circumstances, another type of identity crisis may arise, namely, a sincerity crisis. One may feel unable to develop and enact a proper "daughter-self" when with the parents, or a proper "wife-self" when with the husband. Failure to do this may lead to obsessive self-questioning. And such self-critique may eventually lead to a breakdown of social relationships and psychological collapse. It, too, may cause insanity and suicide.

We now approach a time that sees people suffering from profilicity crises. They may feel that the profiles they project to society are rejected—that they are "dissed" or dismissed. Or they may feel overburdened by the task of curating their profiles. Popular Youtubers, Twitch streamers, and influencers of all kind are increasingly complaining of burnout. The stress to present themselves, and in particular to present themselves constantly anew, may overpower them. They may feel unable to update and innovate themselves and thus feel that they have lost themselves for good, that they are devoid of profile, and therefore have no grounds to live.

Identity technologies are powerful. Just as they can establish value and pride, they can also destroy both. Therefore strategies of sanity are helpful to keep their side effects in check.

6

SANITY

IDENTITY REGIMES

The Emperor of the South Sea was Fast; the Emperor of the North Sea was Furious; and the Emperor of the Center was Hundun. Fast and Furious met from time to time in the land of Hundun, who entertained them most kindly. Fast and Furious deliberated how to repay Hundun's favors: "All humans have seven holes through which they look, listen, eat, and breathe; he alone doesn't have any. Let's try boring them." Every day they bored one hole, and on the seventh day Hundun died.

—Zhuangzi, 7.7

The strange story of the death of Hundun, the shapeless Emperor of the Center, concludes the Inner Chapters of the Daoist classic *Zhuangzi*, which dates back to the third century BCE.[1] One way of making sense of the tale is to read it as a parody of popular origin myths of the time.[2] Such myths explained the origin of the cosmos, the Earth, or civilization with a narrative often involving some royal or superhuman protagonists. Readers familiar with mythological creation stories are led to expect that Hundun, once provided with a face by his fellow emperors, will be properly initiated into society, and then the whole world, from North to South, will be the domain of a graceful and cultured humankind—people with a face. Such expectations, however, are drastically disappointed at the end of the story. What was intended as an act of kindness toward Hundun by his peers turns out to be a brutal murder. Giving Hundun a human face does not allow him to flourish and prosper; it kills him.

Read in this way, the story of Hundun's death is an allegory warning us of the price we may pay for subjecting ourselves to regimes of identity formation. To function in society and to be able to have a sense of self, we need a "face"—a face that others recognize us by and that we accept as ours when looking in the mirror. The chaotic variety of our bodily functions, the incongruities of our mental and emotional experiences, and the diversity of our social engagements have to be integrated into an orderly and distinct unit. This can be a painful process. Everything we do, think, and feel has to be brought into a particular shape, molded according to fixed patterns, regulated with established standards. As Sigmund Freud outlined in *Civilization and Its Discontent*, humans need to repress their vital drives and desires so that they can live together in a peaceful and productive way. Thus some degree of frustration is an inevitable part of human psychology in the state of "civilization." Similarly, the identity work that we undergo when being socialized can require troublesome forms of discipline.

The story of Hundun's death was written in the context of an early Chinese regime of sincerity. Confucian morality prescribed strict codes of propriety and assigned highly specific roles to individuals within the family and in professional and political settings. To this day, there is an elaborate nomenclature in place in China indicating a person's exact position within a kinship group. One is not merely an "aunt" or a "cousin"; there are more specific terms that distinguish each relation—with different obligations attached to them. For instance, the father's younger brothers and older brothers carry different titles, as do each of their wives. To assume identity under such conditions, one must allow society to impose "faces" like "father's younger brother's wife" onto oneself, and to shape one's behavior and sentiments in line with them. This is the kind of identity drill that killed poor Hundun.

A regime of sincerity, no matter if Confucian or not, ancient or modern, can wreak havoc and destroy those whom it is meant to nourish. People sometimes kill themselves because they cannot cope with the pressures of fitting in. To adopt the face they need is simply too much for them. Others may become obsessed with saving face and commit suicide when they feel that their social esteem is taken away from them and their identity no longer tenable. In the case of "honor killings," people become murderers because they fear that someone else makes them, or their family, lose face. These are instances of overcommitting to a role-related identity. An obsessive concern with face can bring about anguish and devastation.

The problem is not exclusive to sincerity. Any technology of identity can produce pathological effects. A teenager's quest for authenticity can drive her into despair or to the brink of suicide. The impossibility of achieving perfect authenticity, given its paradoxical nature, can be a source of insecurity, anxiety, depression, and self-doubt. This impossibility can give rise to a deep— and always to some extent justified—suspicion that others are inauthentic, leading in turn to distrust and a general dissatisfaction with social life, along with an inability to thoroughly relate and bond in society. It can also lead to an overemphasis on individual concerns, or to histrionic displays of pseudo-originality.

Sincerity, authenticity, and of course profilicity, if zealously pursued, can threaten individual and social sanity. A person or a society that tries too hard to be fully sincere, completely authentic, or wholly profilic can end up in an identity frenzy. Suicide attacks are launched and wars fought in pursuit of identity. Identity fundamentalists can be determined to prove their sincerity, authenticity, or profilicity to themselves and others, no matter what the cost.

Hundun died because he could not resist the violent identification that was forced on him. He remained completely passive and allowed his peers to make him "one of us." Under conditions of sincerity, the story of passive acceptance of the face society imposes on a person makes sense. Education in traditional societies often emphasized behavioral drills aimed at implanting a certain role-based ethos in all members. Creative identity formation was not necessarily encouraged. If the story of Hundun were rewritten today to fit the conditions of profilicity, it would need modification. Today, no one is expected to simply accept a given identity profile. Profiles need to be actively curated. They require care and creativity. You need to be invested in them. A Hundun of today would need to "do it yourself": go to the hardware store, get a drill, and start boring.

PROFILE NEUROSIS

Julianna and Mark from Boho Beautiful are not the only ones in need of a break. They provide just one more example of what Simon Parkin describes as "a wave of videos by prominent YouTubers talking about their burnout, chronic fatigue, and depression."[3] The constant pressure to update one's feeds, to present new posts, and to curate one's persona(s) takes its toll. Once you have turned your brand into a successful profile, you need to perpetually display and maintain it. This can soon become exhausting, or worse. Unlike in sincerity, no one is born into a full and stable profilic identity. Society does not do us the favor of fixing our profiles for us. Profiles are work and time intensive; they need a lot of attention, and permanent learning on the job. We have to constantly develop and improve our accounts and continuously hone the skills of doing this. Profile stagnation is identity regression.

Apparently, YouTubers are on the frontline of profile work and feel its stress most forcefully. As Parkin reports, they not only find it difficult to keep up with the speed of social media. Like Boho Beautiful, many run into unexpected difficulties with their audience, the general peer. Matt Lees, who hosts a popular gaming channel, says: "When you've got thousands of people giving you direct feedback on your work, you really get the sense that something in your mind just snaps. We just aren't built to handle empathy and sympathy on that scale." The tremendous amount of attention they get, no matter whether positive or negative, poses a psychological challenge to those with high-profile identities. Rather than mere narcissism, as is sometimes alleged, what results is an almost compulsive concern with how one is publicly perceived. This investment in—and anxiety about—what others think and feel is a common and perhaps necessary consequence of profile-based identity work. Julianna and Mark respond the *next day* when they see numerous negative comments and a slump in ranking. They constantly apply, by their own admission, second-order observation: in order to observe your profile, you need to observe how it is observed. This explains Parkin's point that a YouTuber's burnout typically results from the need to "keep audiences engaged, which includes being active on social media, interacting with fans, and other roles beyond writing, presenting and editing." In profilicity, the validity of one's identity depends on feedback from a mass of anonymous peers. Entering into and living within such social validation feedback loops can be an overwhelming psychological task. Emotionally relating to the general peer and managing one's relation to it can be much more complicated and burdensome than interacting with people with whom one is personally familiar.

As a YouTuber, you want to get as many subscribers to your channel as possible as well as maximize your number of views—the sky is the limit. The mightier the general peer grows, however, the more demanding are the sometimes conflicting or outrageous requests and ever-present desire for more. Viewers might (and often *do*) suggest, "Why don't you just stream all night?" and dozens more volley their agreement. Social media stars may eventually drown in the vortex of the social validation feedback loops they joined. They may lose their sanity as a result of projecting an enormously successful profile.

However, most people who are active on social media will have to face the opposite problem. They must come to terms with the fact that they have only a relatively small number of followers. They are low profile, and their social validation loops are slow and weak. And this, too, can cause great distress. In April 2018 Nasim Najafi Aghdam entered the YouTube headquarters in California with a pistol and randomly shot and wounded three people before killing herself. Her apparent motive, as stated in an Instagram post several days prior to the shooting, was: "All my YouTube channels got filtered by YouTube so my videos hardly get views."[4]

Matt Lees and Boho Beautiful suffer because their profiles get more attention than they can handle. Nasim Najafai Aghdam snapped and ended her life because she felt she was prevented from ever achieving a validated profilic identity.[5] These are extreme cases of in-sanity caused by the pursuit of profilicity. Most people will not experience such extremes, but everyone may be subjected to similar kinds of profilicity stress on a less intense level. Profilicity is prone to breed its own peculiar pathologies.

The German term *Profilneurose* literally translates into "profile neurosis." This folk psychological idea predates social media and is used derogatively to describe the desire to be the center of attention. It used to indicate an excessive concern for the role one plays in the presence of one's peers. A person with a *Profilneurose* would be someone pushing himself obnoxiously to the foreground at social events, always yearning for notability, status, and prestige. Under conditions of sincerity, such behavior can easily be regarded as an improper role violation or immodest—pretended and pretentious. In an authenticity-based context, it can appear shallow and fake—the poser or wannabe—and to indicate a lack of self-confidence compensated for by disturbing appeals for recognition. In profilicity, however, this "neurosis" becomes almost a standard state of affairs. It is the new norm. Constant attention to one's profile and its effects in public is necessary for achieving identity validation. Rather than being seen as a breach of etiquette or sign of phoniness, it is expected. It is no longer considered odd to constantly take selfies in order to send them to as many people as possible. Obviously, profiles are in need of curation, and, of course, one needs to always take care of, care for, and care about them. However, as the professional Magic the Gathering player and popular streamer Louis Scott Vargas, in his advice to a viewer who brags about his recent success, notes: "We are in a world where, like, you are rewarded for people knowing about your accomplishments, and it's good to let people know in a tasteful way about them. But, on the other hand, if you do it too much or inelegantly it kinda backfires."[6] Profilicity is especially taxing because it demands not merely self-promotion but also continuous attention to the degree and means of self-promotion. There is a thin line between the valuable and often necessary publicization of one's achievements and the danger of excessive or "inelegant" promotion, which harms the perception and reception of the very profile being promoted.

We must manage, additionally, the built-in paradox of profilicity that demands we engineer personal profiles that are in a sense "fake" (as everyone knows), in that they are curated to attract the acclaim of the general peer, but nevertheless expected to be "true" in the sense that they provide credible information about one's identity. This contradiction is constantly reproduced when we present profiles, and it constantly needs to be dealt with. This is stressful. We need to post staged photos of ourselves, but at the same time these photos must somehow convey our own desired image of who we are and indicate how we will continue to present ourselves in the future. They are a kind of promise to the general peer. Under conditions of profilicity, "profile neurosis" has become universal; it reflects the common pledge to construct and maintain profiles for validation from the general peer—and then to somehow continually reproduce them. As in sincerity and authenticity, in profilicity, too, overidentification with an ultimately paradoxical identity can damage the sanity of individuals and society. An obsession with getting it right can cause things to go wrong.

GENUINE PRETENDING

Once, Zhuang Zhou in a dream turned into a butterfly, a butterfly fluttering around leisurely, happy by itself, and perfectly content. It did not know about a Zhou. Suddenly a Zhou woke up, fully there. We do not know if then a Zhou became a butterfly in a dream, or if now in a dream a butterfly became a Zhou. But between a Zhou and a butterfly, there surely is a difference. This is what is called the transformation of things.

—Zhuangzi, 2.14

The Butterfly Dream allegory is perhaps the best-known story from the *Zhuangzi*. It was introduced to a wider European and American audience by the translator Herbert A. Giles more than a century ago. Soon it became a stereotypical vignette, ornamenting Western imagination of an exotic Chinese counterpoint to the industrialized and rationalized modern world with picturesque animals and dreamy characters magically uniting with nature. In addition to contributing to the romanticized vision of a mysterious, antimodern East, Giles's translation, somewhat ironically, made the story overly reflective of the "age of authenticity."[7] Giles used the word "I" ten times in his translation of the short passage and has Zhuang Zhou reflecting on "my individuality as a man." Neither the word "I" nor the phrase "my individuality as a man" appears in the original, which our more literal translation reflects.[8]

Rather than being a meditation on authenticity and "my individuality as a man," the Butterfly Dream allegory illustrates the fluidity of identity. Everything is subject to constant change.[9] Every night, humans involuntarily slip away from the identity they spend the day maintaining. When asleep, our consciousness starts to wander and takes on numerous perspectives, including, perhaps, the view of a butterfly. One may revisit past experiences and relive them in a new light, one may enter into adventures that are completely prohibited when awake, or one may relate to people in ways that would otherwise appear grotesque and foreign to oneself. Often, soon after we wake up we completely forget our dreams and slip rather seamlessly into our daytime identity. Thus humans also share a feature with butterflies: both naturally undergo radical identity transformations.

And yet, along with emphasizing the transitory nature of identity, the Butterfly Dream also highlights identity's concrete reality. Dream experiences, however detached from one's "normal" sense of self, are nevertheless physiological and psychological facts. Sexual arousal during a dream actually takes place. The fear experienced in a nightmare can be most intense. Body and mind do not cease functioning during sleep. According to psychoanalysts, the feelings and thoughts we have when dreaming can even be considered more reliable indicators of a person's actual state of mind than what she admits to when fully conscious.

Of course, the events we imagine when asleep do not take place; as opposed to our feelings, they *are* illusions. In waking life, in contrast, both the events and our emotional and physiological experiences of them are real. The Butterfly Dream does not question this: "Between a Zhou and a butterfly, there surely is a difference." What the story suggests instead is that the identity work we perform in our dreams somehow mirrors our identity work when awake. We are able to take on alternative identities in a dream precisely because we can then forget (to an extent) about our waking life. And the same is true the other way around. An erotic dream may well be ruined if the dreamer remembers that she is actually in a relationship with someone else. Similarly, her real-life relationship can suffer from identifying too much with her erotic dreams. We must forget our dream transformations in order to fully identify with our roles, selves, and profiles in actuality. Thus in both our dreaming and waking states, the genuineness and intensity of our identity experience depends on being able to forget the respective other

239 SANITY ⊂ℛ 239

side. The butterfly in the dream can flutter around so carefree only because it does "not know about a Zhou." And once a Zhou has woken up, he can only be "fully there" if his fancy dreams do not linger on.

The paradoxical structure of identity exists both in dreams and when awake. On the one hand, it is contingent and fluid, constituted by many incongruent factors and a merely temporary constellation. It is a temporary make-believe. It is an absolutely essential make-believe, however, without which no individual can exist and no society could emerge. Identity is a make-believe turning into a most intense reality; it is deeply felt and bodily enacted, in waking life much more consistently than in dreams, and in very real community with others who do the same. It is, paradoxically, simultaneously genuine and pretended, like child play that grows into a much more serious and complex life form over time. Erving Goffman already explained the emergence of self and society in a similar way. His analysis of human interaction and the *Zhuangzi*'s understanding of identity are both conceptions of *genuine pretending*.

Genuine pretending is not an ideal to follow. It is not an existential model one can chose or not. It is the mode of human existence that gives rise to the formation of identity and society. Everyone is genuinely pretending all the time. Mothers sincerely committing to their roles are genuinely pretending, just as artists when expressing their authenticity, or YouTubers when curating their profiles. There is nothing wrong with this—and there is no alternative to it. Sanity, at least from our perspective, is best maintained by realizing that personal and social identity can only be genuinely pretended—that one can be a sincere mother or an authentic artist or a profilic YouTuber while at the same time not regarding these identities as binding, essential, or ideal. Truly, they are fluid, temporary, and contingent. Identity participates in the transformation of things. Sanity is challenged when people are either unable to achieve identity at all or when they become identity fundamentalists, disregarding the transformation of identity along with everything else, and over-committing to supposedly "true" roles, selves, or profiles.

DRAFTING WITH EASE

Lord Yuan of Song ordered a figure to be drawn, and all the scribes came. They received instructions and bowed, and then stood in line, licking their brushes and mixing their ink. Half of them had to stand in the open. One scribe came late. Leisurely and in no hurry he received the instructions and bowed. He did not stand in line, and went to the living quarters. When the Lord sent someone to inspect him, he was seen with his clothes taken off, sitting cross-legged, naked. The ruler said: "Alright! This is a real man of the brush."

—Zhuangzi, 17.7

The story of the naked scribe is considered to be one of the many skill stories in the *Zhuangzi* depicting, among other wondrous characters, marvelous bell-stand carvers, fantastic swimmers, and amazing cicada catchers.[10] It is markedly different from the other skill stories, though, by not mentioning any skillful activity or artful product at all. When inspected, the scribe has not even drawn a line—he just sat down in a distinctly relaxed manner. Yet this is already taken as reason enough for his ruler to praise him. We must conclude that the naked scribe's skill lies not so much in his professional talents but rather in the manner in which he approaches his job. He seems to have a social or psychological skill rather than a craftsman's knack.

Like the tale of Hundun's death, the story of the naked scribe has some satirical features that become clear when taking its historical context into account. It too addresses in a humorous manner the early Confucian regime of sincerity. In ancient China professions were largely inherited. There was little social mobility, and most people could not freely choose a line of work. Scribes had to be literate and were therefore part of a small educated stratum. Among this stratum, however, they were among the "lower orders" and had few personal liberties.[11] The profession of the scribe, as an integral part of a system enforcing government regulations and control, was itself subject to tight regulations and controls.

The story depicts the scribes as a uniform group of intellectuals who are nevertheless thoroughly subordinated employees— perhaps faintly comparable to professional academics today. The authorities call them, and they heed the call. Obediently they receive their orders, submissively they bow down, obsequiously they lick their brushes and mix their ink, and sheepishly they queue up one after another in a long row that leaves many of them out in the open.

The image of the long line of servile scribes sets the scene for the second part of the short narrative. Something surprising happens. A final scribe appears, but, contrary to what should be expected, he is neither ashamed nor worried about being late. He is in no rush at all. He, too, picks up the instructions and bows, but he does not line up with all the others outside the hall and instead returns to his living quarters.

While the orderly scribes connote the rigid rule-following of institutionalized Confucianism, the naked scribe combines a range of Daoist attributes: he is calm and his mind is at peace.[12] He shows no specific concern for ritual conventions, and, most notably, he is comfortable being (half-)naked rather than in an official robe. To the reader's surprise, the ruler eventually compliments him rather than his more regular colleagues—as would be expected from a good mainstream Confucian ruler. Tellingly, the ruler calls the naked scribe a *zhen ren* 真人, a "real man," or "genuine," that is, "*zhen*uine" person, an expression used specifically in the *Zhuangzi* to somewhat ironically mirror established Confucian honorific terms of the time.[13]

The naked scribe is neither a rebel rising up against a restrictive system nor an artistic genius—he is not an exemplar of authenticity. He, too, does his job and follows the orders just like his colleagues, and he, too, will presumably contribute to the drawing of the figure like them. As a scribe he is neither better nor worse than any other. He differs from his fellow scribes mostly in displaying a humorously exaggerated attitude of perfect ease in contrast to the satirically caricatured stiffness of his rather stressed out and worried peers. That he takes off his clothes and sits down comfortably signals a capacity to not overly identify with his role. He can deal with social constraints smoothly and resist total role-internalization. He is not overly invested in his (sincere, i.e., role-based) identity. Lord Yuan of Song may envy this servant for his chill attitude. The ruler's surprising commendation of the naked scribe may well indicate that he, too, would wish to share in such ease in the midst of an uneasy regime of Confucian sincerity.

It is difficult to say what kind of "figure" those ancient scribes were supposed to draw. It could be a kind of map, or a ritual chart, or a portrait of the ruler or his ancestors. The Chinese word is *tu* is the same *tu* as in the name of the Chinese app company Meitu: "Beautiful Picture" or "Beautiful Figure." In any case, ancient scribal practices are no longer very much present in contemporary society. Few get called to a lord's court to draw figures. Today the Chinese, like the rest of us, are preoccupied with the drawing of a different kind of image; not of others, but of ourselves. Many of us have joined the ranks of modern-day profile draftsmen and account scribes. In both professional and private contexts, we are constantly expected to carve, recarve, and polish our profiles. We heed the call and diligently get to work; after all, in digital space there seems to always be room for more, and few are left to stand in the open.

A contemporary variation of the old story could be imagined, depicting uncountable masses uniformly engrossed in adding to their profiles—uploading photos, commenting, liking. Zombie-like expressionless faces transfixed by the glow of screens on which eager fingers are typing and swiping. A naked scribe today might do so as well, but not in an obsessed, sheepish, automated manner. He would not overidentify with the unescapably inherited fate of being a scribe.

The most significant Daoist term for social and psychological ease is *you* 游 (pronounced "yo"). It is used more than one hundred times in the *Zhuangzi* in different variations and meanings. The term is related to the words for "swimming" and "journey," and the written character contains the radical "water," associating it loosely with "flow." It expresses the idea of a rather effortless, playful, and not goal-oriented motion. "Rambling around without destination" is how A. C. Graham (2001) translated the title of the first chapter of the *Zhuangzi*: the three-character expression *xiaoyao you* 逍遥游 that ends with *you*. This expression alludes to the movement of children, or animals, like fish. It is important to point out that such movement does not lead to any mystical beyond. Nor is it escapist or antisocial. As in the case of the naked scribe, to be at ease does not mean to do nothing or to eschew one's identity altogether. *You* can indicate the capacity to be highly attentive to one's surroundings, as animals are, or to learn in a nonstrenuous and potentially spontaneous way, as children can. It can also refer to the social ease among people that we experience when engaged in an intellectually stimulating or emotionally enjoyable conversation among friends.

The Daoist notion of *you* explores possibilities for contentment within an often suppressive regime of sincerity. Such contentment can sometimes be found through an approach to identity where one neither overcommits to nor shuns away from enacting one's social personas—a state meditation masters might refer to as "calm emotional detachment." *You* implies the paradoxical flexibility both to critically subvert the ethos of a socially enforced identity and to enjoy having it. Exactly how this is possible under conditions of profilicity remains to be seen. A contemporary version of the tale of the naked scribe has not yet been written.

EXPOSURE

Zhuang Zhou was rambling around [you] Diaoling Park one day when he spied a strange magpie flying in from the south, with seven-foot wings and big eyes an inch around. It grazed Zhou's forehead as it swooped down and went descending into a grove of chestnut trees. "What kind of bird is this?," he thought. "Such huge wings, but it does not get anywhere. Such big eyes, but it didn't even see me!"

Zhuang Zhou hiked up his robe and tiptoed over with his crossbow in hand, preparing to shoot it. There he saw a cicada that had just found a lovely spot of shade, forgetting about (the display of) its own body. A praying mantis was raising its padded hands to seize it. It looked at its gain, forgetting about (the display of) its own shape. The strange magpie had followed the mantis as its catch. It looked at its catch, forgetting about (the display of) its own identity. Zhuang Zhou thought worryingly: "Oh, creatures certainly trouble one another; one kind calls up another." He then tossed away his crossbow and hurried off, a park ranger running behind and shouting curses at him.

When Zhuang Zhou got home, he was gloomy for three days. Matrush Fornow had followed him and asked: "Why have you been gloomy for so long, Master?" Zhuang Zhou said: "As to the protection of my shape, I had forgotten about (the display of my) own body. Looking into muddy water, I lost sight of the clear depths. Also, I've heard the masters' saying: 'When you get yourself into a place with certain conventions, you'll eventually follow these conventions.' Well, I went rambling around Diaoling Park, forgetting about (the display of) my own body. A strange magpie grazed my forehead. Wandering into the chestnut grove, it forgot about (the display) of its own identity. In the chestnut grove, the park ranger took me as his game, and therefore I have been gloomy."

—*Zhuangzi*, 20.8

At the outset, this story demonstrates the brutal law of nature, the cruelty of eating and being eaten. The "transformation of all things," a core Daoist theme, consists not only of cute caterpillars miraculously metamorphosing into beautiful butterflies fluttering from flower to flower, but also of cunning beasts of prey devouring one another. The sudden realization of the bestial violence in the food chain seems to have shocked Zhuang Zhou right at a time when he was at perfect ease, rambling around (*you*) in the woods and enjoying himself. In the blink of an eye the ease with which animals, including human animals, were rambling around turned out to be an animalistic killing circuit. This, it seems, made Zhuang Zhou throw away his bow in anguish.

But this is not the end of the story. In an almost cartoon-like scene, we have Zhuang Zhou himself chased away by the fuming park ranger. He escapes physically unharmed, so the scene ends without bloodshed, but we are led to conclude that Zhuang Zhou, too, was not only hunter but at the same time the hunted. For three days he broods on the event. With his lightness of mind gone, he undergoes an intellectual or perhaps spiritual conversion. His most profound conversion was not the sudden shift from a state of ease to one of horror but the subsequent comprehension that, without exception, we have all got ourselves "into a place with certain conventions"; we are not aloof bystanders. Our standing by, despite what we might have thought, is also part of the game.

Concretely, the story of Zhuang Zhou's hunt is not about eating and being eaten; no eating takes place. As far as the narrative goes, it is about seeing and being seen, and about seeing others see. It is about second-order observation. No arrow is shot, no cicada is caught; instead, we watch others watching others watching others without realizing that they, too, are being watched. We are invited to conclude that while we see what others see and what they cannot see, we are being observed in the same manner. By seeing the blind spot of others, we understand that blind spots are part and parcel of any observation, including the observation of blind spots. The story critically points to the blind spots of others only to invite a self-critical reflection on one's own inescapable blind spot.

Eventually, the story is also about how, by watching others, we present ourselves and thereby become vulnerable. The notion of second-order observation highlights the fact that seeing comes at the cost of being watched. This is the dialectic core of second-order observation. In society, we not only watch others, we are ourselves simultaneously watched watching in return. And the others see more than we can see. They see us presenting ourselves through our observations. Whenever you post something on Facebook, people not only see what you post, they see that you are posting it. This is what makes the story of Zhuang Zhou's hunt—unintentionally, we trust—relevant for understanding profilicity.

Zhuang Zhou's retreat in gloom, we may assume, reflects a deeply felt humiliation on "being found out." At the very moment of perfect ease, of feeling at home with oneself, of comfortably enacting one's identity by focusing in on one's perspective, he had, like the other three creatures in the story, exposed himself most completely and most dangerously. At the very moment when we express ourselves most confidently or state how we see the world, we publicly identify ourselves, bare our profiles, and become a target for others. There is a dialectical connection between self-confidence in one's identity, self-exposure, and self-destruction. We need to learn to be cautious when revealing our profiles.

After having intensely shared their views with an audience, public lecturers can experience a sense of shame and embarrassment, perhaps thinking themselves a fraud (an experience not completely unfamiliar to us). This is particularly true under a regime of authenticity where one is supposed to present one's true self to others. Similarly, authentic artistic performers, after having performed most passionately, may feel psychologically hung over. Such experiences resemble a dream many have: the sudden discovery that one has been naked in public. In profilicity, however, there is a high degree of awareness of being under scrutiny from the start. With its orientation toward the general peer rather than those who are present, we take heed not to show ourselves defenselessly. What is a shock to Zhuang Zhou—the realization of the self-exposure involved in second-order observation—becomes second nature in profilicity. Profilicity comes after the shock of exposure. We know that we are seen. And we settled, however uneasily, into constantly being observed.

In profilicity, it is no surprise that the general peer has been watching. Thus we are alert and careful—we try to protect ourselves. There is little need for censorship in the academic peer review system because it openly operates as second-order observation. Most professors will not violate conventions and the expectations of the general peer in their writing. They will curate their academic self-revelation so that their public "nudity" does not offend. Profilicity encourages highly vigilant self-presentation and identity formulation—vigilant both regarding how we show ourselves and how we watch others. "Political correctness" is voluntarily adopted to make sure that public profiles do not offend too much and are safe.

Under the regime of profilicity, we know that the hunter is also hunted, that the observer is also observed. It is a daily experience: every view can be viewed again. Once identity value is exhibition value, we all become, to some extent, exhibitionists—and thus we learn to carefully monitor, edit, and digitally alter our nakedness.

PRESSURES OF PROFILICITY

It is the "slave" in the blood of the vain person . . . that tries to seduce him to good opinions of himself; and it is likewise the slave who straightway kneels down before these opinions, as if he himself were not the one who had called them forth.

—Friedrich Nietzsche, *Beyond Good and Evil*

Profilicity is demanding: Profiles need constant attention. Identity work is never really finished once and for all. Even your vacations are part of your profile—actually they are especially important. Profiles can cause stress and anxiety, for both high-profile and low-profile identities. We can always be held accountable for the accounts we give of ourselves. And therefore we must be cautious not to expose ourselves too frankly. We need to find a good balance between being opinionated and inoffensive. Profiles make promises—better make sure to promise neither too much nor too little. We are being watched as we watch others, and this fosters mediocrity. We want to be seen as different, but, as Elena Esposito notes, different in the same way as everyone else.

And yet profilicity is neither more suppressive than sincerity or authenticity nor more fake or paradoxical. Arguably, it supersedes its predecessors only in complexity. Despite their tendency toward conformity and mediocrity, profiles are, at the same time, also dynamic, diverse, and flexible. Profilicity is not totalitarian. It allows for the inclusion and coexistence of other identity technologies. There are always opportunities to withdraw from profilicity and to exercise role identity in the family or in a religious community; and one can still experience authenticity in friendship or in art. Often such exercises and experiences will also be put into the service of profilicity. They hardly escape one's profile curation and can easily enter into one's profilic identity. Nevertheless, by accommodating sincerity and authenticity, profilicity allows for a multidimensional approach to identity work.

By adopting second-order observation as its modus operandi, profilicity entertains a good deal of sensibility for the fact that profiles must be staged for exhibition purposes. This allows for a more nuanced, liberal, and, indeed, critical and self-critical attitude toward identity. We understand that identity—both our own and the identity of others—is not that simple, not that easy, and not that stable.

The point of sincerity is to be sincerely committed to one's role so that there is no gap between role and self. In authenticity, the public persona is supposed to be a true representation of the inner aspects of the self. An almost perfect coherence between external display and thoughts and feelings is desired in both sincerity and authenticity. In profilicity, it is understood that there is a need to present profiles to specific audiences, and that this involves feedback processes requiring a marked distance between self and persona. This grants us, to an extent, a little more freedom from our personas—and the personas from us. We reflect more openly on the conditions of the possibilities of profiles. We know that photos are edited before they are posted. We know how Airbnb profiles, academic profiles, or political profiles work. We develop a sense for how they are constructed and for their blind spots. This opens up the possibility for a critical distance from one's own profiles as well, a distance that may bring some relief from the pressures of our investment in identity work. Profilicity grants, at least potentially, more tolerance for the incongruity at the heart of all identity work. We can better accept and live with the inconsistencies hidden in our own identity and those of others.

Any identity technology, once widely practiced, informs bodily, mental, and social regimes. An ethos emerges, along with moral values, social institutions, and ritual practices. The ethos of sincerity sustained and legitimized hierarchical roles, and the ethos of authenticity implanted an individualist ideology in people and societies. An ethos of profilicity is currently emerging. Various kinds of ratings and rankings institutionalize and, typically through algorithms, categorize new standards of excellence. New primary values such as "transparency" or "participation" come to the fore along with profilic exercises, such as writing a mandatory "diversity statement" for a job application. Identity technologies cannot be avoided. Given the increasing complexity of these technologies along with the addition of profilicity their respective limitations and paradoxes become more apparent. Thus it becomes quite possible not to internalize any of them too deeply or too exclusively and to avoid turning into an identity fundamentalist. We can subvert an obsession with profiles by distancing ourselves mentally from them and by critically questioning their absolute validity.

All too often, critics of profilicity phenomena suggest simply replacing one identity regime with another. Advocates of a political new sincerity imply that sincerity-based identity is better than profilicity and that we should return to it. Those who decry the social media as a threat to authenticity take authenticity to be the only correct model of identity. These are problematic idealizations of sincerity and authenticity. Rather than defending any kind of identity as the right one, we recommend a suspicious attitude toward them all. To maintain sanity, strict identity regimes are better kept at a certain distance and met with a good dose of skepticism. The strategy to tackle them should be subversion rather than revolution—which typically ends up in just another regime.

Genuine pretending is not an alternative to sincerity, authenticity, or profilicity. No matter which mode of identity we apply, whenever we do so we are practicing genuine pretending. It is not problematic that identity ideals are inherently paradoxical and unachievable, but it is problematic to demand of oneself or others to wholly commit to them. This destroys personal and social ease. Moral or ideological norms often reify values tied to identity ideals and generate conflicts between different persuasions or creeds. From the perspective of genuine pretending, a preoccupation with the rightness of moral norms does not solve the incongruities inherent in identity ideals, it only serves to escalate them. Rather than insisting on the right way to truly be oneself, genuine pretending allows for deescalation and the reconciliation of incongruent identities. It is therapeutic rather than normative.

The affirmation of genuine pretending is, to speak with Nietzsche, the attitude of the "noble person" who finds the vanity of those who first "try to elicit a good opinion about themselves . . . and who then themselves nevertheless *believe* this good opinion" quite tasteless.[14] The identity mechanism Nietzsche describes here is the same in all identity technologies. In sincerity, one may eventually believe that one is the devoted role bearer that one wanted to be praised as. In authenticity, one may eventually believe in one's uniqueness and originality; and in profilicity, one may in fact "kneel down before" the success of one's profile, "as if he himself were not the one who had called it forth." Unquestioned identity work leads to pretended genuineness, or worse. Rather than finding the identity of oneself and others, including profilic identity, good or bad, or right or wrong, the "noble person" will understand how and why identity is achieved. She will be critical, but not judgmental.

7

CONCLUSION

A SUMMARY

Sincerity demands commitment to roles. The outside is real, and the inside must back it up honestly, otherwise it is considered a dishonest fake.

Authenticity demands the pursuit of originality. The inside is real, and the outside must be an accurate representation of it, otherwise it is considered a hypocritical facade.

Profilicity demands the curation of profiles. The outside is real, and the inside must be truly invested in it, otherwise it is considered a deceptive fraud.

Everyone is genuinely pretending. Every mode of identity makes us experience selfhood, but none really matches up all the incongruent dimensions of human life. To realize that we are genuine pretenders opens up a critical awareness of our contingencies. It eases identity.

YOU'RE STILL MY FAVORITE BROTHER-IN-LAW

"Well, you're still my favorite brother-in-law," says Kate theatrically. We make a few more sarcastic remarks and get off the phone. I'm her only brother-in-law, which is exactly why she likes to call me her "favorite."

Verbalized on the phone, "you are my favorite brother-in-law" is said with an emphasis and an attitude that are strikingly misplaced. The meaning is clear, but it somehow feels strange. At the Tuesday night dinner party she hosts, Kate uses the line in the same histrionic, out-of-place way. Everyone enjoys it, and they've heard it before, but it feels as if it is not really said for the other dinner guests any more than it is said for me. It is said as if for those who are not present: the absent listeners, the nondescript "others" that we post for on social media, that we write Airbnb reviews for, or that we craft our resumes for.

Kate's statement has become typical in our conversations. It plays a fairly important role in our Facebook posts as well. There, this joke is at its funniest. It is exactly what you would expect from an interaction between Kate and me. It shows that we can be entirely, and even exclusively, sardonic with each other. But everyone who knows us already knows that. So Kate's rehearsal of this sentiment really serves as an advertisement for people who are not familiar with our relationship. Feeding our individual Facebook profiles, Kate's endearing comment further curates a profile of our interactions. And like any advertisement, it's not for any one person in particular; it's for a general type. Facebook users know how to read her statement in this manner—as we inevitably read nearly every social media post. That is, after all, the point of the Facebook wall; otherwise we would just send private messages. The wall is about crafting a profile for others, not communicating with anyone in particular.

Today people are increasingly speaking, dressing, and acting as if a video of them might, at any moment, be uploaded for dozens, hundreds, thousands, or even millions to view. Kate calling me her favorite brother-in-law makes the most sense in this context.

Kate often addresses her three daughters in the very same manner, in a similar theatric tone. But of course she doesn't always speak this way. If "bear" doesn't feel well, Kate immediately changes her attitude. As if miraculously adopting a different identity, she comforts her daughter with authentic concern and spontaneous affection. And then, on a Tuesday night, Kate shifts to yet another identity. Effortlessly, she switches from social-media-sounding comments to being a sincerely dedicated host in the old-fashioned manner. She loves to fix her guests' plates, cut and serve desserts, and will make whatever you want next week. This is another side of Kate that we are all familiar with.

There's a difference between what Kate said to her oldest daughter in person when she dropped her off at her first day at college and how she told us all about it rather pensively, almost formally, last Tuesday night. Both are different yet again from her Facebook post: "There are no words to describe how proud I am of this girl. Today we dropped her off at college and she's going to do amazing! I love you honey . . . to the moon and back!"

. . . We did, of course, ask Kate if it would be okay to include this, and if we could use her real name, by posting on her Facebook wall.

POSTSCRIPT

POPE FRANCIS, DONALD TRUMP, BYUNG-CHUL HAN, AND COVID 19

Around the time the manuscript of this book was given to the publisher, the world unexpectedly changed. Covid-19 broke out—somewhat like a war, to which the situation is often compared. A strange war, that is, where many die but no one kills.

The pandemic's domination of society is almost total: in the health system, in politics, in the economy, even in education, everything revolves around the virus. It has changed the daily lives of billions so that in private, too, people talk about it often. The extension of the pandemic into all social spheres, on a global scale, requires permanent attention. Everyone needs to address it in one way or another.

As in a war, those on the front lines—in this case the doctors, nurses, and patients whose lives are at stake—are outnumbered by those in the rear. But in the rear, too, effects can be drastic. Many have already lost their jobs or, worse, lack basic necessities. And yet, despite all such firsthand experience, as in a war we rely heavily on second-order observation to make sense of what is going on and to decide what to do about it. The media tell us about the scale of suffering, inform us about the regulations we need to observe, and let us know what we can, or cannot, expect from the future. Under widespread lockdown, so many of us face the crisis primarily in front of a screen. We see what is happening as it is being seen. And in this virtual lifeworld, we also appear on screens even more than we used to. We have to get on our little virtual stage and present our own self-images, our profiles, with the pandemic lurking in the background.

"Normal" wars invite self-identification along the lines of what we have described here as sincerity: in a war, you can see yourself first and foremost as a member of a nation (that fights another one), or as a believer in a religion (that struggles against infidels), or as someone sacrificing oneself for a greater cause. As terrible as a war is, it can provide opportunities for identifications, for finding meaning in life by developing a strong sense of belonging to "us" rather than to "them." The present pandemic, however, does not establish a clear friend/enemy distinction; there is no specific "other" in opposition to whom we can readily identify ourselves. And yet the pandemic, especially when faced virtually and in the rear, offers chances to boost one's identity— you can profile yourself!

For Pope Francis and, via him, for the Roman Catholic Church, Covid-19 is nature's response to human-made climate change. We, the people on Earth, committed a great ecological sin, he intimates. Now "nature," which, different from God, never forgives, as the pope says, sends us a big warning sign to chastise us and make us change our evil ways.[1] The pope's message is an updated variation of an age-old religious response to disasters. Similar to the Middle Ages, when the great plague was seen as divine punishment, the Catholic Church now implies that Covid-19 is nature's price tag for our misbehavior.

In a completely modern fashion, a traditional religious message is attached to the contemporary green discourse. Very skillfully, the pope connects a powerful, and highly conservative, appeal to religious guilt consciousness with the highly progressive appeal to the widespread sympathies for the movement against climate change. This is efficient profile curation, simultaneously renewing the church's old claim to be the only sure way to salvation and innovating its image by tying it to the present-day ecological cause. Pope Francis aligns his profile, the profile of the church, and the profiles of the faithful with that of Greta Thunberg, *Time* person of the year in 2019.

For Donald Trump, matters are different. Part of the political profile that surprisingly won him the election in 2016 was being tough on China. This very theme can now, thanks to the virus, be recycled with even greater force for the 2020 campaign. The message promoted by Trump and many others vying for votes in America is that China, as manifested in the virus, is a threat to American lives and American well-being. Profiling China as a colossal threat also profiles those who promote this idea as colossal protectors, as political saviors to whom voters can flock. Great opportunities for profile bonding between politicians and the electorate emerge out of the virus crisis. People can build up and sharpen their political identity by expressing their opposition to China.

Byung-Chul Han, the reclusive thinker and writer, came to fame with his public outcries against "transparency society." A whole flurry of new media releases by and on him appeared in major newspapers and on their websites, among them *El País* in Spain (March 22, 2020), *Die Welt* in Germany (March 23, April 17), and *Clarín* in Argentina (April 17).[2] In all these pieces, Han points out how the fight against Covid-19 brought about an even further increase in surveillance of which he had warned all along. It is suggested that we urgently need to heed his call for privacy to save ourselves from the bad social effects of the virus. While Han's apparently somewhat hastily produced texts may be, as David Ownby put it, "a bit repetitive and unstructured" and tend to "recycle buzzwords familiar from his already published work," he was certainly able to reassert himself as a high-profile public intellectual whose thoughts on contemporary events are worthy of global media coverage.[3] The antitransparency warrior is seen as being seen in times of Covid-19, and perhaps more so than ever before.

CARING DEEPLY IN TIMES OF PROFILICITY

In a real war just as during the present pandemic, care is of special importance. People are encouraged, and expected, to care more about one another, and the expression "take good care of yourself" is made ample use of.

Care is central to identity and its different modes. In sincerity, personal identity manifests itself in caring relationships—in caring about, caring for, and taking care of your parents, for example. If this care is "authentic," that is, if you discover or create your "true individuality" in caring for your parents, is quite irrelevant. You truly care for your parents because you are their child.

In authenticity care also extends to others, but it is supposed to be essentially rooted in one's own original self. After all, authentic care for the other cares for her insofar as she is, or can be, authentic as well. Here, genuine care cannot be grounded in the quite coincidental social relations one finds oneself "thrown into," or in the conventional obligations stemming from them. If you are a caring person in authenticity, then you don't merely care for others just because they happen to be your relatives. You care for them because *you* care for *them*.

In profilicity, identity is formed through profile curation. Curation literally means caring, caring in the senses of caring about, caring for, and taking care of. In profilicity, too, people can be caring. Here, what counts is that care is publicly *shown and seen*. Under conditions of second-order observation, we cannot know whether anyone, including ourselves, cares sincerely or authentically. What we have access to is the profile. And you can prove that you are truly invested in your profile by making it deeply caring.

Who is to judge whether Pope Francis, Donald Trump, or Byung-Chul Han cares sincerely or authentically about Covid-19? All of them, however, care about curating their profiles—and the pandemic provides them with opportunities to be perceived as caring. This care extends far and wide and establishes "social validation feedback loops." Pope Francis, by curating his profile and filling it with religious care, reaches hundreds of millions of believers. Many of these follow him and are encouraged to make his care about Covid-19 also theirs. Donald Trump's profile, too, has an almost global reach and touches countless individuals who can display a different type of care about Covid-19 as part of a political self-expression. Byung-Chul Han's crowd of followers may be much smaller than that of the pope or the American president, but his profile, too, connects with people and provides resources and memes for just another possibility of "giving an account of oneself" as caring in times of Covid-19.

Today, people rely on second-order observation to make sense of themselves. Under these circumstances, care, too, cannot but become—not exclusively, but to a large extent—second-order observation care: care on the screen. Under conditions of profilicity, we care deeply about being seen as deeply caring, especially during a pandemic.

ACKNOWLEDGMENTS

Core ideas expressed in this book, and especially our understanding of "sincerity and authenticity," have been inspired by the life and work of Rolf Trauzettel (1930–2019). He published little in English, but the essay "Two Mythic Paradigms of the Constitution of Personhood" (Trauzettel 2012) represents his thoughts well. While thinking, talking, and writing about profilicity, we've gotten substantial help and inspiration from many individuals—from family members, friends, and academics who've been close to us for most of our lives to strangers encountered on planes or at bus stops. In particular we would like to thank the following people for giving advice and critical suggestions, and for commenting on earlier drafts of the manuscript: Henry Allen, Dimitra Amarantidou, Hannes Bergthaller, Lars Clausen, Seth Crownover, Hans-Rudolf Kantor, Luciano Martinoli, Suzanne Murphy, Ryan (Boy) Reisner, Dan Sarafinas, Lidia Tammaro, Wang Fang, Lihuan You (Freezi), and Luka Lei Zhang. Special thanks go to Elena Esposito, who has been an intellectual catalyst for our ideas; to David Stark, who coined the word "profilicity"; to Robert Carleo, who substantially improved the logic of our arguments and their presentation; to the Theme Park Guy Stefan Zwanzger and

Boho Beautiful for generously permitting us to use their artwork; to Wendy Lochner at Columbia University Press, without whose competent support this book would not have been possible; and to Anita O'Brien for her wonderful copyediting. We are indebted to several colleagues who gave us an opportunity to talk about profilicity in academic settings: Anders La Cour at Copenhagen Business School, Gorm Harste and Klaus Laursen at the University of Aarhus, Helmut Heit at Tongji University in Shanghai, Sydney Morrow at Nazerbayev University in Nur-Sultan, Laurindo Dias Minhoto at the University of Sao Paulo, Antonio Florentino Neto at the University of Campinas, Ricardo Evandro Martins at the Federal University of Pará in Belem, and Claudia Lira Latuz and Maria Elvira Rios Penafiel at the Pontifical Catholic University of Chile in Santiago. We are grateful for the constructive feedback provided by the participants at these events as well as at the Workshop on Identity at East China Normal University in Shanghai, the Workshop on Chinese Modernity at the University of Bielefeld, and the seminar on Identity: Cross-Cultural and Contemporary Views at the University of Padova, which was kindly organized by Marcello Ghilardi. We greatly appreciate the support of our work in the form of a Multi-Year Research Grant (MYRG2016-00013-FAH) provided by the University of Macau.

Some sections of chapter 4 are modified from Paul D'Ambrosio, "From Present to Presentation: A Philosophical Critique of Hartmut Rosa's 'Situational Identity,'" *Time and Society* 28, no. 3 (2019): 1061–83. A German version of the postscript has been published by Hans-Georg Moeller as "Die Pandemie als Profilierungschance," in *Corona: Weltgesellschaft im Ausnahmezustand*, ed. Markus Heidingsfelder (Weilerswist-Metternich: Velbrück Wissenschaft, 2020), 247–53.

NOTES

1. THE BIGGER PICTURE

1. We'd like to thank David Stark for coining this term in conversation with us.

2. See Jiayang Fan, "China's Selfie Obsession," *New Yorker*, December 11, 2017, https://www.newyorker.com/magazine/2017/12/18/chinas-selfie -obsession.

3. Meitu's response to these criticisms is documented by Sam Gaskin, "'We Don't Believe Chinese Are Superficial or Narcissistic,' Says Meitu," *Jing Daily*, March 2, 2018, https://jingdaily.com/chinese-meitu/.

4. For a more detailed outline of social media critiques, see Paul D'Ambrosio and Hans-Georg Moeller, "From Authenticity to Profilicity: A Critical Response to Roberto Simanowski and Others," *New German Critique* 46, no. 2 (2019): 1–25.

5. *Facebook Society* is the title of a book by Roberto Simanowski (New York: Columbia University Press, 2018).

6. See Lionel Trilling, *Sincerity and Authenticity* (Cambridge, MA: Harvard University Press, 1972).

7. Trilling, 9–10.

8. See, for example, "20 Things Truly Authentic People Do Differently," *David Wolfe*, https://www.davidwolfe.com/20-things-authentic-people -do-differently/.

9. See Walter Benjamin, "The Work of Art in the Age of Mechanical Reproduction" (1935), in *Illuminations: Essays and Reflections*, ed. Hannah Arendt, trans. Harry Zohn (New York: Schocken, 1969).

10. More a more detailed discussion, see Cathy O'Neil, *Weapons of Math Destruction: How Big Data Increases Inequality and Threatens Democracy* (New York: Crown, 2016).

11. For further analysis, see Genia Kostka, "China's Social Credit Systems and Public Opinion: Explaining High Levels of Approval," *New Media & Society* 21, no. 7 (2019): 1565–93.

12. "Nosedive (*Black Mirror*)," *Wikipedia*, https://en.wikipedia.org/wiki/Nosedive_(Black_Mirror), accessed July 23, 2019.

13. "Nosedive," *Rotten Tomatoes*, https://www.rottentomatoes.com/tv/black_mirror/s03/e01, accessed November 26, 2019.

14. Philipp Löwe, "Selfie vor Krawallkulisse," *Der Spiegel*, July 8, 2018, https://www.spiegel.de/panorama/gesellschaft/g20-krawalle-selfie-bei-randale-im-schanzenviertel-a-1156799.html.

15. "Riot Hipster," *Know Your Meme*, https://knowyourmeme.com/memes/riot-hipster, accessed May 17, 2019.

16. See, for example, "Der 'Riot-Hipster,'" *Stern*, July 8, 2017, https://www.stern.de/politik/deutschland/g20—riot-hipster—antikapitalistisches-iphone-selfie-belustigt-das-netz-7529822.html.

17. "Riot Hipster."

18. Max Stirner, *Der Einzige und sein Eigentum* (Leipzig: Otto Wiegand, 1945).

19. For a further discussion, see Roger Ames, *Confucian Role Ethics: A Vocabulary* (Hong Kong: Chinese University Press, 2011).

20. Bob Dylan, "Beyond Here Lies Nothing," *Together Through Life*, track 1, Columbia Records, 2009, compact disk.

21. See the section on moral profiling in chapter 2 for a further discussion of diversity statements.

22. For more on this notion, coined by Sean Parker, see chapter 2.

23. For a more detailed discussion, see Elena Esposito, "The Fascination of Contingency: Fashion and Modern Society," in *Philosophical Perspectives on Fashion*, ed. Giovanni Matteucci and Stefano Marino (London: Bloomsbury, 2017), 175–90.

2. PROFILICITY

1. For Luhmann, modern society emerged between the sixteenth and eighteenth centuries in Europe when a shift took place from a basic

social division into strata such as "nobles" and nonnobles to the divisions of different "function systems." These systems, such as politics, law, economy, education, academics, and mass media, all fulfill their respective functions in society and establish their own structures and types of communication.

2. Disclaimer: We do not claim to use the concept of second-order observation in exactly the same way as Luhmann did. We are not even sure how to correctly define Luhmann's understanding of the concept since he used it in a variety of ways throughout his extensive oeuvre. We apply the Luhmannian concept freely to outline our understanding of profilicity—which does not occur in Luhmann's work.

3. Niklas Luhmann, *Introduction to Systems Theory*, trans. Peter Gilgen (Cambridge: Polity, 2013), 100 (translation modified). On "orientation" as a broader philosophical concept, see Werner Stegmaier, *What Is Orientation? A Philosophical Investigation* (Berlin: De Gruyter, 2019); for how Stegmaier derives his concept of "orientation" from Luhmann and Nietzsche, see his *Orientierung im Nihilismus: Luhmann Meets Nietzsche* (Berlin: De Gruyter, 2016).

4. See the section on political new sincerity in chapter 3.

5. Similarly, there is no agency completely independent of the observation of others. How one is seen, and seen as being seen, influences decisions and actions.

6. See the discussion of this story in chapter 6.

7. Luhmann, *Introduction to Systems Theory*, 105 (translation modified).

8. Big data organizes and reports correlations, not causations.

9. Using the terminology of Jan Inge Jönhill, it can be said that the general peer consists not of "strangers" (as "outsiders") but of "unknown others" (people we relate to without knowing them personally). Jönhill, "Inclusion and Exclusion—a Guiding Distinction to the Understanding of Issues of Cultural Background," *Systems Research and Behavioral Science* 29, no. 4 (2012): 387–401.

10. Jean-Jacques Rousseau, *The Social Contract*, trans. Maurice Cranston (New York: Penguin, 1968).

11. Elena Esposito, "Artificial Communication? The Production of Contingency by Algorithms," *Zeitschrift für Soziologie* 46, no. 4 (2017): 249–65.

12. For an image of an *American Idol* jury, see Laura Bradley, "*American Idol* Is Officially Coming Back—but Is It Too Soon?," *Vanity Fair*,

May 9, 2017, https://www.vanityfair.com/hollywood/2017/05/american-idol-reboot-abc.

13. Erving Goffman, *The Presentation of Self in Everyday Life* (New York: Doubleday Dell, 1956), uses the expression "front stage" to describe interactive behavior of people who know that they are being watched by others.

14. See Addleton Academic Publishers, https://addletonacademicpublishers.com/review-of-contemporary-philosophy, accessed July 4, 2019.

15. Sean Parker, "Sean Parker—Facebook Exploits Human Vulnerability (We Are Dopamine Addicts)," YouTube video, 2:19, November 11, 2017, https://www.youtube.com/watch?v=R7jar4KgKxs&t=72s.

16. On addiction and social media use, see Nicholas Kardaras, *Glow Kids* (New York: St. Martin's Griffin, 2016).

17. Timothy Mo, *An Insular Possession* (London: Chatto & Windus, 1986), 459.

18. See Niklas Luhmann, *Die Realität der Massenmedien* [The reality of the mass media] (Opladen: Westdeutscher Verlag, 1995). A second, extended and revised, edition was issued by the same publisher in 1996. This second edition was the basis for the English translation, *The Reality of the Mass Media*, trans. Kathleen Cross (Stanford, Calif.: Stanford University Press, 2000).

19. Luhmann, *The Reality of the Mass Media*, 19; translation modified.

20. Luhmann, 20–21.

21. "Meme," *Cambridge Dictionary*, https://dictionary.cambridge.org/dictionary/english/meme; accessed June 22, 2019.

22. Oliva Solon, "Richard Dawkins on the Internet's Hijacking of the Word 'Meme,'" *Wired*, June 20, 2013, https://www.wired.co.uk/article/richard-dawkins-memes.

23. We are grateful to Suzanne Murphy for bringing the profilic relevance of "casting" to our attention.

24. Giovanni Formilan and David Stark, "Moments of Identity: Artists and their Aliases in Electronic Music," unpublished manuscript.

25. For example, see David Lyon, *Surveillance Society: Monitoring Everyday Life* (Philadelphia: Open University Press, 2001).

26. See the back cover of Byung-Chul Han, *The Transparency Society* (Stanford, Calif.: Stanford University Press, 2015).

27. "Why a Surveillance Society Clock?," American Civil Liberties Union, https://www.aclu.org/other/why-surveillance-society-clock?redirect =technology-and-liberty/why-surveillance-society-clock, accessed July 15, 2019.

28. Shoshana Zuboff, *The Age of Surveillance Capitalism: The Fight for a Human Future and a New Frontier of Power* (New York: PublicAffairs, 2019), 202, 20.

29. Elena Esposito, "Elena Esposito: Future and Uncertainty in the Digital Society," YouTube video, 1:56:49, March 15, 2018, https://www .youtube.com/watch?v=zb18MZn9Ies&t=2393s.

30. Amy Webb, "Amy Webb: The Big Nine—Triangulation 387," YouTube Video, 2019, 1:03:34, https://www.youtube.com/watch?v=lrcGrYQc M2g.

31. Tim Wu, *The Attention Merchants: The Epic Scramble to Get Inside Our Heads* (New York: Vintage, 2017), 325.

32. Cathy O'Neil, *Weapons of Math Destruction: How Big Data Increasing Inequality and Threatens Democracy* (New York: Crown, 2016).

33. Frank Pasquale, *The Black Box Society: The Secret Algorithms That Control Money and Information* (Cambridge, Mass.: Harvard University Press, 2015); David Lyon, *The Culture of Surveillance* (New York: Polity, 2018).

34. It is difficult to clearly differentiate between profiles that we curate ourselves and those that are created by surveillance and big data. The two are typically intertwined. Our Facebook profile is curated by us, but also analyzed by algorithms to determine which ads we see. When we publish an academic essay, we can include it in our academic profile or not, but we cannot determine the effect it will have on our H-index.

35. "Byung-Chul Han," *Wikipedia*, https://en.wikipedia.org/wiki/Byung -Chul_Han; accessed June 10, 2019.

36. See "In Orwell's '1984' Society Knew It Was Being Dominated. Not Today," *El País*, February 7, 2018, https://elpais.com/elpais/2018/02/07 /inenglish/1517995081_033617.html.

37. Byung-Chul Han, *The Burnout Society* (Stanford, Calif.: Stanford University Press, 2015), 2.

38. Kylie Morris, "Jussie Smollett Charged with Planning Alleged Homophobic, Racist Attack Himself," *Channel 4 News*, February 21, 2019,

https://www.channel4.com/news/jussie-smollett-charged-with
-planning-alleged-homophobic-racist-attack-himself.

39. "Chicago Police Release Statement on Jussie Smollett Arrest," *Daily Mail*, February 21, 2019, YouTube video, 5:48, https://www.youtube .com/watch?v=zUSnegQd-RQ.

40. "Taylor Swift," *Wikipedia*, https://en.wikipedia.org/wiki/Taylor_Swift; accessed August 1, 2019.

41. Lisa Respers France, "Voter Registration Reportedly Spikes After Taylor Swift Post," *CNN*, October 8, 2018, https://web.archive.org/web /20181009194930/https://edition.cnn.com/2018/10/09/entertainment /taylor-swift-voter-registration/index.html.

42. Reihan Salam, "Taylor Swift Succumbs to Competitive Wokeness," *Atlantic*, October 11, 2018, https://www.theatlantic.com/ideas/archive /2018/10/taylor-swift-kanye-west-and-competitive-wokeness/572716/.

43. Abby Sessions, "Letters: 'Acting Like This Is a Boundless Battle for Wokeness Is Somewhat Absurd,'" *Atlantic*, October 25, 2018, https:// www.theatlantic.com/letters/archive/2018/10/readers-opinions-comp etitive-wokeness-swift-kanye/573754/.

44. Confucius, *Analects* 5:10; Roger T. Ames and Henry Rosemont, Jr., eds. and trans., *The Analects of Confucius: A Philosophical Translation* (New York: Ballantine, 1998), 97–98.

45. Luhmann, *Introduction to Systems Theory*, 100.

46. "Writing a Diversity Statement," University of Nebraska-Lincoln, November 13, https://www.unl.edu/gradstudies/connections/writing -diversity-statement; accessed August 3, 2019.

47. Luhmann, *Introduction to Systems Theory*, 119 (translation modified).

48. For more on this, from a different angle, see Melissa Aronczyk, *Branding the Nation: The Global Business of National Identity* (Oxford: Oxford University Press, 2013). As the Amazon.com description summarizes, Aronczyk investigates how "national governments around the world are turning to branding consultants, public relations advisers and strategic communications experts to help them 'brand' their jurisdiction. Using the tools, techniques and expertise of commercial branding is believed to help nations articulate more coherent and cohesive identities, attract foreign capital, and maintain citizen loyalty. In short, the goal of nation branding is to make the nation matter in a world where borders and boundaries appear increasingly obsolete."

49. Aleida Assmann, "Wir dürfen die Erinnerungskultur nicht ethnisie-ren," *Süddeutsche Zeitung*, February 19, 2018, https://www.sueddeutsche.de/kultur/erinnerungskultur-deutschlands-imperativ-1.3866258-2.

50. River Clegg, "How to Market to Me," *New Yorker*, March 12, 2018, https://www.newyorker.com/magazine/2018/03/19/how-to-market-to-me?.

51. Hannah Drobits, Sam Morris, and Elan Fingles, "Case Study: Mac vs. PC Advertisement Campaign," *Hannah's Media Leap Blog*, July 23, 2014, https://sites.psu.edu/drobitsleap/2014/07/23/case-study-mac-vs-pc-advertisement-campaign/.

52. All ads can be watched at https://www.YouTube.com/watch?v=oeEG5LVXdKol; accessed September 1, 2019.

53. Drobits, Morris, and Fingles, "Case Study."

54. Images of the advertising campaign can be found at "An Oral History of 'Get a Mac,' Part 1," *Campaign*, https://www.campaignlive.co.uk/article/oral-history-get-mac-part-1/1417003.

55. This and the quotes that follow refer to the tenth-anniversary edition: Naomi Klein, *No Logo: 10th Anniversary Edition with a New Introduction by the Author* (London: Picador, 2009).

56. Rejection rates vary from academic field to field and journal to journal. For instance, the average rejection rate of major English-language journals in psychology in 2017 was 70 percent. See APA, https://www.apa.org/pubs/journals/features/2017-statistics.pdf.

57. As an aesthetic concept, the notion of the picturesque is commonly traced back to the influential "Essay on Prints" by William Gilpin, published in 1768, as well as to later publications by the same author. Gilpin and others conceived the picturesque as "aesthetic ideal" that could be distinguished, for instance, from the "beautiful" and the "sublime." Here, we are not tracing the specific meanings of the notion. We are interested in the general use of the term in the literal sense of "resembling a picture."

58. These reflections on profilicity follow an earlier publication by Hans-Georg Moeller, "On Second-Order Observation and Genuine Pretending: Coming to Terms with Society," *Thesis Eleven* 143, no. 1 (2017): 28–43.

59. Anonymous, *Reisebriefe deutscher Romantiker* (Berlin: Rütten und Loening, 1979), 140–41.

60. Rolf Trauzettel, "Landscape as an Aesthetic Person: On the Conceptual world of German Romanticism," in *Landscape East and West: A Philosophical Journey*, ed. Hans-Georg Moeller and Andrew Whitehead (London: Bloomsbury, 2014), 100.

61. Matthew Gibson, "The Impress of the Visual and Scenic Arts of the Fiction of Bram Stoker," in *Bram Stoker and the Late Victorian World*, ed. Matthew Gibson and Sabine Lenore Müller (Clemson, S.C.: Clemson University Press, 2018), 56, 58.

62. Rather than the theoretical aesthetic notion of it—see note 57 on Gilpin.

63. See Tim Milnes and Kerry Sinanan, eds., *Romanticism, Sincerity and Authenticity* (London: Palgrave Macmillan, 2010).

64. First published in 1936 in French, under the title *L'œuvre d'art à l'époque de sa reproduction mécanisée* in *Zeitschrift für Sozialforschung* des *Frankfurter Instituts*. The complex textual and publication history of this text is documented in detail in the German *Wikipedia* entry: https://de .wikipedia.org/wiki/Das_Kunstwerk_im_Zeitalter_seiner_tech nischen_Reproduzierbarkeit, accessed August 18, 2019.

65. Charles Taylor, *The Ethics of Authenticity* (Cambridge, Mass.: Harvard University Press, 1992).

66. Walter Benjamin, "The Work of Art in the Age of Mechanical Reproduction" (1935), in *Illuminations: Essays and Reflections*, ed. Hannah Arendt, trans. Harry Zohn (New York: Schocken, 1969), 13.

67. John Maynard Keynes, *The General Theory of Employment, Interest and Money* (London: Palgrave Macmillan, 1936), 100.

68. Elena Esposito, "Economic Circularities and Second-Order Observation: The Reality of Ratings," *Sociologica* 7, no. 2 (2013): 1–10.

69. Guy Debord, *The Society of the Spectacle*, trans. Donald Nicholson-Smith (New York: Zone, 1994), originally published as *La société du spectacle* (1967). The book is divided into short sections. We quote according to section numbers, not page numbers. An alternative translation (by Greg Adargo) is available at https://www.marxists.org/reference/archive /debord/society.htm.

70. Max Horkheimer and Theodor W. Adorno, *Philosophische Fragmente*, later known as *Dialektik der Aufklärung* (New York: Social Studies Association, 1944).

71. The essay was published in Hans-Magnus Enzensberger, "Constituents of a Theory of the Media," trans. Stuart Hood, in *The Consciousness Industry: On Literature, Politics, and the Media*, ed. Reinhold Grimm and Bruce Armstrong (New York: Continuum, 1974).

72. A Freudian might wonder what sort of psychological mechanism might be behind the probably unintended parallelism between this phrase by Enzensberger and Adolf Hitler's desire, expressed in a 1935 speech, that the German youth ought to be "fast as greyhounds, tough as leather, and hard as Krupp steel."

73. Nicholas Negroponte, *Being Digital* (New York: Knopf, 1995).

74. Jean Baudrillard, *Pour une critique de l'economie politique du signe* (Paris: Gallimard, 1972). The quotes that follow are from the English translation, *For a Critique of the Political Economy of the Sign*, trans. Charles Levin (Saint Louis: Telos, 1981).

75. Sherry Turkle, *Alone Together: Why We Expect More from Technology and Less from Each Other* (New York: Basic Books, 2011).

76. Roberto Simanowski, *Facebook Society: Losing Ourselves in Sharing Ourselves*, trans. Susan H. Gillespie (New York: Columbia University Press, 2018).

77. Ferdinand de Saussure, *Course in General Linguistics*, ed. Charles Bally and Albert Sechehaye, trans. Roy Harris (Chicago: Open Court, 1998).

3. SINCERITY

1. David Kirkpatrick, *The Facebook Effect: The Inside Story of the Company That Is Connecting the World* (New York: Simon and Schuster, 2010), 199–200.

2. Erika Riggs, "Mark Zuckerberg Spends $30 Million on Four Homes to Ensure Privacy," *NBC News*, October 11, 2013, https://www.nbcnews.com/businessmain/mark-zuckerberg-spends-30-million-four-homes-ensure-privacy-8C11379396

3. Mark Zuckerberg, "Mark Zuckerberg & Yuval Noah Harari in Conversation," YouTube video, 1:33:30, April 26, 2019, https://www.youtube.com/watch?v=Boj9eDoWug8; Mark Zuckerberg, "Mark Zuckerberg Talks to Patrick Collison and Tyler Cowen About Accelerating

Progress," YouTube video, 1:09:09, November 25, 2019, https://www
.youtube.com/watch?v=GTlt-pPfLWU.

4. Henry Rosemont, Jr., *Against Individualism: A Confucian Rethinking of
the Foundations of Morality, Politics, Family, and Religion* (Lanham,
Md.: Lexington, 2015), 14.

5. Lionel Trilling, *Sincerity and Authenticity* (Cambridge, Mass.: Harvard
University Press, 1972), 35.

6. Alasdair MacIntyre, *After Virtue: A Study in Moral Theory* (Notre
Dame, Indiana: University of Notre Dame Press, 1981).

7. *Wikipedia* says: "In the 1990s China was among the countries with the
highest suicide rates in the world (above 20 per 100,000), but by the
global economic crisis they kept dropping as significantly (as they were
by the end of 1990s) with the main force having been migration from
rural to urban areas. By 2011, China had one of the lowest suicide rates
in the world, even less than the USA. Between 1990 and 2016, suicide
rates in China fell by 64%, making China the #1 country in the world
in suicide reduction. According to the WHO, in 2016, the suicide rate
in China was 9.7, while the suicide rate in the U.S. was 15.3." "Suicide in
China," *Wikipedia*, https://en.wikipedia.org/wiki/Suicide_in_China,
accessed August 1, 2019.

8. Referring to Samuel Law and Pozi Liu (Law and Liu 2008), *Wikipedia*
states: "A 2008 study—which was based on data from the 1990s—found
that: female suicides outnumbered male suicides by a 3:1 ratio; rural
suicides outnumbered urban suicides by a 3:1 ratio."

9. Wu Fei, *Suicide and Justice: A Chinese Perspective* (New York: Routledge,
2009), 6.

10. We make no comment as to whether contemporary, or past, Chinese
society is "properly" Confucian.

11. Wu, *Suicide and Justice*, xvi–xxi. In cases where a spouse had an affair
or mental illness was involved, sincerity-based understandings still
dominated. Affairs are explained as a matter of shame, and the person
cheated on is left no "face" and thinks they have no choice but to kill
themselves in order to prove the injustice done to them. Those with
mental illness similarly see it as shameful and something that leaves
them unable to fulfill their roles. Unable to live up to familial or social
requirements, they see little alternative to suicide.

12. Giacomo Casanova, *History of My Life*, trans. Willard Trask (Baltimore: Johns Hopkins University Press, 1997).

13. Judith Butler, *Antigone's Claim: Kinship Between Life and Death* (New York: Columbia University Press, 2002); Slavoy Žižek, *Antigone* (London: Bloomsbury Academic, 2016).

14. G. W. F. Hegel, *Lectures on the Philosophy of Religion*, vol. 2, trans. Peter C. Hodgson (Oxford: Oxford University Press, 2008), 665.

15. See for instance, Rosemont, *Against Individualism*. Rosemont demands that we see "ourselves and our fellow human beings not as autonomous individuals, but as fundamentally interrelated role-bearers who *live* those roles, not merely 'play' them" (xiv).

16. Roger T. Ames, *Confucian Role Ethics: A Vocabulary* (Hong Kong: Chinese University Press, 2011), 87.

17. Francis Fukuyama, *Identity: The Demand for Dignity and the Politics of Resentment* (New York: Farrar, Straus and Giroux, 2018), 63–66.

18. The term "new sincerity" is normally associated with a broader aesthetic and intellectual trend exemplified by the American author David Foster Wallace (1962–2008). We apply it here to political theory. See Paul D'Ambrosio and Hans-Georg Moeller, "Political New Sincerity and Profilicity: On the Decline of Identity Politics and Authenticity." *Philosophy Today* 65, no. 1 (forthcoming).

19. Fukuyama's view on identity politics is perhaps somewhat one-sided. We discuss various forms of identity politics in chapter 5.

20. Mark Lilla, *The Once and Future Liberal: After Identity Politics* (New York: HarperCollins, 2017).

21. Kwame Anthony Appiah, *The Lies That Bind: Rethinking Identity* (New York: Liveright, 2018), 27.

22. Cf. D'Ambrosio, "A Sandelian Response to Confucian Role Ethics," in *Encountering China: Michael Sandel and Chinese Philosophy*, ed. Michael Sandel and Paul J. D'Ambrosio, 228–44 (Cambridge, Mass.: Harvard University Press, 2018).

23. Fukuyama, *Identity*, 119.

24. German Lopez, "Donald Trump Can be Weirdly Honest About Lying. The Daily Show Gave a Few Examples," *Vox*, December 15, 2016, https://www.vox.com/policy-and-politics/2016/12/15/13966872/trump-lying-daily-show.

25. Not everyone considers them "less biased." In fact a number of vocal theorists, including Cathy O'Neil (2016), Virginia Eubanks (2018), Safiya Noble (2018), and Ruha Benjamin (2019), have argued that algorithms may institutionalize their programmer's own prejudices.

26. Kashmir Hill, "How Target Figured Out a Teen Girl Was Pregnant Before Her Father Did," *Forbes*, February 16, 2012, https://www.forbes .com/sites/kashmirhill/2012/02/16/how-target-figured-out-a-teen -girl-was-pregnant-before-her-father-did/#48b210456668.

4. AUTHENTICITY

1. Benjamin Franklin, "Letter to Peter Collinson; May 9, 1753," Teaching American History, https://teachingamericanhistory.org/library /document/letter-to-peter-collinson/.

2. Sebastian Junger, *Tribe: On Homecoming and Belonging Book* (New York: Hachette, 2016), 9.

3. Junger, *Tribe*, 12–34.

4. Junger, *Tribe*, 18–19.

5. Jordan Peterson, "INSPIRATIONAL: Jordan Peterson on Western Civilization," YouTube video, 2:30, August 20, 2017, https://www .youtube.com/watch?v=NhgD8pNKlnE.

6. Peterson often talks about his two adult children, his wife, and the bonds between them. He thinks family is extremely important. But like many psychologists, he sees the nuclear family as a den for personal development that the individual must ultimately overcome.

7. See the section on the problem of identity in chapter 5 for more on this.

8. See Theodore W. Adorno, *Jargon der Eigentlichkeit: Zur deutschen Ideologie* [The jargon of authenticity] (Frankfurt: Suhrkamp, 1964).

9. Charles Taylor, *A Secular Age*. (Cambridge, Mass: Belknap Press of Harvard University Press, 2007), 74.

10. Charles Taylor, *The Ethics of Authenticity* (Cambridge, MA: Harvard University Press, 1992), 74.

11. Ulrich Beck and Elisabeth Beck-Gemsheim, *Individualization: Institutionalized Individualism and Its Social and Political Consequences* (London: SAGE, 2001), xxii. xvi. For Bauman's extended argument, see Zygmunt Bauman, "From Pilgrim to Tourist—or a Short History of

Identity," in *Questions of Cultural Identity*, ed. Stuart Hall and Paul du Gay (New York: Sage, 1996), 18–36.

12. Jacob Golomb, *In Search of Authenticity: Existentialism from Kierkegaard to Camus* (New York: Routledge, 1995), 10.

13. Bauman, "From Pilgrim to Tourist."

14. Friedrich Nietzsche, *The Gay Science: With a Prelude in Rhymes and an Appendix of Songs* (New York: Random House, 1974); Allan Watts, *Become What You Are* (Boulder, Colo.: Shambhala, 2003).

15. Sohrab Ahmari, *From Fire, by Water: My Journey to the Catholic Faith* (San Francisco: Ignatius, 2019), 36.

16. Jay Shetty, "Mike Posner: ON How Fame Ruined His Life | ON Purpose Podcast Ep. 4," YouTube video, 127:15, March 14, 2019, https://www.youtube.com/watch?v=gjpB9MXCfOE&t=349s.

17. Elena Esposito, "In and Out: Fashion and the Culture of Transitoriness," YouTube video, 41:39, September 7, 2013, https://www.youtube.com/watch?v=9loww3vyj9o.

18. Rousseau is adamant that he really is a true confessor. At the beginning of his *Essays*, Montaigne tells the reader that he will explore his own self simply and "without artifice." Rousseau scoffs, "I had always been amused at Montaigne's false ingenuousness, and at his pretense of confessing his faults while taking good care to admit only to likeable ones." Jean-Jacques Rousseau, *The Confessions of Jean-Jacques Rousseau*, trans. J. M. Cohen (New York: Penguin, 1981), 478–79.

19. Esposito, "In and Out."

20. "Sherry Turkle," Amazon.com, https://www.amazon.com/Sherry-Turkle/e/B000APEFSI?ref_=dbs_p_pbk_r00_abau_000000, accessed August 21, 2019.

21. See Paul D'Ambrosio and Hans-Georg Moeller, "From Authenticity to Profilicity: A Critical Response to Roberto Simanowski and Others," *New German Critique* 46, no. 2 (2019): 1–25.

22. Marshall McLuhan and Quentin Fiore, *The Medium Is the Massage: An Inventory of Effects*, coordinated by Jerome Agel (New York: Bantam, 1967).

23. Boho Beautiful, "Burnt Out | Milestones & Big Changes for Boho Beautiful," YouTube video, 10:36, March 17, 2019, https://www.youtube.com/watch?v=fAAD8gCgxSk.

24. Tim Peterson, "Creators Are Making Longer Videos to Cater to the YouTube Algorithm," *DigiDay*, July 3, 2017, https://digiday.com/media /creators-making-longer-videos-cater-youtube-algorithm/.

25. Boho Beautiful, "Nothing Will Ever Be the Same ♥ Boho Diary | Nepal," YouTube video, 12:33, June 22, 2019, https://www.youtube.com /watch?v=6yfAt93Ty3A.

26. Boho Beautiful, "I Love Your Yoga Videos, but . . . Subscribers Keep Leaving Our Channel?!" YouTube video, 10:07, June 24, 2019, https:// www.youtube.com/watch?v=-RAyPCbMYno.

27. Eva Illouz, *Cold Intimacies: The Making of Emotional Capitalism* (New York: Polity, 2007), 79.

28. Lionel Trilling, *Sincerity and Authenticity* (Cambridge, Mass.: Harvard University Press, 1972).

29. Goldie Chan, "10 Golden Rules of Personal Branding," *Forbes*, November 8, 2018, https://www.forbes.com/sites/goldiechan/2018/11/08/10-gol den-rules-personal-branding/#2aac095258a7.

30. Emma Sandler, "Supermodel Teaches at Stanford: How to Learn About Personal Branding with Tyra Banks," *Forbes*, June 12, 2017. https://www.forbes.com/sites/emmasandler/2017/06/12/tyra-banks -talks-teaching-at-stanford/#2aecee326965.

31. "Zhang Dayi," *Wikipedia*, https://en.wikipedia.org/wiki/Zhang_Dayi, accessed July 29, 2019.

32. Zhang Dayi, "纪录片《网红》: 真实记录'淘宝第一网红'张大奕的面子, 里子," Bilibili video, 18:52, October 28, 2016, https://www.bilibili.com /video/av6856116/. The original Chinese reads: "因为他本身就是通一张 照片或者是一段视频喜欢你他这个过程也很快你那个生活中你都没有办法做 到唯一和忠诚怎么可能希望网络上的人对你做到一辈子忠诚这更不可的。"

33. "就是我性格那种看上去特别随和其实特别难搞的一个人。"

5. IDENTITY

1. See "Budweiser Super Bowl Commercial 2015," https://www.youtube .com/watch?v=yyVgO_j8vxw, accessed May 29, 2020.

2. Hartmut Rosa, *Social Acceleration: A New Theory of Modernity*, trans. Jonathan Trejo-Mathys (New York: Columbia University Press, 2013).

3. Carol Hanisch, "The Political Is Personal," *Notes from the Second Year: Women's Liberation*, March 8, 1970, 1.

4. Simone de Beauvoir would perhaps make a similar complaint today about the discourse on gender.

5. "The Combahee River Collective Statement," Circuitous.org, http://circuitous.org/scraps/combahee.html, accessed October 27, 2019.

6. Garrett Graham, *The Gay State: The Quest for an Independent Gay Nation-State and What It Means to Conservatives and the World's Religions* (New York: iUniverse, 2010).

7. Paul D'Ambrosio and Hans-Georg Moeller, "Political New Sincerity and Profilicity: On the Decline of Identity Politics and Authenticity," *Philosophy Today* 65, no. 1 (forthcoming).

8. Michael Sandel, *Liberalism and the Limits of Justice* (Cambridge: Cambridge University Press, 1982), 179.

9. Kwame Anthony Appiah, *The Lies That Bind: Rethinking Identity* (New York: Liveright, 2018); Mark Lilla, *The Once and Future Liberal: After Identity Politics* (New York: HarperCollins, 2017); Francis Fukuyama, *Identity: The Demand for Dignity and the Politics of Resentment* (New York: Farrar, Straus and Giroux, 2018).

10. Robert N. Bellah, "Civil Religion in America," *Dædalus, Journal of the American Academy of Arts and Sciences* 96, no. 1 (1967): 1–21.

11. Appiah, *The Lies That Bind*, 77.

12. Sheldon Stryker and Peter J. Burke, "The Past, Present, and Future of an Identity Theory," *Social Psychology Quarterly* 63, no. 4 (2000): 284.

13. Niklas Luhmann, *Social Systems*, trans. John Bednarz, Jr., with Dirk Baecker (Stanford, Calif.: Stanford University Press, 1996), xxiv.

14. Niklas Luhmann, *Theories of Distinction: Redescribing the Descriptions of Modernity*, ed. William Rasch (Stanford, Calif.: Stanford University Press, 2002), 184.

15. Simone de Beauvoir, *The Second Sex* (original: *Le Deuxième Sexe*, 1949), trans. H. M. Parshley (New York: Penguin, 1972), 267.

16. Plato recognizes similar ideas in the *Republic*, and these are also major themes in the *Zhuangzi*, as will be demonstrated in the next chapter.

17. For a more detailed account, see Terry Pinkard, *Does History Make Sense: Hegel on the Historical Shapes of Justice* (Cambridge, Mass.: Harvard University Press, 2018).

18. Douglas Kellner, "Popular Culture and the Construction of Postmodern Identities," in *Modernity and Identity*, ed. Scott Lash and Jonathan Friedman (Oxford: Blackwell, 1991), 141.

19. Niklas Luhmann, *Theory of Society*, vol. 2, trans. Rhodes Barrett (Stanford, Calif.: Stanford University Press, 1993), 22.

20. Timothy Mo, *An Insular Possession* (London: Chatto & Windus, 1986), 459.

21. Luhmann, *Theory of Society*, 2:22.

22. On the concept of identity as developed from a (partly) Luhmannian position, see Werner Stegmaier, *What Is Orientation? A Philosophical Investigation* (Berlin: De Gruyter, 2019). Stegmaier also addresses the connection between identity formation and "profiles" in chapter 11 of his book.

23. George Herbert Mead, *Mind, Self, and Society*, ed. Charles W. Morris (Chicago: University of Chicago Press, 1934).

24. Note that this "social type" is similar to MacIntyre's "character."

25. Stryker and Burke, "The Past, Present, and Future of an Identity Theory," 284.

6. SANITY

1. All quotes from the *Zhuangzi* follow the edition of the text on ctext.org: https://ctext.org/zhuangzi. Translations are ours, making use of A. C. Graham, trans., *Chuang-tzu: The Seven Inner Chapters and Other Writings from the Book of "Chuang-tzu"* (Indianapolis: Hackett, 2001); and Brook Ziporyn, trans., *Zhuangzi: The Complete Writings* (Indianapolis: Hackett, 2020).

2. For a detailed analysis of the story, see Hans-Georg Moeller, "Hundun's Mistake: Satire and Sanity in the *Zhuangzi*," *Philosophy East and West* 67, no. 3 (2017): 783–800.

3. Simon Parkin, "The YouTube Stars Heading for Burnout: 'The Most Fun Job Imaginable Became Deeply Bleak,'" *Guardian*, September 8, 2018, https://www.theguardian.com/technology/2018/sep/08/youtube-stars-burnout-fun-bleak-stressed.

4. Parkin, "The YouTube Stars Heading for Burnout."

5. Millions of (mostly young) people around the world deal with stress, anxiety, and depression directly related to social media. And an increasing number of other psychological problems, as well as suicides, are linked to social media profiles. See Nicholas Kardaras, *Glow Kids* (New York: St. Martin's Griffin, 2016).

6. Louis Scott Vargas, "Modern Horizons—Draft | Channel LSV," YouTube video, 57:23, June 26, 2019, https://www.youtube.com/watch?v=rjbzcRdoB9o.

7. This is Giles's translation as published in 1889: "Once upon a time, I Zhuangzi dreamt I was a butterfly, fluttering hither and thither, to all intents and purposes a butterfly. I was conscious only of following my fancies as a butterfly, and was unconscious of my individuality as a man. Suddenly, I awaked, and there I lay, myself again. Now I do not know whether I was then a man dreaming I was a butterfly, or whether I am now a butterfly dreaming I am a man. Between a man and a butterfly there is necessarily a barrier. The transition is called Metempsychosis" (47).

8. For a detailed analysis of the story, see Hans-Georg Moeller, "Zhuangzi's Dream of a Butterfly: A Daoist Interpretation," *Philosophy East and West* 49, no. 4 (1999): 439–50.

9. From the context of the passage in the book *Zhuangzi*, it is clear that the transition from being awake to dreaming is supposed to allegorically represent the transformation of life into death and vice versa—that is, the "transformation of things."

10. For a more detailed analysis of the story, see Moeller, "Zhuangzi's Dream of a Butterfly." Some passages from this essay are used here in revised form.

11. For a more detailed account, see Robin D. S. Yates, "Soldiers, Scribes, and Women: Literacy Among the Lower Orders in Early China," in *Writing and Literacy in Early China: Studies from the Columbia Early China Seminar*, ed. Feng Li and David Prager Branner (Seattle: University of Washington Press, 2011), 339–69.

12. This is also a key attribute of Confucian sages, as expressed throughout the *Analects*. However, it is not part of the institutionalized Confucianism the *Zhuangzi* rejects.

13. Thanks to Robert Carleo for coming up with the pun.

14. Friedrich Nietzsche, *Beyond Good and Evil*, trans. Marion Faber (Oxford: Oxford University Press), 156.

POSTSCRIPT

1. See "Pope Francis Says Pandemic Can Be a 'Place of Conversion,'" *Tablet*, https://www.thetablet.co.uk/features/2/17845/pope-francis-says -pandemic-can-be-a-place-of-conversion-.

2. "La emergencia viral y el mundo de mañana," *El País*, March 22, 2020, https://elpais.com/ideas/2020-03-21/la-emergencia-viral-y-el-mundo -de-manana-byung-chul-han-el-filosofo-surcoreano-que-piensa -desde-berlin.html; "Wir düfen di Vernunft nicht dem Virus überlas- sen," *Welt*, March 23, 2020, https://www.welt.de/kultur/plus206681771 /Byung-Chul-Han-zu-Corona-Vernunft-nicht-dem-Virus -ueberlassen.html; and "Wir sind längst China—nur wollen wir es nicht wahrhaben," *Welt*, April 17, 2020, https://www.welt.de/kultur /plus207267727/Byung-Chul-Han-Wir-sind-laengst-China-nur -wollen-wir-es-nicht-wahrhaben.html; "El coronavirus bajo el liber- alismo," *Clarín*, April 17, 2020, https://www.clarin.com/cultura/byung -chul-vamos-feudalismo-digital-modelo-chino-podria-imponerse _0_QqOkCraxD.html.

3. Byung-Chul Han, "Asia Is Working with Data and Masks," trans. David Ownby, *Reading the China Dream*, https://www.readingthe chinadream.com/byung-chul-han-coronavirus.html.

BIBLIOGRAPHY

Adorno, Theodor W. *Jargon der Eigentlichkeit: Zur deutschen Ideologie* [The jargon of authenticity]. Frankfurt: Suhrkamp, 1964.

Ahmari, Sohrab. *From Fire, by Water: My Journey to the Catholic Faith*. San Francisco: Ignatius, 2019.

Ames, Roger T. *Confucian Role Ethics: A Vocabulary*. Hong Kong: Chinese University Press, 2011.

Ames, Rogert T., and Henry Rosemont, Jr., eds. and trans. *The Analects of Confucius: A Philosophical Translation*. New York: Ballantine, 1998.

Anonymous. *Reisebriefe deutscher Romantiker*. Berlin: Rütten und Loening, 1979.

Appiah, Kwame Anthony. *The Lies That Bind: Rethinking Identity*. New York: Liveright, 2018.

Aronczyk, Melissa. *Branding the Nation: The Global Business of National Identity*. Oxford: Oxford University Press, 2013.

Assmann, Aleida. "Wir dürfen die Erinnerungskultur nicht ethnisieren." *Süddeutsche Zeitung*, February 19, 2018. https://www.sueddeutsche.de /kultur/erinnerungskultur-deutschlands-imperativ-1.3866258-2.

Baudrillard, Jean. *For a Critique of the Political Economy of the Sign*. Trans. Charles Levin. Saint Louis: Telos, 1981.

——. *Pour une critique de l'economie politique du signe*. Paris: Gallimard, 1972.

Bauman, Zygmunt. "From Pilgrim to Tourist—or a Short History of Identity." In *Questions of Cultural Identity*, ed. Stuart Hall and Paul du Gay, 18–36. New York: Sage, 1996.

Beauvoir, Simone. *The Second Sex*. Trans. H. M. Parshley. New York: Penguin, 1972 (1949).

Beck, Ulrich, and Elisabeth Beck-Gemsheim. *Individualization: Institutionalized Individualism and Its Social and Political Consequences*. London: SAGE, 2001.

Bellah, Robert N. "Civil Religion in America." *Dædalus, Journal of the American Academy of Arts and Sciences* 96, no. 1 (1967): 1–21.

Benjamin, Ruha. *Race After Technology: Abolitionist Tools for the New Jim Code*. Cambridge: Polity, 2019.

Benjamin, Walter. *Illuminations: Essays and Reflections*. Ed. Hannah Arendt, trans. Harry Zohn. New York: Schocken, 1969.

——. "The Work of Art in the Age of Mechanical Reproduction" (1935). In *Illuminations: Essays and Reflections*, ed. Hannah Arendt, trans. Harry Zohn. New York: Schocken, 1969.

Boho Beautiful. "Burnt Out | Milestones & Big Changes for Boho Beautiful." YouTube video, 10:36, March 17, 2019. https://www.youtube.com/watch?v=fAAD8gCgxSk.

——. "Nothing Will Ever Be the Same ♥ Boho Diary | Nepal." YouTube video, 12:33, June 22, 2019. https://www.youtube.com/watch?v=6yfAt93Ty3A.

——. "I Love Your Yoga Videos, but . . . Subscribers Keep Leaving Our Channel?!" YouTube video, 10:07, June 24, 2019. https://www.youtube.com/watch?v=-RAyPCbMYno.

Butler, Judith. *Antigone's Claim: Kinship Between Life and Death*. New York: Columbia University Press, 2002.

——. *Giving an Account of Oneself*. New York: Fordham University Press, 2005.

Casanova, Giacomo. *History of My Life*. Trans. Willard Trask. Baltimore: Johns Hopkins University Press, 1997.

Chan, Goldie. "10 Golden Rules of Personal Branding." *Forbes*, November 8, 2018. https://www.forbes.com/sites/goldiechan/2018/11/08/10-golden-rules-personal-branding/#2aac095258a7.

Clegg, River. "How to Market to Me." *New Yorker*, March 12, 2018. https://www.newyorker.com/magazine/2018/03/19/how-to-market-to-me?.

Commonwealth Club. "Francis Fukuyama: Identity and the Politics of Resentment." YouTube video, 1:06.59, October 8, 2018. https://www.youtube.com/watch?v=I2AUxRQFXY4.

Daily Mail. "Chicago Police Release Statement on Jussie Smollett Arrest."
YouTube video, 5:48, February 21, 2019. https://www.youtube.com/watch
?v=zUSnegQd-RQ.

D'Ambrosio, Paul. "From Present to Presentation: A Philosophical Critique
of Hartmut Rosa's 'Situational Identity.'" *Time and Society* 28, no. 3 (2019):
1061–83.

——. "A Sandelian Response to Confucian Role Ethics." In *Encountering
China: Michael Sandel and Chinese Philosophy*, ed. Michael Sandel and
Paul J. D'Ambrosio, 228–44. Cambridge, Mass.: Harvard University
Press, 2018.

D'Ambrosio, Paul, and Hans-Georg Moeller. "From Authenticity to Profilicity: A Critical Response to Roberto Simanowski and Others." *New
German Critique* 46, no. 2 (2019): 1–25.

——. "Political New Sincerity and Profilicity: On the Decline of Identity
Politics and Authenticity." *Philosophy Today* 65, no. 1 (forthcoming).

Debord, Guy. *The Society of the Spectacle*. Trans. Donald Nicholson-Smith.
New York: Zone, 1994.

Drobits, Hannah, Sam Morris, and Elan Fingles. "Case Study: Mac vs. PC
Advertisement Campaign." July 23, 2014. https://sites.psu.edu/drobitsleap
/2014/07/23/case-study-mac-vs-pc-advertisement-campaign/.

Dylan, Bob. "Beyond Here Lies Nothing." *Together Through Life*, track 1.
Columbia Records, 2009, compact disk.

Enzensberger, Hans-Magnus. "Bausteine zu einer Theorie der Medien."
Kursbuch 20 (March 1970): 159–86.

——. "Constituents of a Theory of the Media." Trans. Stuart Hood. In *The
Consciousness Industry: On Literature, Politics, and the Media*, ed. Reinhold Grimm and Bruce Armstrong, 95–128. New York: Continuum,
1974.

Esposito, Elena. "Artificial Communication? The Production of Contingency by Algorithms." *Zeitschrift für Soziologie* 46, no. 4 (2017):
249–65.

——. "Economic Circularities and Second-Order Observation: The Reality
of Ratings." *Sociologica* 7, no. 2 (2013): 1–10.

——. "Elena Esposito: Future and Uncertainty in the Digital Society." You-
Tube video, 1:56:49, March 15, 2018. https://www.youtube.com/watch
?v=zb18MZn9Ies&t=2393s.

——. "The Fascination of Contingency: Fashion and Modern Society." In *Philosophical Perspectives on Fashion*, ed. Giovanni Matteucci and Stefano Marino, 175–90. London: Bloomsbury, 2017.

——. "In and Out: Fashion and the Culture of Transitoriness." YouTube video, 41:39, September 7, 2013. https://www.youtube.com/watch?v=9l oww3vyj9o.

Eubanks, Virginia. *Automating Inequality: How High-Tech Tools Profile, Police, and Punish the Poor*. New York: St. Martin's, 2018.

Ezra Klein Show. "Francis Fukuyama's Case Against Identity Politics." YouTube video, 1:30.17, October 1, 2018. https://www.youtube.com/watch?v=F7D_mF_siSk.

Fan, Jiayang. "China's Selfie Obsession." *New Yorker*, December 11, 2017. https://www.newyorker.com/magazine/2017/12/18/chinas-selfie-obsession.

Formilan, Giovanni, and David Stark. "Moments of Identity: Artists and Their Aliases in Electronic Music." Manuscript.

France, Lisa Respers. "Voter Registration Reportedly Spikes After Taylor Swift Post." *CNN*, October 8, 2018. https://web.archive.org/web/20181009194930/https://edition.cnn.com/2018/10/09/entertainment/taylor-swift-voter-registration/index.html.

Franklin, Benjamin. "Letter to Peter Collinson; May 9, 1753." Teaching American History. https://teachingamericanhistory.org/library/document/letter-to-peter-collinson/.

Fukuyama, Francis. 2018. *Identity: The Demand for Dignity and the Politics of Resentment*. New York: Farrar, Straus and Giroux.

Gaskin, Sam. "'We Don't Believe Chinese Are Superficial or Narcissistic,' Says Meitu." *Jing Daily*, March 2, 2018. https://jingdaily.com/chinese-meitu/.

Gibson, Matthew. "The Impress of the Visual and Scenic Arts of the Fiction of Bram Stoker." In *Bram Stoker and the Late Victorian World*, ed. Matthew Gibson and Sabine Lenore Müller, 51–76. Clemson, S.C.: Clemson University Press, 2018.

Giles, Herbert A. *Chuang Tzu: Taoist Philosopher and Chinese Mystic*. London: Allen and Unwin, 1889.

Goffman, Erving. *The Presentation of Self in Everyday Life*. New York: Doubleday Dell, 1956.

Golomb, Jacob. *In Search of Authenticity: Existentialism from Kierkegaard to Camus*. New York: Routledge, 1995.

Graham, A. C., trans. *Chuang-tzu: The Seven Inner Chapters and Other Writings from the Book of "Chuang-tzu."* Indianapolis: Hackett, 2001.

Graham, Garrett. *The Gay State: The Quest for an Independent Gay Nation-State and What It Means to Conservatives and the World's Religions.* New York: iUniverse, 2010.

Han, Byung-Chul. *The Burnout Society.* Stanford, Calif.: Stanford University Press, 2015.

——. *The Transparency Society.* Stanford, Calif.: Stanford University Press, 2015.

Hanisch, Carol. "Introduction." Writings by Carol Hanisch, 2006. https://webhome.cs.uvic.ca/~mserra/AttachedFiles/PersonalPolitical.pdf.

——. "The Political Is Personal." *Notes from the Second Year: Women's Liberation*, March 8, 1970.

Hegel, G. W. F. *Lectures on the Philosophy of Religion.* Vol. 2. Trans. Peter C. Hodgson. Oxford: Oxford University Press, 2008.

Hill, Kashmir. "How Target Figured Out a Teen Girl Was Pregnant Before Her Father Did." *Forbes*, February 16, 2012. https://www.forbes.com/sites/kashmirhill/2012/02/16/how-target-figured-out-a-teen-girl-was-pregnant-before-her-father-did/#48b210456668.

Horkheimer, Max, and Theodor W. Adorno. *Philosophische Fragmente* (later known as *Dialektik der Aufklärung*). New York: Social Studies Association, 1944.

Illouz, Eva. *Cold Intimacies: The Making of Emotional Capitalism.* New York: Polity, 2007.

Jönhill, Jan Inge. "Inclusion and Exclusion—a Guiding Distinction to the Understanding of Issues of Cultural Background." *Systems Research and Behavioral Science* 29, no. 4 (2012): 387–401.

Junger, Sebastian. *Tribe: On Homecoming and Belonging Book.* New York: Hachette, 2016.

Kardaras, Nicholas. *Glow Kids.* New York: St. Martin's Griffin, 2016.

Kellner, Douglas. "Popular Culture and the Construction of Postmodern Identities." In *Modernity and Identity*, ed. Scott Lash and Jonathan Friedman, 141–77. Oxford: Blackwell, 1991.

Keynes, John Maynard. *The General Theory of Employment, Interest and Money.* London: Palgrave Macmillan, 1936.

Kirkpatrick, David. *The Facebook Effect: The Inside Story of the Company That Is Connecting the World.* New York: Simon and Schuster, 2010.

Klein, Naomi. *No Logo: Taking Aim at the Brand Bullies.* Toronto: Picador, 1999.

———. *No Logo: 10th Anniversary Edition with a New Introduction by the Author.* London: Picador, 2009.

Kostka, Genia. "China's Social Credit Systems and Public Opinion: Explaining High Levels of Approval." *New Media & Society* 21, no. 7 (2019): 1565–93.

Law, Samuel, and Pozi Liu. "Suicide in China: Unique Demographic Patterns and Relationship to Depressive Disorder." *Current Psychiatry Reports* 10, no. 1 (2008): 80–86.

Lilla, Mark. *The Once and Future Liberal: After Identity Politics.* New York: HarperCollins, 2017.

Lopez, German. "Donald Trump Can Be Weirdly Honest About Lying. The Daily Show Gave a Few Examples." *Vox*, December 15, 2016. https://www.vox.com/policy-and-politics/2016/12/15/13966872/trump-lying-daily-show.

Löwe, Philipp. "Selfie vor Krawallkulisse." *Der Spiegel*, July 8, 2018. https://www.spiegel.de/panorama/gesellschaft/g20-krawalle-selfie-bei-randale-im-schanzenviertel-a-1156799-amp.html.

Luhmann, Niklas. *Die Realität der Massenmedien* [The reality of the mass media]. Opladen: Westdeutscher Verlag, 1995.

———. "Individuum, Individualität, Individualismus." In *Gesellschaftsstruktur und Semantik: Studien zur Wissenssoziologie der modernen Gesellschaft,* 3:149–258. Frankfurt: Suhrkamp, 1993.

———. *Introduction to Systems Theory.* Trans. Peter Gilgen. Cambridge: Polity, 2013.

———. *The Reality of the Mass Media.* Trans. Kathleen Cross. Stanford, Calif.: Stanford University Press, 2000.

———. *Social Systems.* Trans. John Bednarz, Jr., with Dirk Baecker. Stanford, Calif.: Stanford University Press, 1996.

———. *Theories of Distinction: Redescribing the Descriptions of Modernity.* Ed. William Rasch. Stanford, Calif.: Stanford University Press, 2002.

———. *Theory of Society,* vol. 2. Trans. Rhodes Barrett. Stanford, Calif.: Stanford University Press, 2013.

Lyon, David. *The Culture of Surveillance.* New York: Polity, 2018.

———. *Surveillance Society: Monitoring Everyday Life.* Philadelphia: Open University Press, 2001.

MacIntyre, Alasdair. *After Virtue: A Study in Moral Theory*. Notre Dame, Ind.: University of Notre Dame Press, 1981.

McLuhan, Marshall, and Quentin Fiore. *The Medium Is the Massage: An Inventory of Effects*. Coordinated by Jerome Agel. New York: Bantam, 1967.

Mead, George Herbert. *Mind, Self, and Society*. Ed. Charles W. Morris. Chicago: University of Chicago Press, 1934.

Milnes, Tim, and Kerry Sinanan, eds. *Romanticism, Sincerity, and Authenticity*. London: Palgrave Macmillan, 2010.

Mo, Timothy. *An Insular Possession*. London: Chatto & Windus, 1986.

Moeller, Hans-Georg. "Hundun's Mistake: Satire and Sanity in the *Zhuangzi*." *Philosophy East and West* 67, no. 3 (2017): 783–800.

——. "The Naked Scribe: The Skill of Dissociation in Society." In *Skill and Mastery: Philosophical Stories from the Zhuangzi*, ed. Karyn Lai and Wai Wai Chiu, 243–58. Lanham, Md.: Rowman and Littlefield International, 2019.

——. "On Second-Order Observation and Genuine Pretending: Coming to Terms with Society." *Thesis Eleven* 143, no. 1 (2017): 28–43.

——. "Zhuangzi's Dream of a Butterfly: A Daoist Interpretation." *Philosophy East and West* 49, no. 4 (1999): 439–50.

Moeller, Hans-Georg, and Paul J. D'Ambrosio. *Genuine Pretending: On the Philosophy of the Zhuangzi*. New York: Columbia University Press, 2017.

Morris, Kylie. "Jussie Smollett Charged with Planning Alleged Homophobic, Racist Attack Himself." *Channel 4 News*, February 21, 2019. https://www.channel4.com/news/jussie-smollett-charged-with-planning-alleged-homophobic-racist-attack-himself.

Negroponte, Nicholas. *Being Digital*. New York: Knopf, 1995.

Nietzsche, Friedrich. *Beyond Good and Evil*. Trans. Marion Faber. Oxford: Oxford University Press, 1998.

——. *The Gay Science: With a Prelude in Rhymes and an Appendix of Songs*. New York: Random House, 1974.

Noble, Safiya. *Algorithms of Oppression: How Search Engines Reinforce Racism*. New York: New York University Press, 2018.

O'Neil, Cathy. *Weapons of Math Destruction: How Big Data Increases Inequality and Threatens Democracy*. New York: Crown, 2016.

Parker, Sean. "Sean Parker—Facebook Exploits Human Vulnerability (We Are Dopamine Addicts)." YouTube video, 2:19, November 11, 2017. https://www.youtube.com/watch?v=R7jar4KgKxs&t=72s.

Parkin, Simon. 2018. "The YouTube Stars Heading for Burnout: 'The Most Fun Job Imaginable Became Deeply Bleak.'" *Guardian*, September 8, 2018. https://www.theguardian.com/technology/2018/sep/08/youtube-stars-burnout-fun-bleak-stressed.

Pasquale, Frank. *The Black Box Society: The Secret Algorithms That Control Money and Information*. Cambridge, Mass.: Harvard University Press, 2015.

Peterson, Jordan. "INSPIRATIONAL: Jordan Peterson on Western Civilization." YouTube video, 2:30, August 20, 2017. https://www.youtube.com/watch?v=NhgD8pNKlnE.

Peterson, Tim. 2018. "Creators Are Making Longer Videos to Cater to the YouTube Algorithm." *DigiDay*, July 3, 2017. https://digiday.com/media/creators-making-longer-videos-cater-youtube-algorithm/.

Pinkard, Terry. *Does History Make Sense: Hegel on the Historical Shapes of Justice*. Cambridge, Mass.: Harvard University Press, 2018.

Riggs, Erika. "Mark Zuckerberg Spends $30 Million on Four Homes to Ensure Privacy." *NBC News*, October 11, 2013. https://www.nbcnews.com/businessmain/mark-zuckerberg-spends-30-million-four-homes-ensure-privacy-8C11379396.

Rolling Thunder Revue: A Bob Dylan Story. Directed by Martin Scorsese. Netflix, 2019.

Rosa, Hartmut. *Social Acceleration: A New Theory of Modernity*. Trans. Jonathan Trejo-Mathys. New York: Columbia University Press, 2013.

Rosemont, Henry, Jr. *Against Individualism: A Confucian Rethinking of the Foundations of Morality, Politics, Family, and Religion*. Lanham, Md.: Lexington, 2015.

Rousseau, Jean-Jacques. *The Confessions of Jean-Jacques Rousseau*. Trans. J. M. Cohen. New York: Penguin, 1981.

——. *The Social Contract*. Trans. Maurice Cranston. New York: Penguin, 1968.

Salam, Reihan. "Taylor Swift Succumbs to Competitive Wokeness." *Atlantic*, October 11, 2018. https://www.theatlantic.com/ideas/archive/2018/10/taylor-swift-kanye-west-and-competitive-wokeness/572716/.

Sandel, Michael. *Liberalism and the Limits of Justice*. Cambridge: Cambridge University Press, 1982.

———. *The Tyranny of Merit: What's Become of the Common Good*. New York: Farrar, Straus and Giroux, 2020.

Sandler, Emma. "Supermodel Teaches at Stanford: How to Learn About Personal Branding with Tyra Banks." *Forbes*, June 12, 2017. https://www .forbes.com/sites/emmasandler/2017/06/12/tyra-banks-talks-teaching -at-stanford/#2aecee326965.

Saussure, Ferdinand de. *Course in General Linguistics*. Ed. Charles Bally and Albert Sechehaye, trans. Roy Harris. Chicago: Open Court, 1998.

Schlesinger, Arthur M. *The Disuniting of America: Reflections on a Multicultural Society*. New York: Norton, 1991.

Sessions, Abby. "Letters: 'Acting Like This Is a Boundless Battle for Wokeness Is Somewhat Absurd.'" *Atlantic*, October 25, 2018. https://www .theatlantic.com/letters/archive/2018/10/readers-opinions-competitive -wokeness-swift-kanye/573754/.

Shetty, Jay. "Mike Posner: ON How Fame Ruined His Life | ON Purpose Podcast Ep. 4." YouTube video, 127:15, March 14, 2019. https://www .youtube.com/watch?v=gjpB9MXCfOE&t=349s.

Simanowski, Roberto. *Facebook Society: Losing Ourselves in Sharing Ourselves*. Trans. Susan H. Gillespie. New York: Columbia University Press, 2018.

Solon, Oliva. "Richard Dawkins on the Internet's Hijacking of the Word 'Meme.'" *Wired*, June 20, 2013. https://www.wired.co.uk/article/richard -dawkins-memes.

Stegmaier, Werner. *Orientierung im Nihilismus: Luhmann Meets Nietzsche*. Berlin, Boston: De Gruyter, 2016.

———. *What Is Orientation? A Philosophical Investigation*. Berlin: De Gruyter, 2019.

Stirner, Max. *Der Einzige und sein Eigntum*. Leipzig: Otto Wiegand, 1945.

Stryker, Sheldon, and Peter J. Burke. "The Past, Present, and Future of an Identity Theory." *Social Psychology Quarterly* 63, no. 4 (2000): 284–97.

Taylor, Charles. *The Ethics of Authenticity*. Cambridge, Mass.: Harvard University Press, 1992.

———. *A Secular Age*. Cambridge, Mass: Belknap Press of Harvard University Press, 2007.

Trauzettel, Rolf. "Landscape as an Aesthetic Person: On the Conceptual World of German Romanticism." In *Landscape East and West: A Philosophical Journey*, ed. Hans-Georg Moeller and Andrew Whitehead, 93–107. London: Bloomsbury, 2014.

——. "Two Mythic Paradigms of the Constitution of Personhood." In *Selfhood East and West: De-Constructions of Identity*, ed. Jason Dockstader, Hans-Georg Moeller, and Günter Wohlfart, 237–62. Nordhausen: Traugott Bautz, 2012.

Trilling, Lionel. *Sincerity and Authenticity*. Cambridge, Mass.: Harvard University Press, 1972.

Turkle, Sherry. *Alone Together: Why We Expect More from Technology and Less from Each Other*. New York: Basic Books, 2011.

——. "Sherry Turkle: 'Reclaiming Conversation' | Talks at Google." YouTube video, 59:33, October 30, 2019. https://www.youtube.com/watch?v=awFQtX7tPoI.

Varga, Somogy. *Authenticity as an Ethical Ideal*. New York: Routledge, 2011.

Vargas, Louis Scott. "Modern Horizons—Draft | Channel LSV." YouTube video, 57:23, June 26, 2019. https://www.youtube.com/watch?v=rjbzcRdoB9o.

Watts, Allan. *Become What You Are*. Boulder, Colo.: Shambhala, 2003.

Webb, Amy. "Amy Webb: The Big Nine—Triangulation 387." YouTube video, 1:03:34. https://www.youtube.com/watch?v=lrcGrYQcM2g.

Wu Fei. *Suicide and Justice: A Chinese Perspective*. New York: Routledge, 2009.

Wu, Tim. *The Attention Merchants: The Epic Scramble to Get Inside Our Heads*. New York: Vintage, 2017.

Yates, Robin D. S. "Soldiers, Scribes, and Women: Literacy Among the Lower Orders in Early China." In *Writing and Literacy in Early China: Studies from the Columbia Early China Seminar*, ed. Feng Li and David Prager Branner, 339–69. Seattle: University of Washington Press, 2011.

Zhang, Dayi. "纪录片《网红》: 真实记录 '淘宝第一网红' 张大奕的面子, 里子." Bilibili video, 18:52, October 28, 2016. https://www.bilibili.com/video/av6856116/.

Ziporyn, Brook, trans. *Zhuangzi: The Complete Writings*. Indianapolis: Hackett, 2020.

Žižek, Slavoj. *Antigone*. London: Bloomsbury Academic, 2016.

Zuboff, Shoshana. *The Age of Surveillance Capitalism: The Fight for a Human Future and a New Frontier of Power*. New York: PublicAffairs, 2019.

Zuckerberg, Mark. "Mark Zuckerberg & Yuval Noah Harari in Conversation." YouTube video, 1:33:30, April 26, 2019. https://www.youtube.com /watch?v=Boj9eDoWug8.

———. "Mark Zuckerberg Talks to Patrick Collison and Tyler Cowen About Accelerating Progress." YouTube video, 1:09:09, November 25, 2019. https://www.youtube.com/watch?v=GTlt-pPfLWU.

INDEX